The vilest and most odious thing about money is that it confers even talent on those whom it favors. And thus it will be until the end of time.

Dostoyevski,
The Idiot.

At birth we mortals have the same skin, but as we grow, destiny is pleased to differentiate us, as if we were wax, and to lead us along by various paths toward only one end: death. There are men who must take the path of flowers, while others are pushed through thistles and prickly pears. The former possess a calm look and, perfumed with their own happiness, they smile from innocent faces; the others, overwhelmed by the violent sun of the plain, bristle like vermin to defend themselves. Some, to enhance their bodies, use makeup and perfumes; others end up with tattoos that later nothing can erase...

Camilo José Cela,
La Famille de Pascal Duarte.

T0323774

INTRODUCTION

"The crisis of the suburbs," "broken social ties," "the lost concept of citizenship," "the disappearance of civility"—such are some of the recurrent themes taken up at numerous symposia and proceedings of society. Scientists, politicians and journalists appear to agree that social disorder is moving toward a crisis.

Not all social groups are equally touched by this disenchantment. It is especially the cornerstones of popular identity that have given way. If the average families' heritage was always modest, if their possessions—trinkets, pieces of furniture, the small suburban house itself—did not outlast centuries, they still had a collective heritage—the neighborhood, the business, the unions and political organizations—a memory of past struggles that assured the transmission of an identity, generation after generation. This collective heritage is today in ruins. This is the result of a long process of disaffiliation, as Robert Castel wrote—the result of a negative course during which the anchors of society are broken[1].

At the antipodes of this social and human disaster are the great families, those of the monied aristocracy and the haute bourgeoisie—a veritable confraternity, an association of shared interests which does not rule out some secondary contradictions but which essentially assures the solidarity of the group. The interests of each family and the collective interests become confused: the economic, social, cultural and symbolic heritages inescapably have individual, family, and collective dimensions. The con view that equates the haute bourgeoisie with individualism obscures the fundamental cohesion found in the great families. The idea of haut-bourgeois individualism is even more misleading in that this individualism is only, in its manifestations, the transliteration of the habits of the group. By its own social magic, the haut bourgeois is so well adapted to the world in which he lives, that being himself is sufficient to meet the requirements of circumstance and of other people, in the ineffable sense of the achievement of being and of irreducible individuality.

A person's adequacy to his social position, to his social role among his equals is, for a large part, the product of deliberate action of the previous generations. The social stakes are high, and they are eminently collective. It is the conditions for social domination by the group which must be reproduced, and for that to happen there is an absolute requirement of producing heirs capable of covering the costs of the heritage. That is a family responsibility for sure, but also a collective one, in that the heritage to be transmitted and managed, which constitutes the objective basis for the dominating position, is at the same time the common wealth of the group. Real estate, for example, owes its economic and symbolic value to the mutually reinforcing effects of a socially homogeneous neighborhood. In certain seaside resorts and in the residential townships of the Parisian suburb, one can see at work families' awareness of their shared goal of maintaining the value of their patrimony.

Our research follows two main lines of analysis. On the one hand, it is apparent that the heritage of families of the wealthy aristocracy and of the established upper-bourgeois are the object of a largely concerted management effort. There is some collectivism, paradoxically, in the manner in which the grande-bourgeoisie undertakes the maintenance—or augmentation—and the transmission of their fortune and of their dominant position. The greater the heritage, the more it can be attributed to collective management. The complexity of their economic aspects, the day-to-day form of cultural practices, including commerce in art, the decisive importance of social capital that submits daily life to a kind of permanent co-option, are the foundation of this great family fraternity.

The second axis of analysis concerns the accumulation of wealth. This accumulation is not, in any case, foreign to the necessities of relative collectivization of styles of management. No family would be able to exist independent of the group from which it is descended, without tending toward the ineluctable erosion of its various forms of capital. The rupture of the social tie and the process of disaffiliation at work in certain categories of the population oppose the maintenance, not to mention the reinforcement, of the multiple linkages that characterize the great families of the wealthy aristocracy and the bourgeoisie. Wealth opposes poverty in all domains and, at the two extremities of society, there is an accumulation of privileges and of handicaps. Misery and opulence are readily seen, of course, in the material affluence and the market value of the heritage, but also in the educational, the cultural, the social domains, in the symbolic value of all these possessions, materials or nonmaterial. When reand commentary are limited to the strictly economic dimensions of fortune, as too often happens, we do not see the real scope of the social distances and inequalities that affect all measurements of existence.

Certainly, it is otherwise for large sectors of society, situated between these two extreme poles. For them, to take a formula of Pierre Bourdieu's, it is a zero-sum game—fundamental economic and cultural patrimonies have a tendency to be inversely proportional, the one being low when the other is high[2]. But, in extreme social situations, riches or, on the contrary, poverties accumulate in all domains. It is therefore through stocks, securities, property held either for profit or for actual use, through industrial and real estate inheritances, through academic capital and demonstrations of social capital, in the effects of symbolic capital, through the importance of the cultural and artistic patrimony, that we have tried to give account of the social significance of wealth.

From Paris to Bordeaux, passing through Deauville and Biarritz, from the Parisian region, with Maison-Laffitte and the Vésinet, to Monaco and Saint-Jean-Cap-Ferrat, the quality of life and daily existence demonstrate this multidimensionality of wealth. But to manage and to transmit wealth are not as simple as one might imagine, and the whole group finds itself mobilized in these tasks upon which its perpetuation as the dominant class depends.

Patrimony is a decisive element of the "superaffiliation" of the dominant class. Possessions are guarantors of ties and ties assure the permanence and the transmission of possessions. Thus, inheritance constitutes an objective basis for affirming the group. This multiform heritage, economic of course but also symbolic, social and cultural, permits the bourgeoisie to be a class in itself, by affirming their dominant social and economic positions.

But, because it has an effective existence in many other registers besides the market value of the goods owned, this heritage allows the existence of the bourgeoisie and the aristocracy as a class in and of themselves, as a mobilized class. The convergent practices of the dominant classes tend to assure the permanent occupation of their position. Besides, the economic heritage and also the system of alliances and relationships is in large measure international, and cosmopolitanism has long been one of the characteristic features of the aristocracy and the haute bourgeoisie. The Internationale was a fact of the controlling class before it became a hope and a form of organization for the dominated classes. International workers' organizations have disappeared or else are in a very mediocre state. The Internationale of the powerful is doing rather better.

To gather materials that would permit analysis of the different facets of great fortunes, multiple approaches were necessary. Interviews are central in the process of research. Interviews were conducted with several dozen families with only rare guarantees of anonymity. Not all of them are represented among the biggest fortunes. But all share the characteristic of having been wealthy for several generations and having known how to transmit their heritage and to reproduce their social rank. More than one hundred people were interviewed, sometimes for prolonged discussions, and not all could be cited here. But all these interviews enriched our work; they permitted us to internalize the reality that they described. These discussions have been complemented by large amounts of documentation, using available statistical data, and performing original calculations. In addition, parallel interviews of the most diverse interviewees—professional administrators of major fortunes, directors of luxury hotels, specialist in the art market—shed an indispensable light on the data collected. Beyond establishing a perspective, interviews were the point of departure for observations conducted in a great variety of settings and circumstances. Whether one speaks of vast Parisian apartments or of chateaux in the provinces, of holiday resorts or the famous educational establishments—cosmopolitan colleges of Switzerland or France—or of auctions where, in about ten seconds, a Canaletto finds a taker at 66 million francs, the multiplicity of observations corresponds to the multiplicity of facets of patrimony which, far from being reduced to a quantifiable and thus limited material wealth, take on, via their conversions and permanent reconversions, all the appearances of being infinite.

Our objective is to describe and to analyze, on the basis of everyday life of the families who benefit from this state of affairs, the processes that allow them to maintain and conserve their dominant social positions; to show how the lifestyle of the grand-bourgeois is infused with cosmopolitan collectivism, to show, more precisely, the collective and international character of management of class interests which manifest in the most trifling of practices. Power is constructed and managed day by day, even if this daily life is totally out of the ordinary.

Notes

1. Robert Castel, Les Metamorphoses de la question sociale. Une chronique du salariat, Paris, Fayard, coll. "L'espace du politique", 1995.
2. On this "structure en chiasme," see for example Pierre Bourdieu, La Distinction Pari, Minuit, coll. "Le Sens

FIRST CHAPTER

The Great Fortunes: Levels, Composition and Administration

ON THE DIFFICULTY OF MEASURING FORTUNES

"Poverty affects every aspect of life."[1] This observation can be made on the basis of many data, their very number making it credible. Poverty can be measured, plumbed, inventoried, described. It is different with wealth, which appreciates some discretion on the matter of its extent and its structure. Use of administrative and tax records should have rounded out, in a statistical fashion, our information from interviews with families. Unfortunately, the available published data are hardly satisfactory. There was only one serious statistical analysis of the mass of data represented by the tax filings for the Large Fortune Tax (IGF), which became in 1988, after the demise of the first cohabitation, the Consolidated Wealth Tax (ISF). These tax returns first of all include a series of information on the family, the matrimonial status, number of children, and profession. The statement of net worth is organized in three categories: physical buildings (the primary residence being distinguished from other buildings) real estate holdings not comprising buigs (woods and forests, rented farmlands, shares in farming investments, "properties" in the fiscal sense, that is securities or transferable assets (stocks, bonds, trust funds, etc.) and liquid assets.

Now, the only # period that the Tax Office used these tax statements dates from 1986, and concerns the results of FIGF (the Large Fortune Tax) for the years 1982 to 1985[2]. Since this date, the Budget Ministry has been satisfied to publish, in the Blue Notes of Bercy, the number of declarations taxable in the name of the ISF and the corresponding payments received, for the whole of France and for each region and département. The

7

number of people subject to the IGF, then to the ISF, tax went from 117,000 in 1982 to 160,000 in 1993. As for the threshold for imposing this tax, recalculated from year to year, it went from 3 million francs in 1982 to 4.39 million in 1993, and 4.53 million in 1995.

The well-kept statistical secret

The abundant mail and the insistent telephone calls by which we sought to gain authorization to access the ISF tax returns, in order to establish new statistical data, led the service of Organization and Data Processing of the General Tax Administration of the Ministry of the Budget to send a photocopy of the four pages dedicated by the Blue Notes of Bercy, # broken out by département, of the number of tax payers liable, and of amounts paid, in 1992 and 1993. The ministry eluded our questions, thus confirming the confidential and politically dangerous character of disclosing, even in an anonymous form, the structure and the importance of the great fortunes. Wealth remains a mystery, "a taboo topic, even more so than revenue"[3]: little known, hidden, it is at the origin of social fantasies, of more or less well-founded imaginary representations.

This protection of information is all the more regrettable since, as well they know, the patrimony of households, even more than their incomes, constitute a fundamental source of social inequalities. "Well-being," write D. Kessler and A. Masson, "also depends on what one possesses: liquid assets, durable goods and eventual home ownership, # all conditions of present consumption; # accumulated goods, especially, determine purchasing power over the long term and satisfy the needs for security, for preparedness, transmission, and even for power and esteem."[4] Income is insufficient to measure the distance that can separate paths in life, lifestyles, and how families and individuals relate to the world. Wealth has at once the economic, cultural, social and symbolic measurements, and this multidimensionality is one of the essential features of its social significance.

The notion of heritage is complex. The ambition of this work is to restore the social meaning which the fact of owning a significant fortune conceals, by relying on statistics from INSEE, CERC and CREP[5] and on a sociological and ethnographical approach. On the basis of interviews, observations and various documents, the work attempts to establish the relationship between the possession of a significant estate and a way of life or, to put it more ambitiously, between wealth and the constitution of the haute-bourgeois habitus, that ensemble of traits which generates the practices and outward signs proper to this class.[6]

A study of patrimonies must enable one to grasp fortune as that which defines the place of the nobility and the grande bourgeoisie in society and as that which founds the group itself. Indeed, members of the dominant classes can be reduced even less than

8

others to their profession. In distinction from workers, teachers or researchers, whose main form of patrimony resides in their "human heritage," as economists say, or in another vocabulary, in their ability to work, the bourgeois are defined above all by the amplitude and the diversity of their economic capital: direct ownership of industrial or real estate holdings, or indirect ownership via securities. We must also take into account all those possessions that, without offering a direct financial profit, are the source of considerable benefit, such as the fact of owning one's residences. But these revenues are rarely calculated because it is difficult to appraise their monetary value.

Neither does the patrimony displayed in published statistics incorporate the human patrimony. This notion designates everything that has been embodied by an individual, from his physical capital to his cultural and educational capital. But this human heritage is distributed as unequally as material heritage: cultural inequalities are extreme and in part they found the processes of social reproduction. These inequalities constitute the family heritages to the point that, statistically, they transmit themselves between generations with a great probability, as has been shown by certain works which have become classics.[7]

The sources used to evaluate households' patrimonies[8] ignore those durable goods for household use, such as cars, and precious objects on which it would be difficult to set a value, whether one speaks of gold, jewelry or works of art. A survey from CERC in 1975 valued durable possessions at 7% and precious objects at 4% of the total gross value of the household patrimonies.

Furthermore, we know that collectibles and art works are exempted from the ISF tax basis and therefore few statistics have been issued about them. The symbolic, cultural and aesthetic value of these possessions having risen, excluding them from the assessment of patrimonies leads to an undervaluation of the disparities. In addition, they provide the material basis on which the transmission of an essential part of the human heritage operates, that of the qualities acquired by the person, that have no specific price. They play an important role in the inculcation of knowledge and in the formation of the constituent tastes of the cultivated habitus.

A Multiform Reality

Besides the difficulty of access to sources, the assessment of patrimonies comes up against the fact that the economic can not be reduced merely to the economy, nor the cultural to culture: at an elevated level of fortune, the market values and the symbolic values of the various elements of heritage reach an apex. The heritage then forms a whole whose different parts gain significance through their interrelation and their cumulativity.

This totality of a heritage tends to establish a certain analogy between the family environment and the peer group and those global institutions of which Erving Goffman[9] speaks. The individual is involved in a structured set values and required behaviors which spills over from the fields of professional activity to include daily life. Thus, heritage contributes, by the simple effect of its size, but also by means of its cultural and symbolic dimensions, to erasing the individual to the benefit of the group—because the individual is inherited in a way by his inheritance, snatched up by the duty to assume the transmission from which he benefits but of which he, in turn, is obliged to assure the succession. Heirs of prestigious lineages, wealthy aristocrats and the old stock grande bourgeoisie owe more to their inheritances than to their own merits. But an inheritance is earned. You must be capable of managing the heritage that befalls you, or forfeit social stature.

The transmission is in no way independent of that which it transmits. Its conditions are already defined in the very content of the heritages. Among the social effects of patrimonial wealth, there is an accumulation of talents, knowledge, expertise and self-assurance that makes dynasties and their continuation successful. For money does give talent. In other words, material heritage is inseparable from human heritage. Along with financial and material possessions are transmitted acquaintances, knowledge, the know-how and the manners that the accumulation of wealth permitted to collect. Conversely, managing the symbolic capital, conserving and maintaining these talents, presupposes spending the necessary material capital. The different forms of assets, inheritances, capital, and wealth are mutually reinforcing and are indispensable to each other.[10]

CRITICISM OF THE "CHART" EFFECT

What are the great fortunes, which families have the greatest heritages? Is there really transmission? Have today's wealthiest families been the same for several generations? To suppose that money also gives talent is to suppose that it gives the moral and intellectual means to maintain the lineage. Making a fortune would then carry with it both an obligation to transmit it and the means to satisfy this obligation.

The Redistribution of Fortunes?

Several authors, on the basis of the lists of the richest families published by the press, have concluded that wealth is quickly redistributed since they observe that the published lists contained very few names of the famous "200 families" denounced by Édouard Daladier. He, at the radical convention of Nantes in October 1934, had declared that "200 families run the French economy and, in fact, French politics." He was referring to the 200 principal shareholders of the Banque de France, at that time a private establishment, among which were also some sixty legal entities (companies and institutions).

Jules Lepidi finds only about ten of these names among the hundred richest French recorded by Le Nouvel Observateur[11]. Similarly, only ten descendants of the 200 families, according to A. Babeau, figure among the 150 largest personal fortunes listed by L'Expansion in 1988[12]. Such observations would be in harmony with the declaration that French fortunes are deteriorating.[13] The 200 families would have experienced such reverses of fortune, in connection with wars and with disappointing foreign investments, that they would not be represented among the most rich today. The great fortunes would belong to newly rich.[14] But there is a "chart effect" there, which may obscure the most profound and most lasting phenomenon of wealth transmission. Indeed, one cannot infer from the fact that the first in his class is the son of a worker, that all the better students are workers' sons and that it is they who are going to populate the polytechnical institute. By the same token, finding a large majority of industrial leaders and businessmen whose fortunes recently figured among the 200 richest Frenchmen (if not among the 100 or the 50...) does not prove that the old families are ruined and that their descendants are thereby reduced to selling their labor.

Where did the 200 Families Go?

If the old families could be supplanted in the first positions of the old ranking, it is probable that, even in 1993, they are still numerous among the roughly 160,000 who are subject to the ISF tax. Besides, the chart of the 400 largest professional fortunes established by Le Nouvel Iconomiste in 1994 often takes into account the family fortunes and not only the individual, contrary to previous rankings. However, results are somewhat distorted. "Whom does one find today in our ranking of the 400 major professional fortunes?" writes Éric Tréguier. "Of course, the heirs of the grand dynasties: Seydoux, Taittinger, Rothschild, Dassault, Peugeot, Mérieux, Verspieren, Guichard..." Indeed, among the 91 recorded multimillionaires, one notes "the postwar capitalists" and "a few rare examples of new fortunes," but old families or heirs of dynasties also appear: Michel David-Weill (Bank Lazard), the Hermès family (silk scarves), Serge Dassault, the Durand family (Cristal d'Arques), the Bich family (the Bic ballpoint), the Hériard-Dubreuil family (Cointreau), the Guerlains (perfumes), the Vuittons (deluxe luggage), Robert Fiévet (Bel cheese), the Wendel family, etc. In other words, even if there is a certain reshuffling, it is not enough to set the hierarchy of fortunes on its ear.[15]

One can find a strange vanity in the glorification of the newly wealthy, whose advances seem to prove that every French person has only to compete with Mrs. Liliane Bettencourt, the happy heiress who occupies the first rank of fortune since Marcel Dassault gave up that position: her financial assets were appraised in 1994 at some 25 billion francs by *Le Nouvel Économiste.*

If it is true that a certain "turnover" exists at the top of the fortune hierarchy, still it is necessary to avoid limiting these to the first 200, duly listed. According to the VIIIth report of the Conseil des impôts, 0.2% of the 19,588,924 households counted by the census of 1982 had an estate of more than 10 million francs16, which represents more than 39,000 households, by the way. Before concluding that fortunes are changing hands, one would need to verify whether these households include some of these families' heirs.

Especially since, in another hierarchy arranged according to the size of the families' heritages, and not the individuals', one finds numerous family names whose reputation no longer needs to be established. The notes that accompany this chart are illuminating. Jean-Pierre Peugeot, who is definitely the originator of the dynasty (his descendants are located in the third row) was a small steel smelter in the beginning. He lived from 1768 to 1852. The Schlumberger brothers (descendants in the fourth row), Conrad (1878-1936) and Marcel (1884-1953), invented a new means of striking oil. The House of Martell & Cie opened its first account book on August 3, 1720.[17] On the 30 notes on these "richest families," 16 refer to founding dates in the XIXth century, or even earlier. Among the other recognized names represented in this list, and that evoke high finance or major industry, one may mention Vuitton, David-Weill, Rothschild, Michelin, Taittinger, Cointreau, Worms, Hennessy, Vogüé, Chandon-Moët, Wendel, Bouriez and Gichard. No question there of any parvenus. All these families are among the 30 wealthiest of France.

Financial Assets and Heritage for Personal Use

The very manner by which the charts are constructed leaves certain essential aspects of patrimonies in shadow. Indeed, they are mostly based on financial assets. In the brief notes describing the research methodology, only the part relating to the more easily evaluated securities was outlined, starting with specialized publications and expensive data banks, and as far as real estate, landholdings and art works, only passing allusions are made.

Apart from these uncertainties one can entertain, at least as a hypothesis, André Babeau's remark according to which "the taste for money and the power that it confers" constitute a demiurgical aspect of the accumulation of wealth [that] is often present in the motives of the great founders of patrimonial dynasties[19]. This vocation may not always be so strong among those who inherit wealth, some part of the accumulated assets having been converted into heritage for use. Not diminished, as the man on the street would too easily phrase it, but transformed into homes and art works that, while offering an exceptional quality of life, are at the foundation of the attachment to this family heritage whose identification value is thus reinforced over the generations.

However this heritage of enjoyment, whose value can be considerable, is poorly grasped through surveys. Accounting for financial assets, in charts describing the great fortunes, is easier and it favors the most recent fortunes, those where such assets form the major portion. In primitive accumulation, it is the productive assets that take priority among investments.

One might then suggest that the great families no longer occupy the first place in business, while preserving a substantial level of fortune and while having a heritage of enjoyment and a human heritage that assure the permanence of the lineage. It is probable that the process of accumulating wealth passes a peak and then experiences a downturn relative to the patrimonies: they would stabilize over the long term in response to the logic of a life cycle not on the scale of one generation but of many generations. Patrimonial accumulation and its management would therefore be organized not with regard to a term—retirement, old age and death, as in the life cycle theory of Modigliani—but according to a social stake of the first importance: the transmission of the inheritance, the name, the memory and the identity of the family.

The first time winners do not figure in this ranking, at least they do not appear there yet. And this is one of the reasons of the records that these fortunes set. They were recently constituted, and these fortunes are all the more considerable in that they have not been divided yet among heirs. And, besides, it is not for no reason that instead of being evaluated by the press in the family setting, they are evaluated on an individual basis. One doesn't speak yet of family in their case. The family, as a system of alliances and the accumulation of social capital, will be a fact in the following generation. A "great family" is not established by a single generation, and it is the heirs that have to reinforce its foundations while enriching the network of alliances.[20]

These remarks appear to be even more well-founded when we consider that economists specializing in the study of estates have noted that the propensity to adopt a dynastic behavior increased in tandem with the size of the succession.[21] It is enough to start the process: the fortune having been established, the actual principle of passing it down would be consubstantial. Inheritance would be in the very nature of wealth, far from leading toward deterioration. One of the objectives of this work is to show that patrimony carries within itself the factors of its own perpetuation and transmission, and thus that it is at the foundation of social reproduction.

In fact, the very idea of the existence of wealthy dynasties is often disturbing. The ideology of meritocracy, which assumes the probability of individual success, is reassuring because it opens up the universe of possibilities—at least in the popular imagination. Furthermore, the brilliant and rapid success of businessmen whose ascent, in the mind of the public at large, has to do with money, and only money. *A contrario* the existence of dynasties makes one suppose, or rather suspect, the accumulation of other forms of capital, cultural possessions and symbolic powers. In particular for social agents who essentially owe their position to their educational and cultural capital, this competition in the same domain as that which they consider their specialty is intolerable. One could never accept, in the place of economic domination, a cultural domination that one had considered to be the sole dominion of the producers of culture.

Permanence or Fluidity of Elites?

The theme of "fluidity of the elite" has a sociological tradition, too. According to Dominique Merllié, Vilfredo Pareto (1848-1923), who divided society into two classes, the elite and the rest, affirmed that the destiny of elites is to renew themselves, either progressively by integrating some new individuals and rejecting others, or globally when a group, due to a failure to renew itself or for other grounds, loses its dominant position.[22] In addition, the notion of social mobility itself, introduced by Pitirim Sorokin (1889-1968), was formulated on the basis of the problem of elites. For Sorokin, social mobility appeared to be a form of generalization of the older theme of "the mobility of elites". And still long after Sorokin, works on social mobility are in fact fairly often limited to the question of elite recruitment.[23] This tradition returns to an ancient preoccupation in the developed Western societies, that of equality, at least formal, of opportunity. Without being egalitarian societies, North Ameica and old Europe are meritocratic societies, where it is demonstrated and made evident that the dominant positions are not only inherited, but are earned and that they are the object of a valiant struggle whose result is uncertain.

To counter this socially and politically legitimizing picture of an open society, in which competition is possible and permits each person to realize his opportunities, it is necessary to recall some elementary facts. First of all, that "immobility prevails over mobility" as the tables of social mobility show.[24] And then, that social replication does not handle the individual case, from father to son or mother to daughter. This reproduction gains significance on a group scale. It is even more true for the haute bourgeoisie that wealth and power are not characteristics of individuals, nor on the scale of the nuclear family, but on the scale of the extended family and all the families with which, in the course of several generations, they weave ties, loyalties and complicities. The great families intermarry among themselves and, in a veritable collective alchemy, they produce the miracle of the multiplication of the loaves, in every form of capital. But the network of alliances extends past the borders of the families and one would not understand the intense sociability of the grande bourgeoisie if one refused to see it, in part, as a permanent effort to maintain and to develop the great instrument of power that such social capital constitutes.

In their survey on employers, Pierre Bourdieu and Monique de Saint Martin observe that "the criteria in use by the insiders are contrary to the modernist and rational picture that the big technocratic parade suggests to outsiders: this controlling fraction that likes to be seen as entirely focused on the future finds the real principles of its actual selection at the same time as the practical justifications for its privileges in the past, in history and in the seniority of acquired rights.[25] Thus "managers" as the new masters of the economy would in fact mask the weight of the past behind modernist costumes. They would be the indispensable screen for maintaining the illusion of a meritocracy. However, sociologists and economists, at least certain of them, agree in recognizing the property and the family networks that always find themselves in a powerful position. Thus, the authors of the *Dictionnaire des groupes industriels et financiers en France (Dictionary of Industrial and Financial Groups in France)* write that "family ties are one of the means, maybe the principal means, by which the bourgeoisie and in particular the financial oligarchy assures and reproduces over time its control of capital [...] that gives it value."[26] Bernard Marguerite leads to similar conclusions while underscoring the relative permeability of the grande bourgeoisie: "There is not a class of men of means on the one hand and a class of managers on the other, there is a selection-absorption mechanism within the class (or on its immediate periphery) pulling in those who appear best qualified to manage in the collective interest of the class."[27] Daniel Bertaux, in the earliest of all the texts cited here, affirmed that "thanks to some recent studies, [he] saw rather quickly that [the thesis of the manager era] was only smoke in the eyes to conceal the real process from view, which is quite the opposite—the concentration of fabulous wealth and extraordinary power in the hands of a few "big families" all bound to each other by multiple ties of money or marriage, and forming a kind of hard core of very grande bourgeoisie that we call the financial oligarchy."[28] The concentration of fortunes is, by all events, an observable and spectacular fact.[29]

THE CONCENTRATION OF GREAT FORTUNES

Income and Patrimonies

The concentration of patrimony is far more accentuated than that of incomes: half of the households, at the bottom of the ladder, possess only 6% of the total net worth, whereas the 10% wealthiest hold 54%. In absolute value, in 1986 the 10% poorest held less than 12,200 francs, whereas the 10% richest held more than 1,055,000 francs.[30] That would be a ratio of 1 to 87, whereas calculating incomes in the same way, it is only 1 to 6. In 1984, 20% of the homes who owed FISF tax declared an available income of less than 200,000 francs per year, that being the income of a couple with two good careers. 9% of those declaring a combined patrimony between 7 and 10 million francs had no more than this same level of income.[31] So, there is a significant disjuncture between patrimonies and incomes.

This distortion has to do with the fact that the heritages appraised in the tax returns include inherited relationships and a part of the usable estate (certain real estate possessions...). And these latter, which may represent large monetary values, do not produce revenues but do create deep inequalities in the conditions of life. The vast homes in the nicest neighborhoods and the art objects that they house constitute an exceptional living environment. Besides, through the intense socializing proper to high society, these estates for daily use are collectivized, in a way: every member of the group receives and invites guests, the use of status possessions thus being shared, in a certain sense. There is a strong multiplying effect to the benefit of each, and the study of wealth at the family or individual level still underestimates the mass of hereditary possessions to which each one really has access. Limiting the analysis of wealth to monetary measurements impoverishes it. The sociological, or even ethnogc, approach is here a precious complement that allows us to take the measure of what it means in terms of daily life to have a considerable estate at one's disposal.

Thus there is a certain independence between the level of income and the size of the heritage possessed. One can also find the inverse, with very sizeable incomes and a relatively minor heritage, which is the case for fortunes in the process of being made. The relative weight of incomes and heritages, especially if one wants to include in the equation the value of items accessible for use by virtue of the mobilizable network of relationships, may vary far more at the zenith of the social hierarchy than in the less privileged social categories. But, beyond the complexity of some individual situations, there is a remarkable concentration of patrimonial fortunes.

Inequalities of Heritage

The available data makes clear the extent of the inequalities of heritage. On December 31, 1983, the 10% of households having the smallest heritages—the first decile—controlled 0.2% of all household assets, that is 10,653 billion francs.[32] Now, in the

1982 census, a decile represented a set of 1,958,892 households. Thus in 1983, the households of the first decile had, on average, a net heritage of 10,875 francs.

The 9,857 FISFS taxpayers whose heritage is greater than 10 million francs owned 219,177 million together—that is, a mean heritage of 22.24 million francs. The assets of one of these happy owners represented the same amount as the assets of 2,045 of the most modest households.

The wealthiest households, having a heritage of at least 100 million francs, numbered 142. The whole of their heritages added together reached 36,641 million francs, that is 258 million on average.[33] Thus, at the highest level, each fiscal household possessed as many assets as 23,724 modest households, which is the equivalent of the population of the VIth or the VIIIth arondissement of Paris. A great deal in hands of very few; very little in the hands of many: that remains the rule with regard to the distribution of wealth in France.[34]

The phenomenon of the concentration of fortunes thus intensifies progressively as one climbs the ladder of heritages. In 1982, about two thirds of the product of the IGF was derived from 12,000 fiscal households, out of some 100,000 who were subject to the tax.[35] In 1985, those who owed IGF tax, who enjoyed a heritage of over 30 million, represented 1.2% of those subject to the tax, but they possessed 12% of the total the net worth submitted to the IGF.[36] Thus we see there is an enormous disparity in the importance of patrimonies, even more so as one ascends the ladder of wealth. Among the first deciles

Table 1. Composition of Patrimony by Decile (1980)

Deciles of Patrimony	Checking Accounts	Liquid Savings	Primary and Secondary Residences	Securities	Real Estate	Professional Patrimony	Total
Decile 1	81.6	18.4	—	—	—	—	100
Decile 2	64.6	30.2	0.7	—	2.5	2.1	100
Decile 3	41.6	55.4	1.2	1.5	0.2	0.1	100
Decile 4	21.7	67.9	2.9	2.6	2.5	2.4	100
Decile 5	6.6	34.0	49.6	2.1	4.4	3.4	100
Decile 6	5.3	17.8	66.8	2.9	5.0	2.1	100
Decile 7	4.6	12.7	66.2	3.7	6.4	6.4	100
Decile 8	3.1	14.5	64.8	5.1	6.9	5.6	100
Decile 9	3.4	13.1	40.0	8.1	13.9	21.5	100
Decile 10	2.9	10.5	24.0	9.4	26.6	26.7	100
Combined	3.9	13.6	37.7	7.5	18.0	19.2	100

SOURCE: *1980 CREP Survey and A. BABEAU, Le Patrimoine des Français, op. cit.*
Decile 1 corresponds to the 10% of households that possess the weakest patrimonies, Decile 10 to the wealthiest 10% of households.

of distribution, those where one finds the least rich households, the differences are appreciable only in that they concern vital possessions: ownership or non-ownership of the primary residence. Inside the last decile, the wealthiest, the variations are less perceptible when they are seen from the bottom of the social scale, but they are in reality far larger because they concern the number of residences owed, the stylish pieces of furniture and the works of art that they hold, everything that sets the quality of life beyond the ordinary. Wealth is not accumulated for itself, but for all these means and these objects experienced in daily life. This heritage of enjoyment presupposes a heritage of relationships that is even more important than its maintenance and conservation which are expensive. Even though the consolidated tax on wealth has not stopped progrg, reporting 8.3 billion francs in 1994, patrimony remains very concentrated.

Inequalities with respect to inheritance are on the same order as inequalities of patrimony. 10% of successions represent close to half of the heritage transmitted and those who benefit from these inheritances are, in general, already wealthy. The authors of this survey[37] conclude that "the place a son or daughter will occupy on the ladder of wealth will often be near that occupied by the father or the mother." That is the opposite of those findings (made no doubt a little too hastily) on the mobility of fortunes, that the lists of the richest French people suggest too easily. While others skirmish for first place, a relative mass of established fortunes, less spectacular but still quite respectable, quietly live out their happy days. Inheritance creates over time that which the concentration of fortunes creates in the social space. This concentration permits the existence of a network that unifies high society; inheritance allows lineages to build themselves by relying on the permanence, in fact the enrichment of heritages. The wealthy aristocracy and the haute the

Table 2. Composition of Heritages
of IGF Taxpayers in 1985 (extreme categories)

	Total	Real Estate Of which			Total	Other Assests Of which
		Principal Residence	Secondary Residence	Rental Properties		Securities
Less than 5 million francs	63.9	17.0	8.7	38.2	36.4	25.9
More than 30 million francs	15.3	2.6	2.0	10.7	84.7	79.6

SOURCE: The 8th Report of Councel on Imports, and Véronique Sandoval's "La grande bourgeoisie, une planète à explorer", op. cit.

"Financial Products": Some Definitions

CODEVI: Fund for Industrial Development, created in 1983, intended to tap popular savings accounts.
PEL: Plan for Home Savings. Created to facilitate home ownership, it is a fundamental investment choice for individuals (9 million holders of home purchasing accounts plans).
OPCVM: Organization for collective investment insecurities, uniting the organizations that provide collective management of savings in the form of securities portfolios.
FCP: Common Investment Funds. This is co-ownership of transferable securities that can not be assimilated to legal entities. The FCPs are part of the OPCVMs.
SICAV: Investment Societies with Varying Levels of Capital; these open-ended unit trusts are investment societies having the status of legal entities. SICAVs are part of the OPCVMs.
SCPI: Civil Societies for Real Estate Investment (real estate investment trusts). These permit multiple investors to share ownership of buildings. The maintenance and improvement of these buildings are handled by a management company.
Life Insurance: The insurer commits to pay to the subscriber, on fixed terms, a capital amount or a pension. The benefits can be assigned, in case of death, to recipients designated by the contract, but this is not the first objective. This formula presents considerable tax advantages, and specialists readily speak of this as the French "tax shelter."

See:
Bruno PAYS, La gestion de patrimoine, Paris, PUF, coll. « Que sais-je ? », no. 2699, 1992.
Frédéric TEULON, Vocabulaire monétaire et financier, Paris, PUF, coll. « Que sais-je ? », 2628, 1993.
Gérard ATHIAS, Assurance vie, suivez le guide!, interviews with Jean-Luc BENGEL, Paris, E//ditions de Verneuil, 1994.

bourgeoisie thus are formes of two interlacing networks, one of relationships, in synchronicity, and one of lineages, in the diachrony. It is also a manner of making one's mark in time, through family history, ann space, through the extent of relationships made. The heritage of real estate, which in the form of rural retreats or resort locations offer e possibility of overlapping stays and reciprocal invitations, allows the net to be woven more densely and more tightly. The highest patrimonies enroll the individual in a collective that is at once both historic and contemporary.

THE COMPOSITION OF GREAT FORTUNES

The Importance of Transferable Securities, a Characteristic of Wealth

The composition of patrimonies varies with their size. For the 40% of the poorest households, the heritage principally consists of liquidities, available balances in checking or savings accounts such as the savings bank passbook. For households a little better off, the primary residence and a secondary home are listed in the most meaningful way. After that, personal real estate takes a major place in heritage, up to the most comfortable households, the 20% that control the largest heritages. For these, the share of real estate for use takes a back seat to real estate for profit, transferable securities and the professional heritage (see Table 1, p. 37, and Graph 1, p. 38). The higher the heritage rises, the more it is a profit-making heritage, whose goal is to provide a portion of the household's resources. Furthermore, a study on taxable incomes, carried out in 1984, showed that if the revenue from the patrimony represented 6% of the overall income of households, the concentration in this domain was extremnce 18% ohouseholds received 90% of their income from patrimonial assets.[38]

In 1985, within the population that is subject to the IGF tax, the weight of transferable securities increases according to the size of the heritage. For a patrimony between the tax threshold (3.5 million) and 5 million francs, rental properties and real estate represent 64%. This rate goes to 15% when the patrimony passes 30 million francs. Inversely, the weight of securities goes from 26% to nearly 80% for the same slices of heritage (see Graph 2, p. 38, and Table 2, p. 39).

Undoubtedly the goals change with the growth of heritages. "If the small owners and small investors aim above all to insure against the vicissitudes of life, to prepare for their retirement, or to pass something along to their natural heirs, the objective pursued by those holding the largest patrimonies is above all accumulation, for its own sake or for the power that it brings them."[39] In any case changing position on the ladder produces a change in the nature of property. The great heritages have a different social significance from the smaller ones and investment is a multifaceted and varied phenomenon.

20%—picture 2. Composition of heritages
10% of those subject to the IGF in 1985 (the extreme poles)

That a heritage is more and more a revenue-producing heritage when it grows does not prevent it from including a significant heritage of enjoyment as well. Because if property for enjoyment diminishes in relative value as the total heritage becomes greater, it is no less true that in absolute value it continues to grow.[40]

The heritage of enjoyment and income-producing heritage are in fact partly linked. It would be inconceivable to have multiple properties in France and abroad unless the consequent income made it possible to meet the expenses inherent to these possessions: ISF, maintenance, security, insurance. Being rich is expensive. The trap of wealth is ineluctable: enrichment produces the accumulation of a manifold heritage of enjoyment, the maintenance and the transmission of which require the continuity and the growth of income, that can not come from salary alone. Wealth calls for wealth.

The Diversification of Investment Portfolios

Since the diversification of patrimonies increases with their size, it is a very selective criterion of hierarchization because only a minute minority of households possesses a real variety of assets. Thus, a survey founded on the distribution of five types of assets shows that only a quarter of the wealthiest households have a fully diversified portfolio. Inversely, among the most modest households, about one third has nothing to do with any of these assets, and another third has nothing but a savings account.[41] Another breakdown of assets into nine items arrives at the same results: less than 1% of households own 8 stocks and only 0.2% have a complete portfolio.[42] Household wealth does not expand at the same rate across all categories of investment: the richest families are those that possess a very sizeable securities portfolio. No fortune worthy of this name can be established outside of the stock market.

In this sense, Mr. and Mrs. Allières, who live in the Hauts-de-Seine, have a heritage that allocates the majority of their portfolio to securities rather than to real estate

In 1994, they declared to the ISF 8,500,000 francs, of which 6,500,000 come from their personal portfolio. The latter is composed of 1,400,000 francs in securities (stocks and bonds), life insurance policies valued at 4,800,000 francs, and the balance of 300,000 francs remains in the form of liquidities (mutual funds, PELS, savings accounts and cash accounts). This choice is perhaps explained by the fact that, not having any children and "being fond of travel," they prefer investments that assure them of regular and comfortable incomes.

But as soon as one takes a closer look at this breakdown, one perceives the diversity of forms and areas of investments, within the category of securities: OPCVMs, SICAVs and mutual funds, SCPIs, life insurance, etc., reflecting social differences— because their allocation among the various channels is not independent of the volume of the heritage possessed. Thus these financial "products" as bankers and fund administrators say, are extremely varied, but this variety is achieved only in the most elevated heritages.

The Stock Market Opens to Small Shareholders

Nevertheless, the last decades have seen an increase in the number of owners of securities. According to an evaluation by the Commission of Stock Market Operations

(COB), it went from 2,4 million in 1978 to 11,2 million in 1994, with a maximum of 12,4 millions in 1992.[43] This growth is partly due to privatizations. It coincides with a deep change in the representations made regarding share ownership. The ideological context has changed since sixties and seventies. Income from capital tends to be seen today as a just remuneration for savings, even among those of modest means who were, until now, not concerned with the stock market. The success of privatization attests that some forbidden moral and ideological threshold has been crossed. This is a new situation that allows big fortunes to bloom in all legitimacy.

But the structure of investment patrimonies varies according to their size. According to a survey published in 1994, the "small holders," who possess a securities portfolio of less than 100,000 francs, hold 51% of all shares, but 66% of the shares of privatized companies. Inversely, the "large holders," owners of portfolios greater than 600,000 francs, own more than 9% of shares but only 4% of those of privatized companies. One may observe a less pronounced distortion but along the same lines for the OPCVMs.[44] Owners of small patrimonies tend to prefer those assets presented as the most secure, assets managed collectively by professionals or those that are being privatized and which, based on this fact, seem to benefit from a sort of state guarantee.

There is also some disparity among stock portfolios, as a function of their size, from the perspective of how many lines are held—that is, the number of quoted companies of which the shareholder has at least one share. Shareholders overall are invested in 5 companies, but only 2.6 for shareholders of privatized companies. It reaches 11 companies for the largest shareholders and 13 for the most active shareholders. The ownership of foreign asset titles and the number of transactions completed are distributed just as unequally among shareholders.[45] Of the largest portfolio owners, 90% made at least one transaction in 1994, at the time of the survey (between June and September), whereas this is not the case for 64% of owners of shares exclusively of privatized companies. And 93.2% of those whose portfolio passes 250,000 francs made at least three transactions during the first semester of 1994, as against only 17.3% of shareholders possessing a portfolio of less than 50,000 francs.[46]

These results are not surprising: shareholders' stock activity is greater as the portfolio grows. That puts into perspective findings that one might prematurely draw based on the considerable growth of the number of shareholders. In fact, the active shareholders remain a minority, others only coming to feed the financial market. The Banque de France notes, for example, that "in spite of a better distribution of securities, the concentration of portfolios remains strong: about three fifths of the total shares (61%) are still held in something under 10% of accounts."[47]

Recent evolutions show a tendency to diversify the composition of patrimonies in nearly all social sectors. "Households that have a patrimony not including passbook savings, nor a home savings plan, nor securities, nor insurance life nor a savings-retirement account are more and more rare, whereas it is less and less exceptional to hold all these types of investments."[48] But this diversification remains very unequally shared, and, besides, it serves as a basis of marginalization. One can assume that not being concerned when the shares of privatization candidates are put on the financial market, with a great public fanfare, can lead to a feeling of relative exclusion among those who do not have the means to participate in the general movement. By contrast, the economic and patrimonial practices of rich families are now consecrated. They become the new canon of proper and legitimate social practice. Today, to be head of a strong fortune proves one's expertise, it affirms one's dynamism and one's capacities to free market risks, and therefore one's capacity to surmount those brakes on economic dynamism cited by D. Kessler and A. Masson—i.e. ignorance and risk aversion.

In the mind of society, it is also necessary to participate in these ideological turnings. The triumph, temporary or otherwise, of the market economy is also the triumph of the great families who see the economic and social counter-trends disappear from the political and media stage. The dominant position can seem thus more legitimate and more assured than ever. The possession of a large patrimony also has a symbolic dimension and, today, the simple fact of being rich is a confirmation of excellence. It was not always so. But, in these times of "modern dogmatism" where "the unique thought" triumphs, wealth alone is awarded an unprecedented symbolic power.[49]

Some Examples of Great Fortunes

The diversity of heritages can be read through statistics, but it is even more clear in the description of particular fortunes. Take Mr. and Mrs. Duhamel, industrialists, who in 1994 were relieved of close to 200,000 francs in ISF tax alone, never mind income tax. They reside in a 170 square meter, 8 room apartment situated in the XVIth arrondissement, close by the Avenue Foch. They list their assets at 4,750,000 francs. In addition they possess, in joint ownership and under the "nue-propriété" regime, three rental buildings totaling a habitable floor space of 2,040 square meters, plus 2,000 square meters of professional space. These buildings, situated in the Xth and XIVth arrondissements and in Ivry, in the Val-de-Marrie, hold 125 rooms. Add to these real estate possessions an agricultural estate situated in Seine-et-Marne. The total value of these real estate holdings is estimated to be more than 20 million francs.

The Duhamels own woodlands and other undeveloped lots in addition to farms and agricultural lands, for a total of 213,000 francs (before tax abatements). Their securities portfolio is highly diversified, with shares of SICAVs, French and foreign stocks, and debentures for an amount of 4,815,000 francs. The current amounts, savings accounts and treasury bills represent 1,575,000 francs in liquidities. A life insurance contract offers a redemption value of 300,000 francs and the household furnishings are appraised at 254,000 francs. The total constitutes a taxable net worth of 27,800,000 francs, in round numbers, which a liability of 500,000 francs brings down to 27,300,000 francs. Consequently the amount due to the ISF in 1994 was 194,000 francs. Furthermore, this couple's income, the same year, was 580,000 francs, which means they paid an income tax of 91,000 francs. Their tax payment is therefore 285,000 francs, total. The patrimony is considerable, but still under-valued since the professional heritage is ect to the ISF.

In the same way that modest families use the special issue of the CGT weekly, Working Life, to attempt to make the best use of their fiscal resources, those subject to the ISF have the counsel of the guide published by The Figaro. "Every tax rule has its exceptions," as one may read there. "The ways by which the ISF assesses taxable heritage include a certain number of loopholes or reasons for tax reduction that you need to know. You can organize your heritage so as to either benefit from or lose the benefit of these exemptions."[50] But the foreseeable savings are apparently not on the same order of magnitude as those dreamed of by the readers of La Vie ouvriPre.

Take Miss Riloubeau, for example. She belongs with the very rich indeed. In 1994, she paid nearly 3 million francs in solidarity tax on wealth alone. Residing in a small city of Seine-et-Marne where she lives in a modest pavilion of 90 square meters valued at 1.5 million francs, she is landlord in the Oise and in Seine-Saint-Dennis of many residential buildings and boutiques which she values at 43 million francs. She owns some agricultural tracts valued at about 140 million francs. Her securities portfolio is worth about 20 million francs. She reckons that she enjoys the same sum in the form of various liquidities at the bank.

These examples, to which one could add those recently published in the press, of candidates in the presidential election,[51] confirm the very real concern about diversifying investments. By this criterion, the wealthy families appear to be specialists in the management of patrimony. For Pierre Delalande, of the Groupe Crystal, truth is in the diversification of patrimony. But, of course, the more one diversifies, the more one has only an average return. Rates of 11 to 12% are exceptional and rarely apply to the whole of a heritage. When there is a part that earns 10% and more, there is, undoubtedly, some part that makes less than 5%.

These examples also give points of reference: the sums that fortunes can reach would quickly put in their place the wildest dreams of modest Lotto players. Their record winnings remain very much this side of the real fortunes, which are further underestimated by failing to take antique furniture and art objects into account. These lottery winnings, exceptional as they may be, would not suffice to acquire such a painting or a villa in Saint-Jean-Cap-Ferrat. The levels of fortune become unimaginable for the most part. So many figures, like the distances in interstellar space, defy comprehension.

Income from Capital and Income from Work

Profit-generating patrimonies increased in value by 7% per year from the end of 1990 to the end of 1993.[52] This attractive yield is owed to the strong increase in value of the stock market, French shares having recorded a gain of 32% in 1993, whereas liabilities climbed by 13%. These brilliant results contrast with the mediocre salary adjustments that, in the same period, were only 0.5%, considering social contributions, and even negative, by—0.5%, if one counts only the total gross remuneration of salaried employees. Reports from CERC have made this paradox evident for a long time: incomes on heritage grow more quickly than those from work, and they contribute to deepening inequalities.

If, in 1993, in accordance with the general tax management, the recession modified the structure of tax deductions/required payments, it was no such thing for the ISF. Indeed, "some taxes are visibly impervious to the economic situation. That is the case of the solidarity (social security) tax on wealth. From 4.5 billion francs in 1989, these tax returns went to 7 billion in 1992 and 7.2 billion in 1993."[53]

One must qualify these first approximations, however. If one takes the period extending from the end of the year 1990 to June 1994, estimates bring down incomes on patrimony about to 5%. [54]

Results for 1994 on the whole are mediocre, to the extent that on the Paris Stock Exchange, French assets lost 18% in twelve months. But it is well known that the greater their diversification, the less exposed patrimonies are in difficult periods—diversification which in itself depends, as we have seen, on the aggregate size of the portfolios. Whether business is flourishing, or is mediocre or is even poor, the large fortunes are still the better allocated. With the relative distribution of asset portfolios in those social strata that are more modest than the ones usually interested by this type of investment, the phenomenon might be analogous to the school system. Democratization, in the case of all baccalaureates as in the case of all shareholders, only provokes a transfer of inequalities and hierarchies. For not everyone has the same cultural and social resources to play a successful game on the fields of the school system or the financial system.

The poor performance of the stock market during 1994 and the beginning of 1995 points up the decisive importance of knowledge and ability in this complex domain of heritage management. One must be clever to play the formulas to one's advantage, the combinations that limit the risk of losses and amplify gains. For instance, the life insurance formula that one might consider a real national «tax haven» since 1960, is more attainable than the mythical tropical tax havens. Below seventy years of age it is possible to invest capital in this way in reasonable proportion with regard to the total patrimony. At the time of death this capital is, in principle, at the service of the designated beneficiary. Except for death duties, this is an equity equivalent to a high yield. The *ISF Guide* from *Figaro* is not mistaken when it writes that «the other technique for entering or remaining within the limit is essentially to have incomes that are not considered as such by the tax legislation. One achieves this sleight of hand with life insurance contracts.»

Assuring a good yield on the accumulated heritage does not happen by itself but becomes more and more complex as financial products become more sophisticated. The diversification of forms of heritage inherently requires more collective management.

THE COLLECTIVE MANAGEMENT OF PATRIMONIES

The management of patrimonies takes on more and more collective shapes. This process is manifested according to two main modalities.

First of all, shares in OPCVMs represent a growing proportion of securities portfolios. The aggregate net assets of the OPCVMs went from 0.7 billion francs at the end of 1964 to 1,943 billion in 1990. The success of these financial products was therefore considerable—which makes the saver's relationship to his investment more complex. He no longer owns shares of such and such company, of such and such easily identified industrial enterprise, but constituent parts of a portfolio that is highly diversified and collectively owned. It reinforces the role of the professional mediator who, alone, can master these financial products.

So the management of partimonies has generated a new professional sector. Individuals entrust the management of their securities more and more to specialists, bankers, insurers and lawyers, or even of administrators of heritages that proclaim himself such, their profession not making the object of a regimentation again. This sector of activity saw the blossom of the specialized magazines and, in publications for more general practitioners, of categories dedicated to this management. The *La Vie franHaise, Investir, Mieux vivre votre argent, Gestion de fortune*[55] and many of other publications, such as the "Patrimoines"supplement to *Le Figaro*, *The French Income* or *Echoes*, increase advices, suggestions and surveys to facilitate to their readers this arduous task that became the domestic heritage management. There came to exist, therefore, quite a new category of profession whose contours remain still enough fuzzy. The old business banks are still pursuing an activity that they always had, supervising the biggest fortune, whereas a new emerging party of multitudes invests in a sector where the middle savers, in truth modest, make themselves more and more numerous.

Large banks and large fortune management

Contrary to what one might think, it is a large private business bank, the Bank Paribas, that claims a pioneering role, since the early 70's, in managing the securities of large portfolios by OPCVM. "Today," says Pierre de Leusse of the private management of the Bank Paribas, "close to 90% of the assets that we have under our management are in mutual funds. We consider it quite normal to have a portfolio of 10, 20, 30, 150 or 200 million francs managed in OPCVMs." Even if one wanted, for various reasons, to be managed directly, by mandate,[56] he would not be able to do so with Bank Paribas with a portfolio of under 5 million francs. The usual picture associates "SICAVs with public housing projects and individual direct management with private mansions." However, from a strictly financial point of view, collective portfolio management leads to savings of scale on brokerage fees and rights of custody. Remuneration expenses, computer equipment—administrative costs, generally—are absorbed more quickly with large collective portfolios than with a quantity of small ones. "In the matter of taxes," concludes Pierre de Leusse, "the OPCVMs are favored with regard to direct custody of securities and, in addition, when they serve as collateral for life insurance contracts, after eight years of investment, they benefit from almost complete exemption."

In the upscale banks, the various forms of capital possessed by a family enter into this process of collective administration. This is known as total estate management. Administrators at the Bank Paribas are general practitioners who can take action on matters concerning every component of an estate—securities of course, but also art and real estate—while relying on specialized services in each of these domains. According to Bank Paribas' official brochure on private administration, the general advisor, essential interlocutor of the customer, must take into account "family aspirations and emotional requirements. Each patrimony requires a specific management policy which takes into account both needs and intentions, so as to preserve the family's estate, enrich a collection of paintings, increase the capital of a family enterprise, transmit a difficult-to-divide real estate asset or even to ensure something like a regular income over the long term." The real estate advisory team focuses primarily on Paris and the French Riviera, the areas that represent a sizeable market. Total estate management has been helped by the development of data processing and of software that enable one to consider simultaneously the different components of the estate. According to Pierre de Leusse, providing specialized services in such and such domain of patrimony (from works of art and vineyards, to real estate and life insurance) and, at the same time, general tice administrators, assures both total management and personalized service for each customer at Bank Paribas.

The owner of a fortune has at his disposal today a large range of choices as to how his heritage will be managed. Bank estate planning departments, independent estate management consultants, lawyers, certified accountants, insurance brokers and companies on the stock exchange—so many places and specialized agents exist.

The choices, in this domain, are not based exclusively on economic rationale. As is noted by Pierre Delalande, Sales Manager of the Groupe Crystal, which develops estate management products through the management of portfolios by proxy, guaranteed pooled investment funds and life insurance contracts, "in France, heritage management is a very personal thing. One doesn't like to speak of money. The customer is going to go to someone with whom he feels good, in whom he has confidence. The administrator is like a confidant, like a family physician who is unaware of practically none of the fortunes and misfortunes of the family group." Technical considerations certainly enter into the choice of an administrator, but habit as well, strands of connections sometimes woven into the family chain along several generations with a bank that is already familiar with all your business and in which the confidence is total.

There are also some institutional specializations. Bank Paribas was traditionally an investment bank that took in charge "people who at the time they sold their company, for example, were presented with a sizeable packet of securities that required a strategy in heritage management," according to Pierre de Leusse. It is, moreover, because the original core of Paribas was tied to businesses and companies involved in the private management in the Opera district that gave priority to a stripped down decoration—marble and mirrors instead of 18th century paneling, the conference room with its big oval mahogany table and padded leather armchairs that evoke the board room rather than the muffled lounges of other big banks.

A Select Clientele

However, portfolio owners don't choose their partners single-handedly. The administrators themselves, and particularly banks, reserve the right to select their clientele. This selection operates first according to the volume of the patrimony to be managed. At least when it is a question of admitting a customer into the restricted coterie of bank estate planning centers where the privileged families benefit from extraordinary treatment. Within the banking world there exist specialized services where certain important customers are received with added confidentiality. These services bring together experts of all kinds, financial experts, lawyers and managers. Often the bankers and managers who work with the important customers are themselves descended from the bourgeoisie and sometimes hold not inconsiderable portfolios of their own. These experts notably permit a personalized management of the portfolios greater than a million francs. In order to achieve sufficient diversification, the branch will quietly elefor small shareholders, gilt-edged securities and SICAVS.

The rationale of these banks-within-banks is to provide personalization that increases proportionately as the size of the fortune to be managed increases. This is a constant in the social identity of the great families, of the wealthiest people. They are always the object of a very personalized treatment by service providers, their interlocutors always going out of their way to let them know, or have them believe, that they are recognized and that one knows perfectly well with whom one is doing business. This personal relationship between the customer and those who are in charge of his business or his well-being is found in banks as readily as in, for example, the big luxury hotels where one of the essential features is undoubtedly to provide the guests with attentions that indicate a profound understanding of the people who are served. One of the first effects of wealth is to assure you the attention of all those with whom you have a professional relationship. One is never truly an unknown, whoever one may when one possesses a comfortable fortune. This pleasure is psychological, as well, in it that it resides in this insurance of one's being which is procured by the permanent reaffirmation of the interest caused by your person.

It is much easier to persuade oneself of one's importance when banks and the other administrators of fortunes vie with kindness and attentiveness to attract the richest families into their laps. One former industrialist in the agro-food industry, with an imposing portfolio of 50 million francs after selling his business, had the small branch of his provincial bank managing his fortune. Teams of estate management centers from other establishments then vied to attract this interesting customer, and lunches, parties, invitations of all kinds flowed to seduce him. When the executives of a management center learn that an enterprise is going to be sold (and this happens more often in the provinces, where the industrial and commercial fabric is thicker than in Paris), they intervene and propose investments to the selling party. "We, suppliers [of financial products], we often participate in the manufacture of these proposals, for the financial sector that concerns us," says Pierre Delalande. It is a question of attcting these funds into the orbit of the bank, while making the most appetizing propositions to these sellers of industrial or commercial property, who find themselves at the head of considerable disposable financial masses.

Private estate management at the Bank Paribas was originally organized around the heritages of business owners who were giving up all or part of their business, then it expanded to encompass other types of patrimony coming from families with traditional fortunes or those still in formation. "However," writes François Debiesse, Director of Private Management at Bank Paribas, the sum entrusted to us is generally one million francs at the least."[57]

Banks have studied the bill on trusts proposed by the government, a very French take on "trusts," and the opportunities it might present for their patrimonial clientele. But the Tax Legislation Service (SLF) under the Ministry of Economy and Finance required guarantees that prevented the project from seeing the light of day. The French system of taxation on financial products is aligned with the other countries of the Community, Luxemburg especially. "Standard" classic tax avoidance formulas, such as SOFICAs, are subscribed by customers.[58] Sometimes more complex arrangements are proposed for those who are taxed the most. With such investment products one transforms the customer into a merchant, which permits him to generate from the start losses to post against taxable revenue. But there is a risk because, as merchant, the customer participates in business. One finds products of this type on the market in the hotel sector, for example. Prudence is essential in the choice of such an investment and the assistce of savvy professionals is, in this case, quite indispensable.

These a few examples make it evident that the optimal management of a fortune has become an art that requires very highly developed skills. Perhaps it was always so, but today, unless he is an experienced businessman himself, well-acquainted with the mathematical techniques of financial management, with the infinite subtleties of the tax system and assisted by a competent and devoted team, one can not manage his fortune alone, unless he simply invests it all in rock solid "Head of the Family" securities whose profit is very weak.

All those who have investment account of any significance share an awareness of the complexity of the financial mechanism.

So much so that management services have flourished and in a certain way become democratized. That is one of the effects of the entrance of modest or mid-sized investors into the stock market, favored by the creation of OPCVMs ("organismes de placement collectif en valeurs mobiliPres": SICAV and mutual funds) by the highly publicized privatizations of large companies. Small shareholder inflation seems to lead to overbidding in the search for the most efficient and most prestigious administrators. The big investment banks understand very well how to avoid being invaded by the depreciating mass of these small shareholders, at least within their centers of estate management, and conditions for acceptance there have become draconian. In the nationalized institutions, or those that used to be, like the CIC or the BNP, management by proxy has a relatively modest threshold: a securities portfolio of one million, at the minimum, is enough to get you in the door. The great fortunes prefer the prestigious private investment banks, long accustomed to managing the heritages of the old bourgeoisie and the wealthy aristocracy. The same logic pertains in finance as that which leads people to seek out their own kind where they live or where they spend their leisure.[59]

Large Banks Get Publicity

The big investment banks appeal to their potential customers by placing pages of advertising in very specific magazines, such as *Le Courrier du Jockey Club* or *Intercercles magazine*, a publication that, from 1990 to 1993, has been distributed among members of the higher Parisian clubs.[60] "We've been managing fortunes for three centuries."

"Quite Simply," announces the Bank of Neuflize, Schlumberger, Mallet (NSM)[61], adding: "Our concept is simple: to accompany our clients throughout their lives, to counsel them personally, to orient them efficiently; while refusing artifice and false innovations, because we have been anticipating trends for three centuries and others' innovations are our great classics."[62] The tradition proclaimed here is first, essentially, incontestably, not of flaunting wealth but on the contrary, the long tradition of genuine well-being. NSM advertisements are illustrated with a happy property owner tending his rosebushes and the title of the page is, "Our customers know the true value of things." Another NSM advertisement shows a plain purse set on a piece of inlaid furniture, with the title, "Wealthy people have always liked simple ideas." A third variant is illustrated by what is known as a loveseat, which evokes the muffled and confidential conversations in bourgeois living rooms. The advertising text claims both modernity and a sense of innovation, both experience and expertise, including in the most specialized financial techniques. "Every heritage has its history," is the title of a Bank Paribas advertisement composed with a beautiful classical effect in a similar publication. "Maintaining the future of patrimonial families at the height of their traditions," is the proclaimed ambion with care taken to bring together "the required competencies to play a discrete and permanent supporting role: specialists in forestry and wineries, real estate, and works of art, alongside portfolio managers expert in French, European, Asian and American securities."[63] The multidimensionality of patrimonial reality is well affirmed here. As for the Bank du Louvre, "It addresses itself to private individuals whose large patrimony requires a particularly precise and attentive administration."[64] This precision and attention are symbolized by an illustration of the view of reflecting pools of a French flower garden, the rigor and the classicism of which impose the idea of a flawless order and rationality amid calming luxury. The Bank Indosuez, for its part, speaks of patrimonial engineering and a made-to-order concept of management, which is illustrated by a photograph of a fashion model wearing a haute couture gown by Torrente. One could hardly express more clearly that social success provides this privileeo being always considered in one's singularity, originality, irreducible individuality. When one is a member of the haute bourgeoisie, one is always a name, a person, and whether it is a question of how one dresses or how one manages one's fortune, professionals make sure you know that they treat your case as it deserves, custom fit, precisely to your measure, according to the ease you would like to enjoy. That is how the investment banks present themselves when they want to interest the wealthieindividuals and attract them to their management centers: the exact opposite of the agitated, commercial, disorganized and frantic, in any case frenetic, Paris stock market.

Thus the wealthiest families find, to administer their fortunes, agents with whom they are frequently on the same level. That is true of those investment banks where the executives of the estate management departments belong to the same world, but also of many of the lawyers and some of the accounting professionals. Privileged families benefit from personalized service in all domains. Like the director of a grand palace Frédéric Maître, Deputy Chief Executive of the Bank Hottinguer, must identify himself immediately to his customers: it would be unseemly not to show them that they were considered very important. Which is, above all necessary in all the worldly relations: courtesy is a golden rule which distinguishes every social interchange. "I recognize the voice of every one of my 300 clients on the telephone," affirms Frédéric Maître. "Thus I can greet them before they even have a chance to introduce themselves"[65] One finds this family-like welcome in the settings where meetings take place. Stylish furniture is the rule, while bibelots, art objects and paintings recall the home environment, the sitting rooms of the best neighborhoods. This intimate ambiance, at the Bank Lazard, at the Edmond de Rothschild Financial Company and elsewhere, sets estate planning at the level of a family affair, which one deals with within the family, with the help of a better informed and more competent friend.

Required Threshold of Wealth

Now, it is not laxity that presides at the entrance to this coterie, but a certain level of fortune. For the Bank du Louvre to accord you the privilege of direct management by proxy, the level must be 30 million francs minimum. The administrator can effect transactions in the name of his client, according to the style of management desired by the client and agreed in advance with him. A securities portfolio of at least 5 million would correspond to this level of patrimony. This threshold is "only" 10 million francs at the financial company Edmond de Rothschild, for the total patrimony, and 3 million for the portfolio. The cut-off for administration under OPCVM, that is, in the category of collective savings management, in the form of SICAV or pooled investment funds, palpably less personalized, are not necessarily lower: respectively 30 and 5 million francs at the Bank du Louvre, but only 5 and 1 for Edmond de Rothschild. Paribas, which does not provide direct financial management, has set the patrimony thrld at 10 million francs for administration under OPCVM and at 3 million for the portfolio. But it is known that the Bank Indosuez offers its personalized services only to a very restricted elite, those whose partimony is over 200 million. At that level, our happy privileged ones enjoy the benefits of highly sophisticated technical backing: "personnel experienced in financial engineering [...], direct access to top management, made to order financial and judicial arrangements."[66] Furthermore, when the portfolio reaches several tens of million francs, it can be considered an OPCVM in its own right.

Despite the long tradition of administering fortunes through investment banks, some individuals choose to have their fortunes managed by more independent operators. One might indeed suspect the banks' special services administrations of giving preference to the financial products put together by their own institutions, which are not always the optimal investment for their clients. This suspicion can lead wealthy investors to resort to independent administrators.

Newcomers in the Field of Management

One of the oldest of these private offices, that of Jean-François Gareton, was formed in 1971. This office emphasizes its independence from banking and insurance companies, and thus affirms that it suggests financial products and partners with complete freedom of judgement. The independent advisor, explains J.-F. Gareton, is a bit like a physician. His first step is to prepare a diagnosis based upon an indepth study of the heritage, and the prescription takes the following course: the advisor describes an array of solutions that he considers optimal, bearing in mind the diagnosis, that is the structure of the fortune, and the social, family and demographic characteristics of the client. Following up the actual investments is the third phase. The quality of the service provided in the course of these three phases must rival the service provided by competitors—other private estate administrators but also banks and insurance companies—whose rates can be quite competitive: the administration centers of these institutions can afford to be compensated more modestly because they benefit first of all from the funds entrusted to them in the course of this administration. The office of Gareton, and those who are similar, lives on contracts for service where the compensation is based on the amount of the assets entrusted to management. But they are only intermediaries, whereas the banks, insurance companies and other companies on the stock exchange are the depositories of the sums invested. It also sometimes happens that the advisor may be associated with a bill broker, who then serves as banker for the administration firm's clients.

According to Jean-Luc Bengel, director of the magazine *Gestion de fortune*, there are about 800 private consultants in estate management, plus the thousands of consultants working at banks, financial specialists at insurance companies, lawyers who, since the real estate crisis, have mobilized themselves around financial assets, and professional accountants... "You have today about 40,000 people giving advice in heritage management." And according to J.-L. Bengel again, if one judges by what is happening in England and the United States, the future will bring further prosperity to this profession, especially since computer software today makes it possible to research the optimal solutions. "Any advisor can enter a certain number of factors into his computer and turn out a 25-30 page estate plan in a modest amount of time. Whereas in former times, " concludes J.-L. Bengel, "that would have represented a complex, colossal amount of work."

The profession is still very unstructured, since anyone at all can proclaim himself an "estate planner" overnight, and advertise it by hanging out his shingle.

It is true that there is an employers' union that is trying to impose some order on this. But as is the case with all recent professions, it will take some time to put the professional and ethical standards in place. Of course, at the fringes of the profession, those

---

ISF Statistics

The spatial distribution of wealthy families can be understood from the data for the tax on large fortunes (IGF), which became the solidarity (social security) tax on wealth (ISF). The statistics published by the General Tax Division, even in the highly aggregated form, by *département*, provides precious information. From the number of tax returns by département and the amounts of the payments effected, we may calculate an average amount of tax paid. The number of those liable for the IGF per 1000 inhabitants in each département and in each region allows us to assess their demographic weight. Let's consider the Blue Notes, now the Blue Notes of Bercy, published by the Minsitry of Finance, particularly no. 40, from June 1-15, 1993, which give the final results of the ISF for 1992 and the interim results for 1993. Table 3 presents a list of the 5 regions having the greatest number of residents liable for ISF tax.

---

new arrivals whose references and qualifications are not always well established, concern above all the other new arrivals who are the less wealthy buyers of shares of privatized companies, that is, those who hold modest portfolios of OPCVMs. It would appear that this new and often ill-informed clientele was, first and foremost, the target audience of the 10th conference "Buying and Selling Investments," which was held from the 10th to the 12th of February, 1995, at the Espace Champerret in Paris, with 80 exhibitors giving 30 talks. "There is no lack of pensioners," comments one executive from Bank Paribas, "who are fascinated with the stock market. At the end of conferences the questions asked are about stocks, since these are people with time to devote themselves to their favorit game. And

Table 3. The regions with the greatest concentration of households paying IGF and ISF tax

Region	% Households Paying		% Amounts Paid		1990 Population in
	IGF	ISF	IGF	ISF	
	1982	1993	1982	1993	
Île-de-France	41.6	52.3	53.4	62.0	18.4
Provence-Alpes-Côte d'Azur	10.4	9.6	9.5	6.6	7.3
Rhône-Alpes	7.4	7.0	6.8	6.2	9.2
Nord-Pas-de-Calais	4.1	3.2	3.2	3.3	6.8
Aquitaine	3.8	2.7	2.9	2,2	4.8
Total for France	100,0 (104,000)	100,0 (163,125)	100,0 (2,682,000)	100,0 (7,209,262)	100,0

SOURCE: Les Notes bleues de Bercy. Amounts in thousands of francs.

some of them are besides already past masters in following French securities, working almost full-time with the stock maket newsletters." This conference, with its internal hierarchies and by the absence of upper crust institutions, in particular the great investment banks[67] whose reputation is disseminated through more traditional channels, exposes a field of business in the process of formulation. Banks and insurance companies, private offices, newspapers and magazines, thanks to the physical proximity thus effected, display a professional milieu coming together and in the process of being organized. However, the presentations of the different entities showed, by virtue of their disparity, the reality of a hierarchy which would seem hazy only to the eyes of the uninitiated. The fact that the Groupe Patrimoine Stratégie would be located on Saint-Mandé or the Cabinet du Marais, advisors in estate management, on the rue des Archives, in the IVth arrondissement, whereas the Bank Neuflize, Schlumberger, Mallet is situated in the Avenue Hoche, in the VIIIth, the fact too that Bank Paribas greets its estate management clients just two steps away from the Opera, whereas the Indosuez and the Banque du Louvre have their offices on Boulevard Haussmann, in the same arrondissement—that reflects and reinforces the latent hierarchies in this professional field and among the clients involved. However, one of poles of this field is made up of these independent counselors, often originating from the big private banks, who work exclusively in the service of one big family, of which they become salaried employees, and are considered as such.

Since the real estate crisis, lawyers have gotten involved more resolutely in the field of estate management with the objective of making up for the reduction in the number of authentic deeds. By their position they are better acquainted with the composition of the families' patrimonies and can take a more global approach that takes into account the different elements of the patrimony. But they are less well-informed than the bankers when it comes to the financial subtleties of the stock market and they are not players in this market. In order to give these notaries some exposure in this area and more generally in the area of estate management, the profession created a Notaries Institute of Partimony in 1989 which trained 2,000 notaries in the techniques of this field. Led by Jean Aulagnier, professor at the University of Clermont-Ferrand, this institute provides an education in the area of economics and the various financial investment products.

The advent of lawyers into this sector, limited as yet, is nonetheless not neglible. They are in any case potentially well-placed to play an important role in that their relations with their clients have always been characterized by the confidentiality and familiarity which the great families highly appreciate. However, lawyers are limited by their status. Sophisticated financial arrangements are risky for them because their capacity as ministerial officers does not allow them to cause their clients to run the risk of a tax audit, motivated for example by an abuse of law, especially given that courthouses are rarely indulgent with lawyers, emphasizes master Jacques Larmandes.

And he gives as example the case of a change of matrimonial status followed too closely by the gift/division of property in favor of the children. "There is a risk that the IRS will say you have made your gift only to get a tax break, that it is an abuse of the legal system." There could be no more persuasive way to instill prudence among lawyers that is far greater than that among independant consultants and in the banks.

Increasingly Sophisticated Financial Products

But whatever kind of administrator is involved, whether from a company on the stock exchange, a law office, independent counselors or bank officials, the central tendency seems to be to give to heritage management an increasingly technical twist that requires recourse to collective methods of defining and realizing objectives. Thus, independent consulting firms can also take the form of financial institutions which, without being banks, can whip up financial "products" which it then recommends to its clients directly, or to administrators of fortunes. Among these wholesalers of financial products one may cite the Groupe Cristal, whose services include analysis and advice on financial matters, portfolio managment by proxy, and FCP management. To complete the range of possibilities, a life insurance contract and a retirement plan have been created. Cristal Gestion, which manages FCPs, gives banks, insurance companies, independent advisors on patrimony, and private individuals, techniques that enable them, indiates Pierre Delalande, its sales director, to guarantee their capital. "Furthermore, due to a ratchet effect, the gains are acquired for good." The techniques, which require a very great financial competence, allow the creation of guaranteed financial products. "Through a risk/return analysis and a systematic use of derivatives on margin [Cristal Gestion] guarantees the capital and obtains all or part of the rising market." Such sophisticated products require collective supervision, they are beyond the capacity of a private individual.

That is, in any case, what Jean-Philippe Bouchand, an engineer with the Atomic Energy Police, denounced in an article that appeared in Le Monde.[68] According to him, mastering derivative products requires "a mathematical arsenal at once elegant and efficient, but at the same time difficult to achieve since one needs to reach at least a third scientific cycle to have practiced it!" Derivatives are negotiated contracts whose risks are pegged to securities, but it is the contract that is bought and can be sold. With derivative products, we seem to have reached a new level in financial abstraction and insubstantiality, all taking place as though the world of high finance was wrapped up in an automation enclosing it in its own speculative logic.

The administrators and the producers of these financial products can belong to an employers' association which has been bringing together since 1961 all the managers of SICAV and of the pooled investment funds at the heart of the CNPF. The ASFFI (Association of French Investment Companies and Funds) is an achievement of the president of the Compagnie financière de Suez who wished to protect and inform professionals, and through them, investors, about this type of investment. "The ASFFI represents the profession of collective management before the public powers, the tutelary processes (Management of the Treasury, Commission of Stock Exchange Futures...) and the Market. It is consulted regularly on the range of problems having to do with OPCVM or likely to concern them. It gives its members and its various corresponding members permanent support in the judicial, tax, accounting and technical domains."[69] The trend is converging toward a rationalization of heritage management, taking place due to the reliance on qualified professionals and a more and more advanced collectivization of the forms and methods of management. The great families, surpassed by the sophistication of the products, the internationalization of finance and the complexity of judicial and legal texts, particularly with regard to taxes, are forced to turn themselves over to the knowledge and expertise of the professionals in these matters. But these professionals are most often escapees of the same seraglio, of the haute bourgeoisie itself. From this standpoint, the personalized and individualized administration of large fortunes is in fact the product of multiple interactions and reciprocal observations, exchanges of information and advice, in all a social task confined within a group of equals—work that, at the same time, supports that intense sociability that characterizes high society families.

THE SPATIAL DISTRIBUTION OF LARGE FORTUNES: THE WEIGHT OF ÎLE-DE-FRANCE

Not only are the large fortunes distributed among just a few hands, but they are also strongly concentrated by location. By favoring contacts, this concentration is a factor in the accumulation of other forms of capital—social capital of course, but also cultural, educational, and symbolic capital. The richness of the others, in these diverse modalities of capital, reflects upon each other and has a multiplier effect on the richness of the individual. One is richer in the vicinity of richer people, physical proximity having the effect of increasing the potential of each fortune if it were considered in isolation. By how well equipped they are, by their esthetic qualities, the cultural and social environment— neighborhoods that are very distinct sociologically strengthen those who correspond to the locally dominant group. They plunge people a little deeper into misery, in the poorer quarters, and they magnify the opulence in the richer quarters. Whether one thinks of the disinherited suburbs to the north of Paris or of Marseilles, or the wealthy areas of the west of Paris or the French Riviera: in all these cases spatial proximity exacerbates the features inherent to every family.

The proportion in Île-de-France is astonishing: the region represents 18% of the total French population, but 62% of the sums due for ISF tax in 1993, and 52% of the people liable for the tax. Whether by proportion of those paying the tax, or of the amount to be paid, this percentage increased from 1992 to 1993. Of course, the importance of mobile securities means that the location of the taxed possessions does not correspond exactly to the location where the tax is paid. Still, it is not an indifferent matter to know where the principal domicile of the taxpayer is located. That provides an indication of the usage value of an important asset, the principal residence, and of the means of spacial regiestration of the existence of these families.

The average sum owed by taxpayers subject to the solidatrity tax on wealth in 1993 was 44,195 francs for all of France, but 52,419 francs in the Île de France. It reached 72,313 francs in Paris-Ouest, that is to say in the VIIth, XVth and XVIth arrondissements.

If the data were accessible, one could chart the wealth far more precisely. The Paris region spectacularly concentrates fortunes, well beyond the effect of its demographic weight.

Outside the Île-de-France, 12 départements are above the average national amount of the ISF.[70] The list is fairly surprising: you will not find there certain regions such as the Rhône or the Gironde, despite the long-time presence of a wealthy bourgeoisie, nor the départements well-known for the secondary residences of those privileged by wealth, such as the Alpes-Maritimes, le Var, or the Pyrénées-Atlantiques. Lyon, Bordeaux, Nice, Cannes, the Côte dAzur or Biarritz could have given these départements remarkable scores. But that is not the case. The average payment made, per taxpayer, fluctuate there between 23,000 and 34,000 francs, far from the national average, and very far from the Paris average.

On the other hand, this list also includes the North, an old industrial region whose once famous textile fortunes are largely redeployed by now; Marne, where champagne still flows as a source of wealth; Charente, which no doubt owes its excellent score to cognac; Oise, with its huge agricultural estates and the proximity of Paris. But it is hard to understand how Orne and the Indre made it onto this list, even if, with Normandie and Sologne, they figure as hunting grounds and recreational areas frequented by those with great fortunes. One understands even less the presence of Haute-Saône, Haute-Vienne and Savoie (although the presence of Haute-Savoie, which borders on Lake Geneva, would surprise us less). It would be worthwhile to clarify these unanticipated results of the geographic dispersion of fortunes. But only investigations within the départements in question, or access to the tax documents, would allow that.

The over-arching fact remains of the exceptionally disproportionate weight of certain arrondissements in Paris and of certain départements of the Île de Paris. The average payments of Paris-Ouest (VIIth, XVth and XVIth arrondissements) and of Paris-Nord (VIIIth, XVIth and XVIIIth) are above or in the neighborhood of 70,000 francs. Only the arrondissements of Paris-Est (XIth, XIIth, XIXth, XXth) find themselves below the national average at 29,500 francs. Hauts-de-Seine also scores high (68,800 francs for the north of the département). But if one considers the legal residences of the members of the great social clubs (Automobile Club of France, Cercle de l'Union, inter alia...), one would see far higher averages with the definition of a geographic area considerably more relevant.[71] Thus the Center-West of Paris, the VIIth, VIIIth arrondissements, the north XVIth and the south XVIIth, to which it would be logical to include the township of Neuilly) should reach sums, and numbers of assessed households, at higher than those constituted by the grouping by arrondissements—which are all we have at our disposal. Analyses of studies touching on the patrimonies of the French would show that their concentration was particularly strong at the two extremes of distribution, which an analysis of the data for the IGF and ISF have confirmed for the greatest fortunes. This concentration in the distribution of wealth is paralled by the geographic concentration of its beneficiaries.

While on average, for France as a whole, 2.6% are assessed for ISF, the tally is 7.4 for the Île-de-France. It is 15% for Paris-Sud, 19.7% for Paris-Nord and 49.2% for Paris-Ouest.[72] One can estimate that the number of those who owed ISF tax was considerably over 50% in the arrondissements of the center/west where otherwise the members of the great social clubs are concentrated. Even in Paris-Est, the tally of the assessed remains at 5%, that is close to double the average for France overall. Three other départements in the region are above this number. Hauts-de-Seine, of course, but also Yvelines and Val-de-Marne. Now, nearly all the départements are below this average and vary between 0.6 and 1.8%. Only four départements outside the Île-de-France have more people subject to the ISF tax than the national average—the Alpes-Maritimes (7%) and le Var (3.3%), that is, the residential Midi which one would have expected to present higher average payments, and which makes up for it with the number of people assesed. The Rhône and Haute-Savoie are in the same position.

Two conclusions can be drawn from this data. On the one hand, the demographic weight of the Île-de-France decisively influences the national average, especially as its scores on the two variables studied herein are far above those of the other regions. For France overall, excluding the Île-de-France, the number of people liable for ISF fell to 69,919, which represents 1.5% assessed, rather than 2.6% and an average amount paid of 32,000 rather than 42,000 francs. The role played by the Île-de-France is thus disproportionate in relation to its demographic weight.

On the other hand, there is a fairly cleancut independence between the number of those who owed the tax, and the average amount to be paid. Thus, in Orne, with 0.9% of those assessed, each of the 273 assessed taxpayers paid an average of 56,000 francs. In the same way, rates of assessed taxpayers are especially low, 0.3 or 0.4%, in départements overseas—Guadeloupe, Martinique and Guyana—but the average amount collected exceeds 44,000 francs. Conversely, the number of taxpayers liable in the Alpes-Maritimes is high, at 7%, but the average tax paid is relatively low (31,000 francs). These erratic aspects of the distribution would probably be reduced if one could slice the data more finely. The situation in the Alpes-Maritimes must have to do with the presence of many retirees who are well-to-do, but not so well-to-do that they can retain their Parisian residence. This all leads us to think that the very large fortunes are Parisian, and that the age of retirement, or rather the fact of "retiring from business" as the INSEE so nicely phrased it in its former "nomenclature for socio-professional categories," does not mean, for them, abandoning a second or third residence.

There is only one place that could really be called the chosen land of wealth, and that is Paris. The places mentioned in Table 3 are merely a bit less unfavored than the others. This means that fortune, in common with power, has at the least to sacrifice to French centralism. That makes capitol rhymes with capital. And that is a rich rhyme. Fortunes, which used to be land-based, are less and less so. Economic gambling takes place elsewhere: in the city, in the financial districts, in the Parisian clubs and the great restaurants of the capital, the swank new offices of the La Défense business district or the fine old paneled halls along the boulevards and the avenues of the best neighborhoods. Where the residences are placed geographically is one of the dimensions of the usage value of partimonial possessions. The complete measure of inequality does not stop at the specific and rare benefits that are obtained from being rich among other rich people. It is a lack of privacy that is enriching. The concentratiof wealth among neighboring families facilitates the management of these patrimonies, through the accumulation of social capital which it allows. Meetings, parties, social gatherings, dinners, clubs, boards of directors: the most elevated patrimonies find the most favorable conditions for full expansion in the aggregation of fortunes. The grand fortunes influence urban dynamics by creating the best neighborhoods, prestigious addresses, the "designer" space which, in turn, attracts the covetous attention of business establishments. Rich families, not much interested in re-taking old neighborhods such as Marais, have always been prime movers in the urbanization of western Paris, clearing virgin lands when the pressure of those prestigious activities that spur them on become too strong. After the "Grand Boulevards," there were the Faubourg Saint-Honoré, then the Champs-Élysées and the Avenue Montaigne, then the northern part of the XVIth arrondissment and Neuilly. The desire to be among people of the same bckgroun, and the quality of the spaces thus created, will always be in conflict: these areas are too beautiful and too expensive for company headquarters and luxury trade offices not to try to move in.

The homes of the wealthy nobility and haute bourgeoise are at the same time social prestige, economic value, and cultural asset: they manifest, perhaps more than any other element of patrimony, the multi-dimensionality of fortune.

PATRIMONY FOR PERSONALUSE AND JOINT TRANSMISSION

Patrimony for personal use, that patrimony which, without bringing in any monetary revenue, performs a service that one might compare to natural revenue, supports the practices, the images, the world views that are essential to successful transmission. Patrimony of possession, in the great families, is the solid basis of the "joint transmission" of which economists speak.[73] The château, the great family homes, fashionable furniture, paintings and art objects, antique jewelry, all this patrimony stuffed with knowledge and with symbolic value must, in order to be "appropriated" by those who will also have to pass it down, become integrated culture. The patrimony of enjoyment is at the heart of transmission because the inheritor identifies the family saga through it. One does not form himself as an heir spontaneously. It takes knowledge and ability. "If inheritances allow one to stay well up in the hierarchy of patrimonies over time, then it is probably because there exists a certain complementary relationship between having and knowing. When it turns out otherwise, the human partimony or the cultural patrimony having been inadequate, the traditional patrimony can serve for a while as a 'parachute' but not for many generations."[74]

Money also confers talent. At least the talent for assuming the management of the fortune, of knowing how to face the demands of wielding a considerable fortune. There is technical mastery, of course, in regard to the diverse forms of investment and the choices to be made, depending on their various rates of return. One must also be able to maintain and nurture the social capital accumulated by the preceding generations, to extend the network of relationships in the various domains of social activity. But wealth enables something priceless to dominate—having time. For fortune allows leisure time that is put to use in nurturing the different forms of capital, in particular through the high society life. There again, André Babeau puts forward the idea that the level of financial information and building of capital are probably linked in a positive way to the level of wealth and that, as a consequence, the return for a given type of asset is likely to vary as a function of the volume of assets owned. These considerations could, over time, justify the poll-tax based electoral system on the grounds that wealth was a guarantee of competence. Jules Lepidi cites Benjamin Constant, who favored this system during the Restoration. "Only property," wrote Constant, "provides that leisure which is indispensable for the acquisition of insights and rectitude of judgement. Only property makes men capable of exercising political rights."[75]

At the level of fortune that we are analyzing, one might think that there could be no other model in these families than the "dynastic" model of economics. Learning to be an heir worthy of its name, is also learning to transmit it, and above all to internalize the moral requirement of transmission. The theory of a life cycle, which reduces the plans and actions of each actor to the level of his own sole existence, certainly does not pertain in these aristocratic and bourgeois lines where the first duty is to assure the continuity of the generations. Why do these households adopt this behavior, this relationship with time? The answer lies within the patrimony itself. There are forms of wealth that carry within themselves the requirement of being transmitted.

Notes

1. André Villeneuve, "Les formes multiples de la pauvreté et le rôle des difficultés de jeunesse," INSEE, *La Société française. Données sociales 1993*, p. 363-369.

2. Tax Council, Eighth Report to the President of the Republic relating to the taxation of capital, Paris, official newspaper of the French Republic, no. 4063, 1986.

3. Alain BIHR and Roland PFEFFERKORN, (French) Deciphering Inequalities, Paris, Syros, 1995, chapter vii, "Inequalities of Inheritance," p. 242. See also, by the same authors, "Wealth, Statistical Terra Incognita." Economic Alternatives, no. 25, 3rd Quarter 1995 (from the series: "The Rich"), p. 8-12.

4. Denis Kessler et André Masson, "Le patrimoine des Francais : faits et controverses", INSEE, Social Data 1990, p. 156-166.

5. INSEE (Institut national de la statistique et des études économique) publishes the survey Logements et actifs financiere, as well as an accounting of inheritances, in collaboration with the Banque de France. These data are the basis of our approach to questions of household wealth. CERC (Centre de l'études des revenues et des cofts, "The Center for the Study of Incomes and Prices") and CREP (Centre de recherche économique sur l'épargne, "Economic Research Center on Savings") published and continue to publish certain specific surveys. CERC was suppressed in 1993 by a discreet amendment of the 5-year law on employment. Very independent, CERC, whose studies gave evidence of increasing inequalities, had annoyed more than one government. It has been replaced by CSERC, the Conseil supérieur de l'emploi, des revenus et des cofts (the Superior Council on Employment, Incomes and Prices).

6. For a systematic exposition of the habitus notion, see Pierre BOURDIEU, Le Sens pratique, Paris, Minuit, coll. "Le Sens commun," 1980, especially Chapter III: "Structures, Habitus, Practices."

7. See Pierre BOURDIEU and Jean-Claude PASSERON, *Les Héritiers. Les étudiants et la culture*, Paris, Minuit, 1964, and Pierre BOURDIEU, *La Distinction, op. cit.*

8. Comptes de patrimoine (INSEE and Banque de France), // get French///

9. Erving GOFFMAN, Asiles, Paris, Minuit, coll., "Le Sens commun," 1968.

10. Lottery winners, at least those of very modest means, would provide a very interesting test population from this point of view: how do people manage a fortune for which nothing prepared them, and for which they do not have at their disposal the necessary specific resources?

11. Jules LEPIDI, La Fortune des FranHais, Paris, PUF, coll,. "Que sais-je?" No. 2424, 1989, p. 80-84, and Le Nouvel Observateur, No. 1197, October 16-22, 1987.

12. André BABEAU, Le Patrimoine des Franc\ ais, Paris, La Decouverte, coll "Repe\ \ res," 1989, p. 44-45, and L'Expansion, no. 340, September 23 to October 6, 1988.

13. "The total of private fortunes in 1954, expressed in germinal francs [that is to say brought back to their value to the 17 germinal year XI, either April 7 1803, the date of the establishment of the modern monetary institution], barely reaches its 1913 total, diminished by the losses of two wars," notes J. LEPIDI (*Op cit.*, p. 18). In 1908, private fortunes represented 5.7 times the national income; the corresponding figure was only

1.4 in 1953 (ibid., p. 19).

14. *L'Événement de jeudi* also published an analysis of the "nouvelles 200 familles" (no. 372, December 19-25, 1991). L'Expansion had published two reports prepared by Pierre Beaudeux on the 50, then on the 100 "Richest People in France" in its numbers 274 of December 6-19, 1985 and 301 of January 23-February 5, 1987. Le Nouvel Iconomiste of October 14, 1994 (no. 967) gives the ranking of the 400 largest professional fortunes, the survey itself appears in No. 1017, October 5, 1995.

15. *Le Nouvel Économiste*, no..340, p. 68-69.

16. Conseil des Impôts, op. cit., Table 11, p. 20.

17. See *L'Expansion*, no. 340, September 23-October 6 1988, p. 128.

18. See L'Expansion, no. 340, p. 114, or Le Nouvel Économiste, 967, p. 76,

19. A. BABEAU, Le Patrimoine des FranHais, op. cit., p. 31-32,

20. Furthermore, a lack of male descendents may be a factor in some of these old families disappearing from the lists. To appreciate the real meaning of the absence of certain names from the list of 200 families, one must verify that the lineages are not continued under another name, for lack of male heirs.

21. Dennis KESSLER and André MASSON, "Qui possPde quoi, et pourquoi?", Revue d'economique financiere, no. 10, 1989.

22. Dominique MERLLII, Les EnqueLtes de mobilitJ social, Paris, PUF, coll. "Le Sociologue," 1994, p. 23.

23. Ibid., p. 23-24.

24. See A. BIHR and R. PFEFFERKORN, DJchiffrer les inJgalitJs, op. cit., chap. XII, 3rd part, "La reproduction des inJgalitJs," p. 518-546.

25. Pierre BOURDIEU and Monique de SAINT MARTIN, "Le Patronat," Actes de la recherche en sciences sociales, no. 20-21, March-April 1978, p. 65.

26. P. ALLARD, M. BEAUD, B. BELLON, A.-M. LÉVY and S. LIÉNART, Dictionnaire des groupes industriels et financiers en France, Paris, Le Seuil, 1978, p. 19.

27. Bernard MARGUERITE, "Crise du syste//me financier et reproduction de l'oligarchie financiere//,Le Seuil,1982. See also Michel BAUER and Bénédicte BERTIN-MOUROT, Les 200. Comment devient-on un frand patron?, Paris, Le Seuil, 1987, and L'Acce//s au sommet des grandes entreprises françaises (1985-1994), Paris, CNRS, 1995.

28. Daniel BERTAUX, Destins personnels et structure de classe, Paris, PUF, 1977, p. 66.

29. Pierre BIRNBAUM's analyses on "the myth of rich people" are based on the record of political speeches and attitudes. It is true that "the Rich" and "the 200 families" are sometimes rudely caricatured there, and that this "mythology" is very distinctly tinged with anti-semitism, including in the old texts emanating the French Communist Party. Furthermore, Pierre Birnbaum does not deal with real fortunes and the family or other networks: the mythical character of the rich is established only through such data as voting to the right of the social categories with average or modest means. The reasoning is that opinions and electoral behaviors are fluid and present themselves as a continuum, sufficiently so that the recurrent opposition of "the people" and "the rich" appears to the author to raise a representation, both erroneous and biased, of the social world. If it is true that this opposition is in part something of a myth, by reason of its strong symbolic charge, it is hoped that the present work will shhe size of the social distance that separates the most privileged factions of society from the masses of the middle and popular strata in their lifestyles, their resources, their access to culture, their opportunities for social promotion, etc. See Pierre BIRNBAUM, Le Peuple et les gros. Histoire d'un mythe, Paris, Hachette, coll. " Pluriel ", 1995 (Ire édition: Paris, Grasset, 1979).

30. Stéfan LOLLIVIER and Daniel VERGER, Le Patrimoine aujourd'hui. Beaucoup entre les mains de quelques-uns..." INSEE, DonnJes sociales 1990, p. 167-170, figure 1, p. 169. These figures can be estimated in today's francs using the consumer price index. But that would be somewhat deceptive: all of the CERC's

studies have shown that during the last two decades income from capital increased far more rapidly than income from work. Bringing the values given here uniformly up to date would still conceal the growing concentration of wealth. It is sufficient to take into account the structures of distribution while knowing that they underestimate the inequalities that one would find today.

31. Véronique SANDOVAL, La grande bourgeoisie, une planPte à explorer." La Pensée, no. 290, November-December 1992, pp. 65-74.

32. This number corresponds to the net worth of households, less debts, and gold, jewelry, precious objects and art objects—assets which are in any case scarcely to be found in the less well-endowed households. Professional assets are included. Source: Conseil des imp^ts, Huitième Rapport..., op. cit., table no. 1, p. 12.

33. This is again referring to net taxable assets, but without taking into account collectibles and art objects, including professional possessions. Source: VIIIth report of the Conseil des imp^ts, op. cit., table 135, p. 124. Thus it reflects a seriously underestimated heritage.

34. A. BIHR and R. PFEFFERKORN, Déchiffrer les inégalitées, op. cit., Chapter VII, "Les inegalit//es de patrimoine", p. 246.

35. A. BABEAU, Le Patrimoine des Franc//ais, op. cit., p. 117.

36. VIIIth report of the Conseil des imp^ts, table 134, p. 123. In 1993 the number of those subject to the tax had increased considerably, passing 160,000. This growth can be imputed to various factors, including the increase in the value of real estate, particularly in the Île-de-France region, and the advances of the stock market since 1985-1986. But these two factors reversed themselves in the recent period. We have no detailed analyses of the structure of the greatest patrimonies liable to ISF after 1985. As far as the discussion of the possibility of a heritage tax since the end of the 1970's, one may consult the Rapport de la commission d'étude d'un prélèvement sur les fortunes, Paris, La Documentation française- Union général d'éditions—10/18, 1979.

37. D. KESSLER and A. MASSON, Le Patrimoine des Français, op. cit., p. 159-160.

38. A. BABEAU, Le Patrimoine des Français, op. cit., p. 87, and G. CANCEILL, "Les revenus fiscaux des ménages en 1984", Les Collections de l'INSEE, series M, no. 139, 1989. Unfortunately, more recent tax returns that would show the composition of heritages according to their level are not available. Amounts by socio-professional category, published by the INSEE, show that in 1988 the categories that controlled some of the largest heritages are also those for which the patrimony of profit is largest in relative (and absolute) value.

39. V. SANDOVAL, "La grande bourgeoisie...", op. cit., p. 72.

40. Which is confirmed in the study 'Financial Assets' from INSEE. See S. LOLLIVIER and D.VERGER, "Le patrimoine aujourd'hui", op. cit., figure 1, p.169. To do that it would suffice to apply the breakdowns used in Table 1 above, to the sizes of the patrimonies given in the study.

41. Jean-Jacques MALPOT, Véronique PAQUEL and Daniel VERGER, "Que possèdent les diverses catégories sociales?" INSEE, Données sociales 1993. The assets studied are savings accounts, investment in homes, transferable assets, life insurance and retirement savings, and finally, home ownership. The patrimony of these modest households was 20,000 francs lower in 1992, the wealthiest households having been defined as those that controlled a heritage of over 1,500,000 francs—that is 10% of households.

42. D. KESSLER and A. MASSON, Le Patrimoine des Français..." op. cit., p. 161. The authors publish results that concern the following assets: checking accounts, savings accounts, bonds and time deposits, mortgage accounts, residential real estate, life insurance, stocks and bonds, investment properties, professional assets.

43. Banque de France, COB, SBF, Les Porteurs de valeurs mobilières,, op,. cit.

45. Ibid., p. 93. The largest shareholders are defined as those having a portfolio greater than 250,000 francs—about one million shareholders. The most active shareholders made at least six transactions, purchases or sales, in a semester—about 650,000 people.

47. Monique CHOCRON and Lydie MARCHAND, "Les portefeuilles de titres des personnes physiques à fin 1993," Bulletin de la Banque de France, no.10, October 1994, p. 109.

48. J.-J.MALPOT, V. PAQUEL and D. VERGER, "Que possèdent les diverses catégories sociales?", op. cit., p. 392.

49. See Ignacio RAMONET, "La Pensée unique", Le Monde diplomatique,No. 490, January 1995.

50. Le Figaro économie, Guide de l'ISF 1995, p. 10.

51. One finds the same patrimonial diversity in M. and Mrs. Chirac's tax return, with real estate holdings in Paris and in Corrèze and a securities portfolio in the amount of 3,500,000 francs. One can estimate their total heritage at about 7,300,000 francs since they paid 13,707 francs to the ISF in 1994, according to their statement to the press in March 1995.

Mr. and Mrs. Balladur paid 124,150 francs for the solidarity tax on wealth. Their patrimony is real estate, with a large apartment in a beautiful neighborhood of Paris, a villa in the center of Deauville and a chalet in Chamonix, but it also encompasses valuables with a securities portfolio valued at 4.5 million francs. Mr. and Mrs. Balladur cannot pretend to the status of a "large fortune" as it is defined by the private services office of the Bank Paribas, whose floor is fixed at 50 million francs, since a tax payment of 124,150 francs corresponds to a taxable estate of 22 million francs—more or less.

52. According to calculations performed at the request of the Conseil supérieur de l'emploi, des revenus et des cofts (The Superior Council on Employment, Incomes and Costs), CSERC—which replaced the CERC—that take into account profit-generating patrimonies overall, that is "the ensemble of physical and financial investments that individuals make when they put buildings, money, or land at the disposal of other people in exchange for a monetary remittance," which excludes the patrimony for personal use, and professional tools. This increase in value is calculated based on revenues (interest), and also on possible appreciation or depreciation of the assets.

53. Laurent MAUDUIT, "Un bilan de la Direction générale des imp^ts", Le Monde, January 4,1995.

54. According to INSEE, incomes on profit-generating patrimony reached 4.2% per year from the end of 1991 to the end of 1994, less inflation. See Laurent MAUDUIT, "Les revenus du patrimoine continuent de prospérer," Le Monde, September 15, 1995.

55. The monthly magazine Gestion de fortuneis intended for estate planning professionals who are independent counselors or bankers, notaries and certified accountants. Yet 40% of subscribers to this magazine are individuals. «It is an upscale magazine," considers its editor in chief, Jean-Luc Bengel, "which intends to be at the same level of information as the best professional. » Created three years ago, Gestion de fortunesells as many as 20 000 copies. But magazines like Investir, or Mieux vivre votre argent, have press runs of several tens of thousands.

56. That is to have a portfolio composed of stocks, not mutual funds, but under the portfolio management service of the bank.

57. 1995 ISF Guide, op. cit. This "manual" starts with an interview with François Debiesse, "Private Management: Objective Quality," and closes with an article entitled, "Management by Objectives, a Scholarly Weighing of Security vs. Appreciation," by Alain Leclair, Vice-president of Paribas Asset Management.

58. Companies for the underwriting of film and audiovisuals (SOFICA), created in 1985, were intended to divert savings toward this sector. The amount invested can be deducted from taxable income, up to 25%.

Profitability depends on the commercial success of the works produced. The Malraux Law, which dates from 1962, permits the deduction from taxable income of work undertaken on historically significant real estate that represents something of historic interest. Of course it is mainly the rich families who live in residences of historic interest. They alone have the means to have such work done; it is they who benefit most from this Malraux Law. See F. TEULON, Vocabulaire monétaire et financier, Paris, PUF, coll. « Que sais-je ? », No. 2628, P. 66 et 112.

59. On this theme, see: Michel PINÇON and Monique PINÇON-CHARLOT, Dans les beaux quartiers, Paris, Le Seuil, 1989.

60. L'Automobile Club de France, le Cercle du Bois de Boulogne, le Cercle de l'Union Interalliée, le Polo de Paris, le Jockey Club, and a few others.

61. « NSM was at first the largest bank of the protestant bourgeoisie. The Peugeot family and their allies, are, for example, clients of this establishment." Jack DION and Pierre Ivorra, Sur la piste des grandes fortunes, Paris, Messidor, 1985, p. 185.

62. In Le Courrier du Jockey Club, XV, June 1993.

63. Ibid., XVI, December 1993.

64. Intercercles magazine, n' 13, Winter 1993.

65. Armelle ORY-LAVOLLEE, " Gestion de fortune: quelle banque choisir " La Vie Française, December 31, 1994 to January 6, 1995, p. 36-38.

66. Ibid.

67. In 1995 Paribas did not have a stand at the conference, but one of its representatives gave a presentation.

68. « Marché dérivés: pour une pédagogie du risque », Le Monde, Tuesday March 14, 1995.

69. ASFFI, OPCVM 1994, Paris, ASFFI, 1994, p. III. This is in reference to a directory of all the OPCVMs.

70. In descending order: Charente, Savoie, Orne, Indre, Haute-Vienne, Haute-Saône, Martinique, Guyana, Marne, Oise, Nord, Guadeloupe.

71. Dans les beaux quartiers, op. cit., chap. II. p. 25-29.

72. These tallys were calculated based on ISF returns for 1991 (Les Notes bleues de Bercy, n' 18, 1-15 July 1993) and the census returns for 1990.

73. A. BABEAU, Le Patrimoine des français, op. cit., p. 97.

74. Ibid., p. 101-102.

75. J. LEPIDI, La Fortune des Français, op. cit., p. 59.

CHAPTER II

The Fief, or the Rural Roots of the Great Families

Time, as materialized for several generations (sometimes for several centuries) in the family mansion, and inscribed in the family registers, is the recorded lineage in a local space where it weaves itself into complex social relationships. The wealthy families of the aristocracy and the old bourgeoisie appreciate all signs that escape the wear and tear of time, because they depend on time, symbolized by the succession of generations, to assure and to legitimize their dominant positions. For these families, the past is both collective and familial. The heritage is not attributed, in representations or practices, to such and such individual but to the lineage. The lineage exists over time, the only thing that can establish legitimacy. Through the permanence that it establishes, time is an ally with the name, but also with the heritage and its transmission. The composition of family heritages is a translation of the requirement of denying the ephemeral.

The castle in the family's provincial cradle, the family seat of the 18th century in the town of Saint-Germain or the old city of Grasse, the large bourgeois apartment from the turn of the century, all these habitats constitute what we will call patrimonial capital in that these real estate possessions combine economic capital, cultural capital and symbolic capital. They are recorded over a long period, unlike the Île-de-France style house that is expected to be held only for the span of one generation. There is no castle without fief, without those relationships created by grants and counter-grants between the lord and villagers—because one cannot be rich alone, by anonymous means. Wealth, at least to endure and be transmitted, must be rooted in the social relations with the group of peers, but with all categories of the population as well. This recognition, the more easily acquired since the game of condescension and paternalism has been mastered better by the dominant class than by others, is necessary to legitimize the unequal relationships that would not last without this guaranty.

IMMOBILE TIME

In the 18th century, Urban des Monstiers married Quitterie du Fraisse, the only daughter of the Lord of Fraisse, a domain situated close near Angoulême. Since that time, the des Monstiers have been the successors of the Fraisses. In 1994 Louis des Monstiers, 27 years old, knows that he will have to assume the burden of maintaining the family's presence, and he prepares himself to do so. This is a family whose alliances, throughout the centuries, have permitted them to diversify the heritage. To carry on into the 20th century François des Monstiers-Mérinville, the present landowner, grandfather of Louis, married a Miss Darblay, whose fortune was founded on the paper industry. Land, real estate and securities are thus mingled in the des Monstiers' fortune.[1]

The approach to Fraisse is majestic. A vast court, enclosed by buildings forming a U, precedes the Renaissance castle constructed around 1550. To the left, the outbuildings are extended by stables constructed in the 17th century, along the length of the former moat. To the right, one can see what remains of the "old castle", as Marquis François des Monstiers-Mérinvilles calls it.

That is the ch>teau constructed in the 15th century (the primitive 13th century ch>teau having burnt during the Hundred Years War). This old castle is in oblique line with regard to the main body and it includes two towers. The large building that completes the U on the right is more recent and is used for agricultural purposes. The estate's Director of Agrculture lives there with his family.

The whole ensemble of ancient buildings is registered in the Supplementary Inventory of Historic Monuments. The exterior doors of the Renaissance building and two interior doors (which open onto the main staircase), as well as the fireplaces, are classified. These elements, in the Italian style, are decorated in polychrome marble. Inside, feminine busts of porcelain decorate the doorways giving onto the main staircase.

Long passageways lead to rooms on various levels. Parquet floors, some dating from the time of construction, are composed of large boards of oak, extremely worn but perfectly waxed. There are a considerable number of rooms and an even more significant area if one takes into account the attics, out buildings, the stables, and barns. Some spaces are under-utilized and some activities are dormant. No one practices horsemanship any longer and there is not a single horse at the ch>teau. The stables are empty and, in the tack room, saddles and harnesses are disappearing under dust and cobwebs. In the castle itself, some chambers are abandoned to the marginal role of storage room, where various objects that have fallen into disgrace are piled on top of each other. In one of them are piles of books that no longer fit in the library. Everywhere, on furniture, on doors, are locks, in such great number that everyone simply leaves the keys on top—which is fun for the children but causes the parents a great deal of worry. No doubt these locks and keys have the power to stimulate the childish imagination and to maintain the magic of such a house. These old homes are very efficient supports for the memory of childhood years. All those who have spent part of their young years in such a setting retain a very lively memory of that time.

A bust of Bishop Jean des Monstiers, who built the Renaissance castle, adorns the rear faHade of the main building. With his beard trimmed short, his hat and his sagging neck, he reminds one of Henri IV. In all the rooms, portraits and mementos of forebears abound. Members of the family and of personalities from distant epochs are represented in miniatures collected on a panel in the grand summer salon.

There is a summer palace and a winter palace, for reasons of economy—to heat such a space in its entirety is unthinkable, it would take a fortune every winter. Consequently, the whole family moves into the left wing when the frosts come. The main building is given up to low temperatures. The hallways and staircases are unheated, so that to get to one's room one must face the risk of getting a severe chill. This is only one of less agreeable aspects of the life in a castle, which is not always as one might imagine, even though there have been some improvements. The adults still remember long dark passageways where, on evenings with a full moon, the pallid light let show portraits of forebears and trophies of deer or boar that, under this lighting, took on fantastic appearances—impressive decor that was necessary to face before making to one's familiar, reassuring room. Electricity has only attenuated this magic forever engraved in memory.

Summer, on the other hand, is pleasant. There is plenty to do, considering the immensity of the place. Those reception rooms, dining room and salon that are heated in the winter are already vast. The grand salon that is only used in summer is two times larger, with a monumental chimney (registered on the protected site list) that hardly works, and many portraits of forebears.

Even the family members sometimes have the impression, when they visit the castle, of rediscovering forgotten places, of forsaken places where old furniture, papers, disdained trinkets wait that one would very much like to go through. There is plenty of space.

The Château as a Place of Memory

The castle of Fraisse overflows with memory, like so many of its counterparts—it is memory crystallized, especially given that the same family has lived there since the 13th century. In addition to several hundred old bound books and more recent books, the library, refurbished in the 19th by the grandfather of the present landlord, contains a few dozen cardboard boxes where the family archives are filed. Classified by themes (wills, marriage contracts...) and by geographical region (Fraisse, but also Languedoc, where a branch of the family lived for several generations), these archives represent a mass of information of a rare wealth on one same lineage.

Louis, the eldest grandson of François, Marquis des Monstiers, to whom the domain will devolve, undertook to reclassify all these old books and these more or less abandoned documents. He protects the venerable leather bookbindings with a fungicidal and insecticidal wax patented by a laboratory of the CNRS and made from beef hooves. Gradually, this part of the family memory is taking on a more pleasant aspect. But the richness of that which has thus far been preserved of the domestic past seems to be far greater than free time and the taste for dusty old papers, available in unequal measure, has allowed to be exploited. In any case, there was a student outside of the family who has written a paper on the history of the château and of Jean des Monstiers.[2] However, Marquis François des Monstiers puts his leisure time to use in typing up the family's history as it was penned by his grandfather, who thus made a work that is both a memoire and a genealogy. As difficult as it may be to come up with anything significant beyond the grandparents' generation in most French families, still, in the case of the nobility and, to a lesser degree in the families of the old bourgeoisie, the accumulated memories are considerable.

The ancestral portraits that decorate many walls in the receiving rooms were labeled by Marquis François des Monstiers and his grandson after they had identified each one with the help of inscriptions on the back of the pictures or on the ancient plaques. Louis des Monstiers remembers that, as a child, living under the omnipresent gaze of his forebears worried him a little, as if he had felt already weighing upon him a moral obligation: to continue keeping the family alive by preserving its ancestral home. From time to time he finds resemblances between one or another living relative and such and such portrait of the 16th or the 17th Century. He points out these resemblances with an obvious pleasure: they are one of the signs of continuity over the centuries. Besides, the ancestors are well enough known that jokes and stories about them still circulate.

One of walls of the "winter" salon is covered with seven pictures painted in the 19th century, representing the château de Voisins, in the département of Yvelines, of which the maternal grandparents of Marquis François des Monstierses had been the owners. They sold it to come closer to the domestic cradle by purchasing the château of Sannat, a few kilometers from Fraisse, where some cousins of the des Monstiers still live today. These requisite pictures reveal the importance conferred upon the family home. In every family it figures among portraits of ancestors, whether in the form of paintings, engravings or photographs. As if the château itself were part of the family, as if objects and bodies should be as one.

The relationships with the local population

Proximity between the lord's domicile and those of the farmers or agricultural workers allows for looking back and forth, a certain mutual surveillance. Each lives permanently under eyes of the other.

At Fraisse there is a certain evolution since the estate passed into direct stewardship, which means that the lands are work by salaried employees, certainly interested in the results of the estate, but who see their principal remuneration in the form of salary. Once, sharecropping was the rule. After the law of 1946, which made the maximum share of the landowner 33% rather than 50%, the sharecropping formula was no longer so profitable[3] and Marquis François des Monstiers took over the management of the estate, which is carried on today by his son, Jean-François, Louis' father.

The effects are felt in the social relations between owner and peasants. The latter saw the change to salaried employee as a deterioration in their social standing. The domain employs 5 salaried employees, of which 3 are unmarried. They live in the ancient farmhouses that were occupied once by whole families, and Marquis François des Monstiers complains about the emptiness thus created. He regrets the absence of children that once enlivened the courtyards of the farms and of the castle.

But, in spite of his relative remoteness, since he no longer directs the estate and spends most of his time in Paris, Marquis François des Monstiers remains a local personality. While passing through Nouic, a village on the territory where the domain is situated, he is recognized and greeted by a villager who tips his hat upon seeing him, although he is in the passenger seat of a car that is not known in this area. In the bakery at Mézières-on-Issoire, the next town, a conversation takes place between the baker and the Marquis, who asks him for news of his father: he had once been in the service of M. des Monstiers, who uses his first name. A public works employee walks in and greet him with a

"Hello, Monsieur Marquis!" that appears entirely natural. The lord preserves the status of a notable, and relations with the locals remain imprinted with a certain paternalism, a magical relationship, familiar and at the same time unequal, that traditionally governs relations between master and servant. [4] The lords must maintain good relations with the village and insinuate themselves as much as possible into its social fabric, as much for material purposes, by making funds available for certain tasks, charitable or otherwise, as for symbolic reasons, in establishing the legitimacy of domination. Without this presence in the mesh of local life, there can be no lords worthy of the name.

Privatization of the School and the Church

The des Monstiers family built a Catholic private school at Nouic and Quitterie, today aged forty-two, was a pupil there. She remembers putting a friend in her place when she was bothering her, by reminding her that her father owned the school and that she should respect the daughter of the master of the place.

But the family's ubiquity especially makes itself felt in relations with the church. The château was the place for family ceremonies not long ago. Quitterie was baptized there and made of her first communion there. During the Marquis des Monstiers' childhood, Mass was said there twice a week, on Thursdays and Sundays. In a small vestry annexed to the chapel one can still find the ministerial gowns and the chalice. Some of M. des Monstiers' ancestors are buried in this chapel.

The family also has a small private chapel in the modest church of Nouic. Occupying a part of the transept, this chapel is maintained by the family. M. des Monstiers changed the 19th century stained glass window that illuminates it. In the Saint-Sulpice style, this stained glass window really did not go well. The new ones, in an abstract style, integrate better. The 19th century stained glass window had already been a gift from the family. The new one is dedicated to Saint Quitterie, a forename valued by the des Monstiers since it is through Quitterie du Fraisse that the palace became part of the family heritage.

While the church was being restored, M. des Monstiers replaced the parquet which covered the floor of this chapel with tiles similar to those utilized in the other parts of the building. The family's involvement extends beyond the private chapel. So M. and Mme des Monstiers donated a granite statue of the Virgin, found during a stay in Brittany where Mrs. des Monstiers had a large family home on an exceptional piece of land at Dinard. At the end of the 19th century, the des Monstiers family offered a statue of Saint François, whose pedestal carries a plaque with the inscription, "offered by the Marquis and the Marchioness des Monstiers-Mérinvilles." This statue is now surrounded with plaques engraved with the names of victims of the last wars.

The des Monstiers chapel is reached by a small side door, to which the family does not have the key, in any case. That is left with someone whose house faces the church. During services, no one takes a seat in the chapel unless he is extremely wealthy and there are available seats "at the des Monstiers'."

To the right of the small altar decorated with a pietà, an old wooden panel bears the names of the family members buried in this chapel. Urban and Quitterie des Monstiers come first. Their interment is mentioned as having taken place before 1280. The last members of the family mentioned were buried shortly before the Revolution.

Thus, religion is deeply integrated in the family life. Like culture, it is inseparable from the life of the lineage and the daily existence. By these two chapels, the one at the castle and the one in the church, by the very presence of the burial places within the religious sites, there is a very strong interpenetration between religion and the family—it contributes intensity and depth to an existence that no doubt finds a certain serenity there.[5].

Local roots were also a factor for families of minority religions, such as certain families of the Jewish haute bourgeoisie. Caroline de Ricqlès, whose paternal ancestors, originally from Amsterdam, made a fortune in the beginning the 19th century in Lyons, manufacturing and merchandising drinks and candies with a mint base (the Ricqlès mint), had for maternal ancestors a family in the wool industry at Elbeuf. The brothers Maurice and Théodore Blin founded the enterprise in Bischwiller, Alsace, in 1827. They left Alsace, which had become German, and reinstalled themselves at Elbeuf. "The workers followed on foot," reports Caroline de Ricqlès. The enterprise was largest in the city and at the beginning of the century employed 1200 workers. The social relations were imprinted with paternalism. The Blin ancestor had "created a sort of social security within the factory, at a time when social welfare absolutely did not exist. He constructed dwellings for workers. I remember that my grandmother used to bring cand to every worker who had just given birth." Even though its inhabitants were Jewish, the "château" (or, rather, a large bourgeois house) that accompanied industrial success at that time was therefore very well embedded in its social environment, here more urban than rural. This integration did not prevent the Blins from maintaining the Jewish tradition since these industrialists had a synagogue built, which one supposes was utilized only by some related or allied families, the Fraenckels, Bernheims or Herzogs (the family of André Maurois). But one sees the same process of integration of large fortunes into the local scene, be they land-based or industrial, and supporters of the dominant Catholic religion or members of a minority religion.

Fraisse is an old and respectable castle, but it is not a luxurious place. Its owner pays the solidarity tax on fortune; yet Fraisse doesn't come across as a high status home. The symbolic value of Fraisse does not lie in an obvious magnificence, but in time itself, which is crystallized there. In the abundance of space also—the inimitable assurance conferred by its perfect integration into the landscape, its old stones so deeply rooted. Comfort is not the castle's strong suit, even though it is not lacking in modern amenities. For all that, this is not a home hit by obsolescence like those mentioned in the Sixties when the spectacular destruction of towers attracted idlers and television reporters. At Fraisse, time has been defeated and it has become the vassal of lords. Without meaning decay and deterioration, it offers the priceless patina of centuries passed, the memory of the lineage. Now it only needs to be maintained. The profit-making heritage is therefore mobilized to permit the upkeep of this irreplaceable, invaluable asset. Other resources are necessary to keep alive the domain whose estate now runs a deficit. The revenue from the patrimony is thus converted into symbolic capital, into a symbol founding a part of the family legitimacy and the assurance to members of the group of the need to continue.

A PRACTICALLY NEW CASTLE

Fraisse is an extreme case, being the family's domain since the 13th century. There are certainly other châteaux, such as the Arcangues family's, in the eponymous village close to Biarritz, which have been in the same family for close to one thousand years. But fortunes and roots can be more recent without the symbolic stakes associated with the real estate heritage. The château de Contenson, in the Forez hills, provides an example.

Memories of a Girl

Although Contenson is less laden with history than some other places, it is rich enough in memories to have fed the Memoirs of the Countess Jean de Pange, born Pauline de Broglie. These exceptional real estate heritages are still capable of providing the prestigious decor of the recitation of family sagas, economic capital, cultural capital and symbolic capital being thus inextricably mingled. Mrs. Pange tells in her memoirs how her family was allied to the Rochetaillées. Her brothers, Maurice and Louis, were famous physicists, the second receiving the Nobel price in 1929 and both having been members of the Academy of Sciences and the Académie Française. "I knew," she writes, "that to save the future of Broglie [the family castle, situated in the Eure] my parents wanted a very large dowry. It was Camille de Rochetaillée who brought it, by marrying Maurice de Broglie. A very young widow, the Baroness of Rochetaillée, born Rochefort, had been able to manage and increase her fortune in the Saint-Étienne coal mind to use her considerable income with intelligence [...]. She owned, in addition to the Saint-Étienne coal mines, extensive lands in the Monts du Forez where her husband had bought the Contenson family a superb castle all in pink granite, which I immediately imagined as an Elsinor or a Holy Rood." [6] Today it is the 1500 hectares of forest and peat bogs that assure the revenue necessary for the château's upkeep. The Saint-Étienne mines were nationalized during the Liberation, which was, according to the present Baron de Rochetaillée, a good transaction for the family. "We were indemnified at a time when mines were no longer profitable; the state, actually, made a very bad deal."

The young Pauline de Broglie was invited with her mother and her Maurice brother for a stay in the Monts du Forez. "They arrived at Contenson around nine o'clock in the evening. Our servants and the trunks came a little later in the night. Here was a new dazzle; the castle was illuminated by electricity! Few private houses in 1903 had such lighting; I had never seen it. Mrs. De Rochetaillée took advantage of natural waterfalls in her park, as a good home maker." The Baron de Rochetaillée had rebuilt and enlarged the castle in 1885, a short time before dying in an equestrian accident. Around the primitive dungeon, an enormous building was raised with four façades and a tower crowned with a high roof that was pointed from every angle. Ogive windows in the purest Cluny style, balconies with stone balustrades, turrets, watchtowers, a loggia with stained glass windows, all in pink granite alternating with the gray stone of the local region.[7] A large reflecting pool, by the entrance, adds to the majesty of the place.

The Château and the Mines

Contenson exemplifies the dominant representations of a "castle," an old home that presents all the characteristic features of a long past, architectural "defense" features whose pointlessness is so charming today. But which, also, shelters life in the castle, as those who are not knowledgeable about it can imagine all they want—that is, the "beautiful" life, the "grand" life. Contenson, the better maintained since it was recently constructed, offers a perfect setting for life, comfortable and at the same time showing all outward signs of a long existence. Visible from afar, but well sheltered from intruders thanks to a vast park, it manifests all the majesty necessary to affirm an incontestably dominant position.

Looking at it from up close, one notices that Contenson suffers the same syndromes as the other ch>teaux. The size and the tremendous maintenance costs end up transforming into a heavy burden these "heritages of enjoyment" that, sometimes, ill deserve their name. Vast, Contenson has some forty main rooms.

"But of the forty rooms, only twenty are lived in today," confides the Baron de Rochetaillée, who inherited it as nearest relative of Maurice de Broglie and Camille de

Rochetaillée.[8] And further, these rooms are only occupied in summer, "because we spend the winter in one of the other buildings." The main building cannot be heated, due to the cost that would represent—a cost that was considerably less when the energy came from family enterprises. "Once, there was a stove, a system for blowing hot air, since my grandmother was owner of Saint-Étienne's coal mines. There was a train that brought us coal directly from Saint-Étienne to Saint-Just-en-Chevalet."

That was the family's birthplace and the old home seemed to work together with ownership of the coalmines to establish a local reputation. The father of the young Camille, who was also christened Camille, was there at the beginning of the development of the Saint-Étienne coal deposits. He bought the swampy meadows, which no one wanted, he dug and he found coal, as his descendant enjoys telling. The grateful city dedicated a street to him.

It is true that the family already had its place in local history. One of the baron de Rochetaillée's ancestors, Jean Bernou, consul of Saint-Étienne, became famous for his courage during the terrifying plague of 1643;[9] later a Rochetaillée was named by the king to Saint-Étienne's provincial assembly and was designated to represent the nobility in the assembly of the 10th département.[10]

History and industry, old stones and mine pits, aristocratic distinction and daily labor form the canvas in the background of this family saga. Elsewhere the founding elements will be different, but the ancient aristocratic and bourgeois families know the same formative processes. To the primitive accumulation of a heritage of profit are progressively added the heritage of enjoyment, which has a major role in forming the identity of the lineage. Saint-Étienne's history is partly intermingled with that of the Rochetaillées—as is the history of the Parisian bank with that of the Neuflizes or the Rothschilds, and with their homes, the individual town houses and castles that fortune enabled them to acquire or have built. At a certain level, business is family business and residences are places for managing social capital, places for circulating information and for negotiation among people of good company.

A Fragment of the National Heritage

It is not an indifferent matter to inhabit a historic monument. Being listed, or registered in the supplementary inventory, designates the building as remarkable, offers it a badge authenticated, what is more, by the state. "The interest in historic monuments, abbeys, churches and castles took off in the beginning the 19th century. It is at this moment also that Napoleon's architects, Percier and Fontaine, announced their aesthetic theory: what is beautiful is what the eye is accustomed to. It was essentially a strong moment for the law, with the establishment of the civil code. The registration of historic monuments led to the creation of a specific law, often called the law of aesthetics, that indicates to the public what it is interesting to look at."[11] It remains to be seen, as Yves Aguilar implies in his conclusion, whether the procedure of registering, instead of creating an objective measure of what is beautiful or of which historic sites merit preservation, "this ineffable category that purports to be pure talent," would not actually be reduced to the social judgment of the moment, by the social class that has the right to it, and also, probably, as a function of the economic and symbolic interests of this class.[12] When the State, by various means, favors the maintenance of historic private patrimony (while requiring an opening of the doors to the public), it allows of course for the preservation of a national patrimony—but at the same time it contributes to the conservation of a certain social order, and even to the perpetuation of the architectural forms that symbolize it. And this is even more so since descendants of these famous families still occupy these buildings.

Fraisse is in part classified, in part registered in the supplementary inventory. Contenson, more recent, is registered, "which means you can choose your architect," as the Baron of Rochetaillée consoles himself. It is certain that being classified or registered offers considerable advantages to owners that can benefit from subsidies for maintenance work amounting to 20 to 80% of estimates, for classified monuments, and up to 40% for those that are registered, which is still substantial. These benefits are not tied to any requirement for opening to the public, that being necessary only in order to benefit from tax abatements for the work performed. But then, classification and to a slight degree registration in the supplementary inventory create liabilities when it comes to authorizations to be requested and precautions to be taken for any work to be undertaken on the building and even on its environment. But there are other lords, such the Count and the Countess Philippe de Chenerilles, for the château of dquote Arbieu B Bazas, in Gironde, or Michel d'Arcangues, for the château of Arcangues, in the PyrJnJes-Atlantiques, who find the countervailing demands of the state to be overly burdensome. "Having a château or a historic home classified," regrets Michel dArcangues, "does not allow the landlord, if he wants to undertake restoration or repair work, to choose his own architect, if (of course) he wishes the benefit of state subsidies. The architect is designated by a commission of the Buildings of France, upon presentation of a file, a long and difficult process. This work can prove more expensive than if it were done by the landlord with local manpower since, in the case of a house classified on the supplementary inventory, these subsidies never go over 2% of the total estimate. We are very far from the theoretical figures of 40% to 80%, which probably pertain to the big châteaux that are open to the public or those transformed into museums. Finally, they propose some help to us, but with such requirements as to make our house no longer our own." "I wantto remain master of my home," concludes Mr. Philippe e

Chenerilles. Again power is needed: the family strategies in this domain vary according to the available resources and the foreseeable solutions. But they all have one thing in common: to preserve the family home is a very strong need, a priority, and for that one accepts, if necessary, much effort and many constraints. Often it comes down to behaviors whose economic irrationality appears obvious. But, beyond that, the symbolic value of these buildings is such that maintaining them within the heritage of enjoyment has some very positive effects on other forms of capital—the social capital and symbolic capital. Maintaining the lineage on its own fief is one of the surest signs of its everlastingness.

There is therefore a substantial symbolic gain inherent in the fact of inhabiting a classified home. Owners are promoted to the title of guardians of the [national] heritage. They are responsible for it and, if that includes certain duties, it is also a way to fulfill the family responsibility to transmit an asset. Which asset, the longer it has been in the family, the more provisionally one holds, with, at the extreme, the idea that the family has the usufruct of part of the national heritage. Classification or registration basically amounts to recognition of this duty and this honor. There are two associations of owners that follow the interests of those who own buildings having a historic value, "Historic Home," and "Old French Houses." These associations bring support, advice and information to their members. Thus there is a collective organization managing the interests of owners of old homes.

The Local Record of the Family Saga

At Contenson, traces of the past and of the previous generations are carefully preserved. The office of Maurice de Broglie is devoutly kept. Under his painted portrait an academician's sword is displayed, decorated with a medal symbolizing Hertzian waves and a marine motif that recalls his passion for physics and his brief career as a naval officer. This sword was given to him by members of the *Cercle de l'Union*[13], of which he was President from 1915 to 1960, scientific work not being, at this level of the social universe, antinomical to a life in society. Mrs. Rochetaillée Senior had her son-in-law's office set up in a tower. One also finds there a photograph of him taken by Nadar, and boat models, which were his second passion. On the desk, the old telephone always seems ready to ring.

The big dining room with the decoratively painted ceiling holds a large Aubusson tapestry in colors that are still fresh and lively. The chapel enjoys a high quality organ, built by Aristide Cavaillé-Coll, who rebuilt the one at Saint-Sulpice in 1862. The altar is dominated by a crucifix sculpted by the grand prix of Rome of 1866. The authority to say Mass at Contenson was granted by Pope Léon XIII, and the framed document recording this decision is prominently displayed. Prior to 1914, chaplains lived permanently at the castle where they assured the offices. The billiard room houses a table that has been restored "by a French champion," as the Baron of Rochetaillée likes to emphasize, happy to have the riches of his family's home discovered. By successive layers every generation has brought its contribution to the formation of this unique heritage, fruit of the tastes and passions of various groups and individuals. Having the cash value of all these assembled possessions would not enable one to recreate suca collection. It took a great deal of wealth to achieve and to maintain such a home; but time was also necessary, and what wealth made possible was the maintenance of a living memory of centuries past. Wealth is therefore also a means of mastering the flow of time and associating around a house not only the members of one family, but all the local history.

That takes money. At the end of the 19th century, according to the vow of her dying husband, Mme. de Rochetaillée [the mother of Camille, who married Maurice de Broglie] made a gift to the township of Saint-Just-en-Chevalet of a large church like a cathedral, a vast school as well as a house of charity. The ensemble forms a whole religious district.[14] Today this architectural ensemble of red bricks is still out of proportion to the modest borough. At the entrance of the church, a bas-relief represents Camille, Baron de Rochetaillée. His effigy, circumscribed in a medallion, is surmounted below by a baronial crown and is inscribed: "To Baron Camille de Rochetaillée. The thankful Saint-Just-en-Chevalet Township. Étienne Pagny, 1894". So the trace is there, indelible, and memory will not forget the generous donor.

Reduced means—or loss of interest in a patronage whose profitability appears less obvious today? In any case, if the Rochetaillées pursue their policy of helping nearby parishes and church schools, it is by other means. "Taxes of all sorts, including the ISF, represent 85% of our income," explains the Baron de Rochetaillée. "So one has bazaars, and charity feasts that help us to maintain schools and churches. One can no longer be as generous as my great-aunt was. Patronage is no longer within the reach of the individual, it is not possible anymore except at the enterprise level."

If a certain erosion of fortunes limits the possibilities of direct charitable support, still the renunciation of engagement in the local social life is to be avoided. So Mr. de Rochetaillée, if he does not hold any local elected office, is president of the Union of Foresters of the Loire.

It is not possible to have a great fortune without maintaining some specific relations with the local population, built on the model of an exchange of gifts and favors, each coming into the exchange on the basis of his means, economic or otherwise. Can one say that "richness oblige" as one says that "noblesse oblige"? That is to say that one must hold onto his rank and give himself the means to maintain it, to assure its reproduction—which presupposes that the dominated group will go along with this. Then this local paternalism based on grand fortunes would have the effect, probably not consciously planned, of assuring the tacit renewal of dominating positions. According to Maurice Halbwachs, "Society respects wealth because it respects wealthy people; and it respects weathy people by virtue of the moral qualities that it supposes them to have."[15] In any case the Rochetaillées adhere to this rule of exchanges, even though circumstances force them to evolve new means of expressing it: 800 hectares of the estate are made available to hunters from the town for free. To express their appreciation, for this generosity and for others, the inhabitants, explains the Baroness de Rochetaillée, "used to come on the feast day of Saint-Just-en-Chevalet, the last Sunday of August, to bring me brioche. Then they would offer a performance in front of the castle, for inhabitants of the castle. It could be "les gilles de Binche." But now that is too expensive for the township."

Whatever the level of wealth, a castle would be nothing without the territory on which it is situated. The territory is a space encompassing agricultural lands, but also vineyards and sometimes mining or industrial areas. But it is also the people who live on it and by means of it. A castle is nothing if it is not on its fief. The latter may be reduced: what is important is the privileged ties between the lords and the common people. Which is why we see the granting of charitable works and all possible forms of support given to the local life, which calls forth gifts in exchange, in the form of recognition and gratitude, but also acceptance of the social order.

STRONG INTERVENTIONS IN THE LOCAL LIFE

The Village, the Castle, the Golf Course and the Family Arcangues

"Arcangues is a village of 2,500 inhabitants that was shaped by my grandfather," says Michel d'Arcangues. "He renovated the church in the fifties, he constructed the theater, he did a lot for his village. Uncle Jean, my father's brother, was mayor of Arcangues. His son Avelino has just been elected town counselor at the first try, with all its candidates." The village and the family of Arcangues, deep-rooted in Basque reality, have existed since 1150. The coat of arms displayed on the public buildings, the school and the town hall, are at once those of the two entities whose histories are intimately intertwined. All this would not be very original if the family of Arcangues had not recently had a 100-hectare golf course constructed that, like a moat, surrounds the whole village and the castle. "Because the Arcangues golf course was made on our lands to preserve our house and the village. Three holes, 13, 14 and 15, are right nearby the castle itself. [...]. In the view of my grandfather, who had already been considering the creation of this golf course for thirty years, it was a matter preserving the village of Arcangues from the real estate invasion that was imminent, considering the proximity of Biarritz, Anglet and Bayonne. He already wanted to create a green belt to protect the heart of the village from an unavoidable speculative assault. However, the initiative for constructing the golf course at Arcangues fell to my father, Guy d'Arcangues, the present owner of the castle and former captain of the French golf team." The golf course was the chosen solution because it presents a potential return considerably greater than the corn farming that it replaces. By freezing the lands, it limits real estate construction to service buildings and villas and a few small housing units whose clientele will be provided by golfers, the lords retaining control over the development of the operation.

A landscape that so strongly associates the castle and the village inscribes within its structure, in a pretty clear way, a symbolization of the local social relationship. There may have been sociological and not only ecological grounds for the heated opposition to the golf course—because even though the practice of this sport has become widespread, it remains no less marked by social and class distinctions. Enclosed in its hectares of cool trimmed lawn and its artificial undulations, the village has become a place of leisure for wealthy sportsmen. However, Michel d'Arcangues clarifies, "The golf course is open to those who want to play there, in return for an entrance fee at the same rate as at other golf courses in this country, according to a subscription plan. Besides, children of the village have the right to free courses there every week with the trainer."

At Arcangues, since the lords were the owners of the agricultural land that surround the village, they were able to effect this real state transaction, the management and the development of which depend henceforth not only on the lords, but also on golf course member-shareholders. But, due to inheritances, subdivision and sales, there are castles today without lands of their own. In the vicinity of Biarritz, a vast property of the 18th century dominates the hills that, little by little, are taken over by vacant lots and by construction sites for small individual houses, or again by traffic corridors that slowly nibble away the landscape. "A property of this magnitude," confides the current inhabitant, "with its view of wastelands and housing developments, is no longer worth the trouble. A part of its inherent interest resides in the beauty of the view." The deterioration of the landscape makes one conscious of the common cause held by lords and farmers, tied to one another for reasons that are both different and yet identical, in maintaining agricultural activity. Agricultural work not only brought the domain a significant source of revenue, but it also assured the upkeep of the aesthetic and hence symbolic quality of the location. With the agricultural crisis, one is also witnessing a real crisis of the landscape, a threat to the economic and symbolic security of heritages.

In an urban milieu

In the city, the spatial expression of social relationships is less readily seen. But one can read according to this logic the nobility's and the haute bourgeoisie deploring the urban evolution that, in the best neighborhoods, unravels a social fabric that might have recalled those that exist between the village and its castle. In the VIIIth precinct of Paris, the disappearance of small local businesses, under the pressure of luxury business and trades, has forced all the personnel and the tradesmen that assured a very personalized service to the grand families of the district to leave. [16] This infrastructure of daily vocation, replaced by the great fashion houses and jewelers, has suppressed the bakers and grocers, the pharmacist and the florist, on whose services one relied and with whom interpersonal relations, frequent and cordial, could enjoy something of the richness of relationships in the village. The transformation of the districts of west Paris, about which the wealthy families who reside there complain so much, is also the disappearance of this ordinary, daily paternalism, that forms the habitual framework of relationships of the dominant ones with other social groups. Without doubt its absence has the disenchanting effect of leaving the privileged ones alone with their heritage, with possessions that do not amount to much if they are not legitimized, enhanced and reinforced by the social relationships that can bring to life the happy feeling of having escaped the common lot by having before one's eyes the recognition of those whom one dominates.

The private townhouse of the Fontmichels, in the heart of the old city of Grasse, imprints the family's identity profoundly upon the local reality. An historic monument of the 17th century, the building, together with other more modest buildings, is mentioned in the tourist guides and is one of the highlights shown to groups that visit the old city. The Fontmichels, who have lived here since 1774, have accumulated a not inconsequential heritage of works and objects of art in a listed home that shelters as well the law offices of M. Hervé de Fontmichel. The latter, a former mayor of Grasse (as were several of his ancestors, even before the Revolution) is now regional councilman. Thus he still lives in a patrician house set amid the more modest dwellings of the area he used to administer. One finds in an absolutely urban setting these relations of proximity-distance that are the principle of the farming fief, that is deeply inscribed in the local social fabric of old families.

Once one could also attain nobility through the exercise of local power. During the 18th century, the "corps de ville," which correspond to the present town councils, were among the prestigious institutions and the municipal functions sought out by the opulent families, which in certain towns thus acceded to nobility (noblesse de cloche, "landless nobility") [17]. Even though the village of Courson, in Île-de-France, had grown much larger, Patrice Fustier, who married Helen de Nervaux-Loys, owner of the castle there, noticed that, as a long time mayor-adjunct, he was always placed to the mayor's right. "My opinion was always the first solicited, no matter what the nature of the problem might be. The 'château's' opinion was wanted, and I was simply its representative."

A family's position in the local social fabric symbolically consolidates and legitimizes the dominant social positions. They also inter-relate with all forms of capital, and in this case a particular form, the political capital whose basis can be found in the local roots of certain families.

HERITAGES OF ENJOYMENT AND HERITAGES OF PROFIT

On the ground, it is sometimes difficult to distinguish the heritage of usage from the heritage of revenue. The castles of Bordelais—the château de la Brouchetière à Joeuf, in Meurthe-et-Moselle, in steel-making country, the château de la Verrerie (Glass-Making) at Creusot, Contenson in the midst of its forests, Fraisse, surrounded by its agricultural fields—form a whole with the estates and the enterprises which enable them to exist. This conjunction between the patrimony of enjoyment and the patrimony of revenue is at the root of the symbolic capital of the families in question, because in this proximity appear the social relations of domination that organize the local economic life. The different facets of the heritage are closely interdependent.

The Bordeaux Vineyard

The Bordeaux wine country constitutes a particular form of territorial heritage where real estate capital, economic capital and cultural capital (because wine and its science have their place in the dominant culture), social capital and symbolic capital are all intermixed. For the vinicultural bourgeoisie from Bordeaux, a heritage of this nature has an important symbolic dimension. It is sometimes very difficult to isolate the economic dimension, in that the vineyard is, also, a certain social relationship with a territory, and the materialization of the history of this relationship.

The Lur-Saluces are land-owners of two castles in the Sauternais, Yquem for the elder branch and Malle for the younger branch. For four hundred years Yquem has belonged to this same family. This wine of Sauternes was classified as premier grand cru—the only one to get this honor in its category—by the brokers of Bordeaux, at the demand of Napoleon III and on occasion of the 1855 global exhibition in Paris. Numerous homes are concentrated in this region, many of which are listed, all of which conceal antique furnishings and objects of art. Around these castles, the vineyards pruned in straight lines are like the velvet cushion upon which a diadem would rest. All is elegant and refined, the castle and grapevines. The mythological and cultural dimensions of wine ennoble an economic activity whose transfiguration allows wealth to show off here without restraint and without bad conscience, without that aggressiveness typical of the newly rich. There is a homology between grapevines, the fruits of an ancestral work, wine, which time improves, and the great winegrowers of Bordeaux, where such families as the Cruses and the Rothschilds are counted among the lineages. "A sign of this capacity to register time, the vintage—a rare, even unique, plant product to be marked by the year of its origin—wine derives from the vintage a double value, age and identity."[18] Buildings are ranked even as the wines are; even cellars are susceptible to being thus honored. At les Cruses, at the Ch>teau la Dame Blanche, in the township of Taillan, "the cellars date to the time of Henri IV: half buried, they include two levels and are surprising for the quasi-mystical atmosphere that reigns there, fruit of their monastic origin, but especially of the mysterious alchemy of the alcohol that, over the centuries, has blackened and embalmed the vaults." [19] Henri Cruse bought Taillan at the end of the 19th century and assembled there "astonishing collections, saving [a] retable from the Manufacturers' Hospital which was at risk of being lost forever when the Palais Descas en Paludate was built, and giving it a choice location in the gardens of his property."[20]

In the midst of these accumulated material and symbolic riches, the alchemy of wine is created—because there is magic in the work of wine and it is the old cellar masters who make the good wines. Experience is decisive and it is highly valued. Bernard Ginestet, former proprietor of Château-Margaux, describes the paternalistic relationship that ensues between the cellar master and the owners, the brokers and the traders. A paternalism whose foundation rests on a reciprocal esteem among all parties, for their expertise and their ability in the domain of winemaking and the economy of wine [21]. Wine, in its development and its merchandising, is the support of complex relations that mingle groups that are socially diverse, and unites them in a special space.

The Horse and the Racing Stables

The horse is at the origin of a similar overlapping between heritage of profit and heritage of enjoyment, a combined form of capital that seems to be highly meaningful for the wealthiest social categories. Mr. Castilla inherited the stud farm of the tile works at Silly-en-Gouffem, in Orne. As much on the paternal side as on the maternal side, the families have a tradition linked to the horse. The father of M. de Castilla rode in equestrian competitions. The family home, an old master's house very well preserved is adjacent to the stud farm and the stables are not far away. The life of the stud farm sets the rhythm for life at the house.

And above all the horse is a living heritage that "nourishes the dream" and that is the product of scientists' calculations on breeding and their efficiency. "It is all an adventure, every horse gives you hope." Hope, for example, of finally producing one ace and to win back a few big prizes. A racing stable or, more modestly, raising horses for competition, constitutes both heritage of profit, whose profitability is uncertain but can be considerable, and especially a form of heritage of enjoyment whose interest lies in the strong symbolic value of this type of activity. The symbolism resides in the size of the network of relations that can develop around the horse. That may be on the local level, with all the magical relationships made possible by the rare expertise shared between agents who are far removed from one another in social standing. But also by all the magic of race courses that mingles bettors of every social rank and owners, trainers, jockeys and lads. The equestrian world forms a part of heritages with high symbolic value, as may be seen at race tracks with tribunes of owners and those reserved for meers of the high class clubs (Jockey, Cercle de Deauville...). The Grands Prix (Grand Prix de Diane, Grand Prix de Deauville) are lie social events that allow the haute bourgeois to appear in such a group. At the same time, a well-run racing stable is a heritage of profit quite competitive with other forms of investment. Thus it is an extreme case of the overlapping of various forms of capital.

Châteaux on Industrial Lands

In the same way, the château de la Brouchetière, belonging to the Wendels, or La Verrerie, which belonged to the Schneider family, were real estate assets for profit, principal residences, and vacation homes, but also an important part of the professional patrimony: steel-making plants in Lorraine and metallurgical plants at Creusot. These homes, by their pomp and above all by their location, just at the necessary distance from the workshops and workmen's cottages, participated in forming the social legitimacy of the bosses.

The ambiguity between patrimony of revenue and patrimony of enjoyment is sometimes reinforced by the very origin of these constructions. The castle may once have been the main building of a large farm. Or, in the case of La Verrerie, an ancient glassworks that functioned from 1787 to 1837, and that was bought at that time by Eugene Schneider in order to make it his residence. At the beginning of the 20th century, Eugene II, as the heirs of long lineages like to be called, using an ordinal number to distinguish the generations that take forenames of ancestors, undertook the transformations that proved necessary for La Verrerie to play its role in the management, weighty and complex, of a social capital which has become considerable over time. In that case it is the receiving rooms and ceremonial spaces that are given the most work. It is necessary to appear worthy of the great ones of this world that the family of forge masters is called upon to receive. Thus one arranges large sitting rooms on the ground flo, transforms one of the ancient kilns of the glassworks, an imposing conical construction, into a replica of the Petit Trianon of Versailles. So the castle of La Verrerie became the emblem of the economic and social success of the Schneiders. In the haute bourgeoisie, it is not easy to separate private life and business: the residence is a major place of socializing, of a life of relationships that constitutes a part of the accumulation and management of social capital.

The Patrimony of Enjoyment Becomes a Patrimony of Revenue

Because of a relative decline of fortunes, but also because maintenance costs have gone up, with the benefits claimed by salaried employees, families sometimes find it difficult to maintain these vast, ruinous and inconvenient homes with no domestic importance. A process has appeared that has led to the conversion of some of these castles into heritages of profit. Today, a large number of castles are open to the public so that their owners can benefit from tax remissions. But each example, after opening for the statutory minimum of a few dozen days per year, is a candidate for being open permanently, such as, for example, the Château de Chenonceaux, in Indre-et-Loire. The patrimony of enjoyment thus blurs into the patrimony of revenue. The lord furnishes the outbuildings and withdraws to them, abandoning his ancestors' home to the curiosity of tourists or to families lacking a prestigious place to unite their progeny. Or to seminars and other symposia whose social importance is measured by the majesty of the location rented. The Marquis de Breteuil, president of the association "Historic Home" (the goal of which is to help owners of classified monuments to maintain them and to keep them within the family's heritage), succeeded by this means in converting a symbolic heritage into an economic heritage. It is understood that this conversion is not absolute: the castle, as a form of work and as a producer of resources, remains nonetheless laden with symbolic and emotional value, an identity. There was just an inversion of the main aspect. [22]

Overlapping Forms of Capital

Here is an example of the blurring of boundaries and categories that appear to be one of the characteristics of socially dominant environments. The different forms of capital are closely intermingled and one passes imperceptibly from a symbolic aspect to an economic dimension, without abandoning the cultural tonality. Power is also power over categories. The ordinary social agent is classified, listed, accounted, recorded. The aristocrat or the haut bourgeois is much harder to categorize: for proof, one might emphasize the fact that official figures, the socio-professional categories of INSEE, are inadequate to define them. And more: social rankings, according to careers or professions, are misleading. One can never reduce an haut bourgeois person to the definition of his professional activity. First of all, he often has several of them. But whether he is a marketing executive in an enterprise, a general in the army, CEO, farmer or academician, it goes without saying that his real social standing results frois profession, certainly, but also from all the closely maintained ties with his counterparts in other socially dominant positions. In other words, a grand bourgeois is a grand bourgeois by virtue of the systems of relationships that involve him in the networks proper to his own background. A worker, even a misanthrope living withdrawn by himself, will remain a worker. A grand bourgeois can not be a grand bourgeois by himself. His power is not individual but collective. It is his social class that assures him his dominant position. There is no need to belong to a club if you want to be a housewife. But one cannot be grand bourgeois without intense socializing.

One finds this ambiguity in other aspects of social existence. The notion of a secondary residence, which is also a statistical category used by INSEE to categorize residences, is inadequate for categorizing aristocratic or grand bourgeois habitats. The Duke de Brissac would be quite surprised if one asked him whether he intended to spend the weekend in his secondary residence, the Château de Brissac. There is in fact in these families an exceptional pluri-territoriality. The family roots are maintained by these properties and castles that are like many deep anchors in a farming reality, founding the identity of the lineage. The heritage integrates these dimensions. It is because these families are provided with all forms of capital that they also have some unclassifiable possessions. The accumulation is not only economic: memory, prestige, symbolic capital are also accumulated.

However, the reduction of family enterprises in favor of anonymous portfolios of undifferentiated securities is an evolution that can lead to a certain rupture with this diagram. This autonomization of the economic sphere seems to imply the possibility of a greater liquidity of fortunes. But that is only a recent tendency, and one supposes that the grand bourgeoisie could convert part of its economic capital in such a way as to recover its symbolic, even cultural dimensions, which at the same time assure the dominant position in society, its legitimacy and its transmission. The subtleties of heritage management and the personalized character given it by the money managers go in that direction.

One may contrast this degree of integration of the different forms of capital to the one that characterizes the popular classes. Today at least, in working class neighborhoods, it is exceptional to find such an interpenetration between professional activities, the system of relationships, and ethical and aesthetic values. Young people from the poor outskirts accumulate social and spacial rootlessness. Without real professional or territorial toeholds, they consume the city, and therefore society, as if it were simply decor in which they can no longer really record their life. Some speak of life as a spectacle,[23] others speak of the city-as-a-museum—"the centers of towns would then be doomed to a patrimonial destiny and would be deserted[24]" —that is, they would become non-places. "If a place can be defined as giving a sense of identity, relational and historic," writes Marc Augé, "a space that can be defined neither as giving a sense of identity, nor as relational, nor as historic, must be a non-place."[25] In other words, a relationship to a space is constructed socially and if some people have the material, symbolic and cultural means to appropriate places, more are deprived of spaces that are not made for them and for which they do not have the resources needed to appropriate them. One of the most flagrant privileges of the privileged class is to be able to transform most spaces into fiefs: by their symbolic capital, and by their material comfort too, they can invest in a place and become socially dominant there.

THE CONFRATERNITY OF FIEFS

The great families of the wealthy aristocracy and the bourgeoisie prefer to keep to themselves. They like to live among their peers, in spaces away from the ordinary, which they shape and fashion in their own image. These families do not reconquer spaces already occupied. They create their habitat *ex nihilo*, on virgin land. All the history of the good neighborhoods of Paris is that of an urbanization whose initiative and the motor are to be found in high society. At the same time these families are always highly concentrated in space. Being at the start of the urbanization of new districts has permitted them to stay grouped together even when, under the pressure of business and luxury trades that covet the good addresses that they created, they left their former districts to retire to the west side, which was quieter and sociologically more homogeneous.

The great families' space is not limited to the west of Paris, nor to upper crust neighborhoods of provincial cities, such as the Jardin Public in Bordeaux or the Parc de la Tête d'or in Lyons. Since the end of the 18th century, noble families have distinguished themselves by their double or triple residences: they live in the city or the countryside according to the social rhythm, more or less based on the rhythm of seasons. This practice uses castles and mansions. Since the 19th century, vacation regions such as Dieppe and Deauville offer the opportunity to extend still further the possible living places. Multi-territoriality is so linked to the aristocratic way of life that, when the bourgeoisie tries to merge or join with it, they acquire several homes, in the city and the countryside. Conversely, Claude Brelot observed that in the 19th century "being reduced to one single residence characterizes those elements of the nobility that are threatened with becoming bourgeois. In other words, having just o hou clearly characterizes a loss of class and threatens the ability to reproduce one's social status."[26]

Everyone has to live somewhere and every family has, in principle, one home. But having a second, not to mention a third and fourth home, denotes social strength and signifies a certain power over space. For, with the nobility or the grand bourgeoisie, it is not a matter of secondary residences but of an ancient patrimony, bequeathed from generation to generation, which has sheltered family life for many decades. Multi-territoriality is consubstantial with the definition of dominant social positions. *Le Bottin Mondain* of 1995 attests to this: the families who indicate just one home are very rare. The des Monstiers live in the VIIIth arrondissement of Paris and on their estate in Limousin. The Rochetaillées note, aside from their address at Neuilly, in the quartier Saint-James, two other homes in the provinces. Two years ago they lost their fourth residence, the Château de Nantas, in the Saint-Étienne region. "It had been in the family for three hundred years. It was sold; one can't keep everything," regrets the Baron de Rochetaillée. The estate of Captan, in the Landes, was given as a gift from M. de Rochetaillée's mother to one of her grand-daughters. "It's an agricultural property that does not make a profit, but it doesn't lose money either. That's pretty good." In managing family patrimonies, the burden of this real estate for enjoyment, which has become excessive when you consider the changes in lifestyle and, sometimes, in revenue, is considerable. Some families reorganize their activities in relation to the heriage to one home, which they try to keep going on its own resources in order to keep it within the family patrimony. That, for example, is the case with the Marquis de Breteuil, who has made the château which carries his name into a revenue-bearing patrimony from which the income enables them to preserve the patrimony of enjoyment.

In Bordeaux, according to their involvement in the commerce of wine or of pine, families possess a château in the wine country or a beautiful home in the forest of Landes. But they also own a mansion or a vast apartment close to the Public Garden or on the Court of Xavier Arnozan, and a villa at Arcachon or the Cap Ferret as well as a chalet in the Pyrenees, for winter sports. This double or triple territoriality is definitely a component of a dominant position. Marking one's place socially seems to require being able to mark geographically as well. But the "true homeland" of these uncommon families, as Norbert Elias says, is "their society" to which their "attachment is unshakable", and no matter that this requires "frequent changes of residence."[27]

The example of the Ganay family shows what this multi-territoriality means when the different branches of the family and the networks of friendship proliferate. Jacqueline Sébastien was Pierre de Ganay's nurse for eighteen months, in the Fifties, and she preserves a living memory of this experience. Pierre de Ganay, eldest son of Victoire de Montesquiou Fezensac and Michel de Ganay, lived the first days of his life in a mansion on the Esplanade des Invalides. "I used to walk Pierre in the gardens of the Rodin Museum," says Jacqueline Sébastien. "Mrs. Ganay had taken a membership for me, which was very pleasant because it was a very quiet place. No one was there, at least as I remember it, except nurses with their babies." When summer came, "We left for vacation to the various châteaux. First of all the Château de Montrozier, close to Rodez. It was a château that belonged, I believe, to the godmother of Mme de Ganay. It was really in the countryside. And then we went to Gers, at Marsan, to a castle that belond to the Montesquiou family.[28]

I had a room on the first floor, an immense room which I occupied with Pierre, for I did not leave him for one second. The room was so large that my current house could fit inside it. The month of September was spent at the Château de Courances, at Victoire de Montesquiou's parents-in-law, in the Île-de-France.[29] Courances, they told me at the time, is a replica on a smaller scale of Fontainebleau. The stairway, the architecture, it is a marvelous château which really struck me. And then when one lives in such a place, when one can walk through all the rooms... there were splendid paintings, and the library! I was really impressed. It was all so grand!" Some years later Michel de Ganay and Victoire de Montesquiou, Pierre's parents, moved to the Château de Fleury at Fleury-en-Bière, in Seine-et-Marne, a few kilometers from Courances.

One could find many examples of families who, like the Ganays, have at their disposal directly or indirectly, whether they are owners or recipients through the network of family and friends, of various homes, whose very variety is in line with that of the seasons and circumstances. Summer in the châteaux of the South, the fall at Courances for the opening of the hunting season, winter in the Faubourg Saint-German. But still in exceptional places, charged with history, very often classified places, always out of the ordinary. Places that contribute to having the young heir internalize his position far from usual standards, and the inherent right of his group to occupy space, to take up all the room. All these châteaux that sheltered the wonder of Jacqueline Sébastien do not belong to the same person, nor to the same family. But throughout the national territory they form a network that quickly trains those involved: the world belongs to you, it is made for you, you never travel as a tourist but as an owner—or a friend of the owners.

The predilection of high society families for rural living disperses them across the entire territory. There are other places where they gather collectively, recreating in a certain way the ghettos of big cities. Holiday locations, high society always knew how to set aside for themselves. Just as they were at the origin of the most beautiful parts of Paris, Society built resorts, whether warm, beach areas, or for winter sport. For relaxation, too, for time in the countryside, in the mountains or by the sea, the great families prefer, as a general rule, to urbanize for themselves a piece of virgin land rather than to reconquer a habitat that has already served. The small fishing port where one buys an old house without being sure of the neighborhood is not at all how it is done in the most comfortable category where, again, they prefer to decide on their environment and to construct in their own image, the shell that will shelter their leisures. Deauville, as we will see, is an exemplary case of such a town pned by certain individuals to the benefit of high society families.

So the wealthy families have, through their heritage of enjoyment (which, as we have already seen, is not so simple to distinguish from the heritage of profit) the possibility of living in a space that is not anonymous, that is not that interchangeable space of rootless city-dwellers. It is not a fluke if the homes that allow this connivance with a native soil are also, very often, a part of the national heritage. These family heritages are interwoven with family and national histories. Space and time are reconciled in the same fullness of the unified space and the length of time mastered.

The social significance of such a family universe is so profound that national borders are scarcely meaningful to the higher classes.

Notes

1. According to the Catalogue of Nobility by Régis VALETTE (Paris, Laffont, 1989), the des Monstiers-Mérinville family figures among the oldest in France. They can trace their lineage, through direct descendants by name, back to 1350.
2. Annick TULASNE-MOENECLAEY, Jean des Monstiers et le château du Fraisse, Poitiers, Faculté des Lettres, mémoire de maîtrise d'histoire, 1970.
3. The ne rights of the landowner limited those of the proprietor. For example, there had been a right of preemption for the sharecroppers who could obstruct the proprietor in his plans, which were liable to being signed away by the new rights of farming and sharecropping between supervisor and worker, between landowner and farmer.
4. There are many such examples. A documentary by Marianne Lamour, La Famille la Rochefoucauld, une famille millénaire, distributed by Planète in May 1994, shows the family in relations with the church that dominates the village of that name. The family's thousandth anniversary was celebrated in August 1992, and villagers went up to attend festivities alongside the lords. Tradesmen in the village reproduced maxims of François VI de La Rochefoucauld in their shop windows with the Romanesque decor of the small church.
5. The bells of churches built with a family's gifts are baptized with the children's forenames. This, for example, was the case at Montfort, in Sarthe, at the initiative of the great grand-parents of the Nicolay family.
6. Countess Jean of PANGE, "How I saw 1900," Paris, Grasset, 3 vol.., 1962, 1965 and 1968 (t. 2: Confidences of a girl, 1965, p. 89-90).
7. ibid., p. 104-105.
8. The only child of Maurice de Broglie and Camille de Rochetaillée died at the age of ten.
9. Jean-Noël DESPOYEAUX, Foreword to the book by Henri de JOUVENCEL, L'Assemblée de la noblesse

du baillage de Forez en 1789, Lyons, 1911, p. v.

10. Ibid., p. vi.

11. Yves AGUILAR, " La Chartreuse de Mirande. Le monument historique, produit d'un classement de classe ", Actes de la recherche en sciences sociales, n'42, April 1982, p. 77.

12. Ibid., p. 85.

13. This is an aristocratic club, housed today in the same mansion as the "Cercle de l'Union Interalliée," rue du Faubourg-Saint-Honoré, in Paris.

14. Comtesse Jean de PANGE, Comment j'ai vu 1900, op. cit., table 2, p. 108.

15. Maurice HALBWACHS, Les Cadres sociaux de la mémoire, Paris-La Haye, Mouton, 1976 (1st Edition 1925), p. 257.

16. Michel PINÇON and Monique PINÇON-CHARLOT, Quartiers bourgeois, quartiers d'affaires, Paris, Payot, 1992, p. 138-153.

17. Jean-Louis HAROUEL et al., Histoire des institutions de l'époque franque à la Révolution, Paris, PUF, 1987, p. 472. On the elective responsibilities of the nobility, see Monique de SAINT MARTIN, L'Espace de la noblesse, Paris, Métailié, 1993.

18. Georges DURAND, "La vigne et le vin", in Les Lieux de mémoire", under the guidance of Pierre NORA, Paris, Gallimard, (t. III: Les France, vol. 2, p. 786).

19. Janine GRAVELINE, Châteaux et manoirs d'Aquitaine, Éditions Minerve, 1988.

20. Paul BUTEL, Les Dynasties bordelaises, from Colbert à Chaban, Paris, Perin, coll. «Histoire et fortunes», 1991, p. 349.

21. See Bernard GINESTET, Les Chartrons, Paris, Acropole, 1991.

22. For more important development on this point, see our work "Dans les beaux quartiers," op. cit., chap. IX, "Châtelains de toujours, châtelains d'un jour", p. 119-142.

23. Guy DEBORD, La Société du spectacle, Paris, Gallimard, 1992 (New edition). "Society that rests on modern industry," writes Guy Debord, "is not casually or superficially built around a spectacle, it is fundamentally a society of spectators. The sectacle, an image of the reigning economy, the end is nothing, development is everything. The sectacle is not going to become anything more than it already is." (p. 8).

24. Olivier MONGIN, La Peur du vide, Paris, Le Seuil, 1993.

25. Marc AUGÉ, Non-Lieux, Paris, Le Seuil, 1992, p. 100.

26. Claude-Isabelle BRELOT, "Itinéraires nobles: entre ville et château, la noblesse et la maîtrise de l'espace au XIXe siècle," in Noblesses et villes, 1780-1950, Tours, Éditions de la Maison des sciences de la ville, 1995.

27. Norbert ELIAS, La Société de cour, Paris, Champs-Flammarion, 1985, P. 21.

28. The Château de Marsan is today the property of Aymeri de Montesquiou Fezensac, Mayor of Marsan and Deputy of Gers.

29. The Château de Courances, in the town of that name, is found in Essonne. The current owner is the Marquis Jean-Louis de Ganay.

CHAPTER III

Sterling Cosmopolitanism

The heritage of enjoyment is also an instrument for managing and accumulating social capital, that system of relations that is part of the power of the family group. Announcements in the magazine *Properties of France*, published by *Le Figaro*, carefully mention the square footage of reception rooms and the number of bedrooms of the properties offered for sale. The houses and apartments of friends, independently, are emphasized as assets: big homes in the countryside or by the sea must be able to provide a worthy welcome to family and relations.

And this real estate heritage cannot be limited to the status of 'heritage for personal use' except by a reductive vision. In a more global conception of the economy, one sees that this heritage plays a role in the accumulation of social capital and symbolic capital, capital that is not taken into consideration in the accounting of heritages. Certainly, there are no units of measure that would enable one to include these forms of capital in the assessment of heritages and their distribution. However, in an analysis more qualitative that quantitative, one can distinguish the social impact of these other forms of capital and can show the multifaceted and complex forms and effects of heritage.

It is therefore important to take into consideration the cumulative effects these enjoyment heritages shared and exchanged between members of the extended family and networks of acquaintances and relations. In a closed social circle that is constantly undergoing renewal, members of high society frequent the same places in a dance set to a rhythm that varies according to the seasons, age, or professional obligations, but still to a sustained rhythm. It begins with the Parisian apartments and the dinners that are daily events: when one isn't receiving, it is because one has been invited. In these exchanges, apartments, with their large reception halls, are indispensable settings for the socializing that would not blossom without being thus harbored in the best conditions. As guests overflow the borders of family, one has a sort of collectivization of real estate heritage. The right of ownership is not an issue. But the dining rooms and the salons of Paris end up almost forming a sort of ensemble of public ps where the good society lives, with the same ease and the same pleasure that it finds in the clubs or the big restaurants

THE COSMOPOLITANISM OF THE HIGH CLASSES

This collectivization doesn't limit itself to the narrow confines of Paris. The castle, the yacht, the chalets are also places where this life of relationships can blossom. However, these excrescences of the beautiful Parisian districts, or of the large provincial metropolises, may be situated beyond the national borders. If the château is generally on the national soil, it may be otherwise for the chalet, which may be in Switzerland or Austria. As for the yacht, she is essentially a voyager, and cruises on foreign seas. The Tunisian palace, the villa in Marrakech or Marbella, the Argentinian estancia, are forms of family heritage that are mobilized for this life of sociability whose intensity is proportional to the social standing. Patrick Guerrand-Hermès invited "some amateur polo players to share his passion for this elite sport in the sunny setting of his sumptuous house in Marrakech."[1] Seen among the happy elect were Anne d'Ornano, Mayor of Deauville,Marquis Arnold de Contades and his wife, Alain Carignon, Mayor of Grenoble, and Alain Boucheron, jeweler from the Place Vendôme. Marrakech is one of those privileged of privileged places anda certain number of the wealthy families possess sumptuous homes there. So the countess Charles de Breteuil, who received there a messenger from the magazine L'Éventail. "A young and pretty servant," relates the journalist, "opens the entry door, immense and heavy, curiously fluted, and you enter, astonished by the beauty of the hall where the portrait of a baron of Breteuil is enthroned, surrounded of two immense vases from China... Never has the alliance of Europe and the Orient been so successful."[2]

Matrimonial Alliances and Economic Interests

The group of equals thus has at its disposal a space that is collectivized in its use, even though each of its elements remains one family's private property. The territory is certainly first of all national butit is also international. There are, in any case, solid objective reasons for this de-localization of the heritage of enjoyment.

Matrimonial alliances with foreign nationals are frequent in this milieu, and for centuries the aristocracy has practiced internationalized marriages. Through memoirs, examples of international marriages abound. Prince Jean-Louis de Faucigny-Lucinge has been married twice to Brazilians. Count Cahen d'Anvers, also twice married, chose two Argentinians. The mother of Michel d'Arcangues, Eugenia-Maria of Ouro-Preto, was Brazilian, a descendant of a large family from Minas Gerais and daughter of the Brazilian Ambassador in Paris. Some of her ancestors were Spanish; her grandmother was Bolivian. The maternal grandmother of Christel Baseden, descendant of the wealthy shipowner from Bordeaux wed a Chilean when she married for the second time. And so, still today, the month of August sees "the Chilean tribe" arriving at the vast family villa at the sides of the Arcachon basin. Thus is the matrimonial alliance network extended beyond national borders.[3]

Similarly, some fortunes are created abroad. With possessions overseas, one has at his disposal residences whose exoticism is part of their appeal. To find oneself in a country and a region where one has interests is, at another level, like returning to one's lands for the yearly inspection visit to the domaine. One is a local personality when one is the landlord or the main shareholder of a factory essential to the life of a region. Count Cahen d'Anvers remembers that, on a pleasure trip in Morocco, he took advantage of the opportunity by visiting Glaoui and stopped in at some canneries, properties of the family, which he had never seen. Of course everyone made haste to have him visit them.

The collectivization of this exceptional and international real estate heritage, by virtue of being available to the whole network of the family and friends, is analogous with arrangements of a social group that prefers collective institutions. High society has always cultivated structures for coming together, such as theCNPF (Conseil national du patronat franc/ais, the National Council of French Employers), created in 1946, but whose origin goes back at least to the Committee of Forges, created in 1864. As for the grand Parisian clubs, for most partthey date from the 19th century, or at the latest, the beginning of the 20th. These networks of relations and sociability have always had an international dimension: power has a vocation to cross borders and to make ties with those that are in similar positions abroad. The Parisian clubs maintain relations with their counterparts in other countries and often sign conventions that share membership privileges with members who are traveling. The Cercle de l'Union Itlliée is thus in contact with 121 clubs through 32countries.[4] The choice of given names for infants appears to be less susceptible to foreign influence, even in the case of international marriages.

Thus a member of the Jockey Club will be welcomed with the greatest courtesy at the Knickerbocker in New York, an analogous club on Fifth Avenue. Accordingly, the integration in France of foreigners belonging to the dominant spheres does not pose a problem, since it is true that the first "Internationale" was that of power.

There are clubs such as the Travellers that institutionally cultivate this international capital: "Statutorily, the club, international in scope, is composed 35%of Americans, 25% British, Spaniards and Turks, and only 30% French."[5] For a French person to pretend to membership in this club, created in 1850 and occupying the last private mansion on the Champs-Elysées (number 25 on the avenue), he must be in business and speak English fluently. Of course, as in all other grand clubs, the sponsorship requirement and the procedure of induction are in place to assure control over the social quality of incoming members. As for the French-American elite, they can find each other in another club, France Amérique, situated not to two steps away from the Travellers, in a private house on the Avenue Franklin Roosevelt. Through price discounts, conferences and dinners, this club maintains and develops relations between the French and American elites at the highest social level. Again on the Champs-Elysées, Roger de Persuy's club, the Society of Sons of the American Revolution, was created by the descendants of noble officers who had participated in the War of Independence. The current president is Hélie de Noailles, Duke d'Ayen.

Worldwide Worldliness

There are many other clubs for foreigners, such as the International Yacht Club of Antibes, which offers its 19 members a pleasure harbor for yachts larger than 60 meters—some of them over 150 meters. "Stavros Niarchos, Adnan Kashoggi, John Latzis, King Fahd of Saudi Arabia, Robert Maxwell, Terry Gleg, so many names of giants of worldwide business, finance and politics you may meet in one day on the shore," write X. Périssé and D. Dunglas,[6] who must, however, be aware that the club's harbor is private and that access is especially difficult. Patrice Fustier belongs to an English association specializing in rare plants, Count Robert Léotoing de Anjony, owner of the Anjony castle in Cantal and permanent secretary of "Historic Home," is also an administrator of the association Europa Nostra Ibi, presided over by Prince Henrik of Denmark, which is concerned with defending heritage and the environment on the pan-European scale. There is also an association of Friends of Old French Houses that brings together "friends" of French heritage across the Atlantic. Examples of these associations and international clubs abound.

The cosmopolitanism of relations, and multi-territoriality extended across foreign countries, these are two essential components of the specificity of high society. The Le Petit

Mondain, which categorizes families on the social list according to their places of residence, mentions about a hundred foreign countries in which families on the list indicated they have residences.[7] One finds in Argentina the great names of the French aristocracy, with the Countess de Castellane, Count Emmanuel Clermont-Tonnerre, the royal family of La Tour d'Auvergne. But Belgium is by far the country that houses the most families of the worldly list. This is due, in part, to proximity but also to tax reasons, as is true for Switzerland. Also there have been numerous alliances between Belgian families and French families. Blue blood has never had borders and "Noblemen were the first Europeans. With a cousin in each country, their networks have been functioning for centuries."[8]

"While the 19th century may be known for mounting nationalism, the French nobility saw, rather, the apogee of a social order that is essentially cosmopolitan," affirms Claude-Isabelle Brelot, who sees many reasons for this cosmopolitanism. "The persistent endogamy of Gotha, the fidelity to the diplomatic career and the communality of a way of life [...]. Networks of lineages of international character appear thus like a first anticipation of pan-Europeanism. But the cosmopolitanism of the nobility is founded on the concept of the clan, far more than on the universality of human rights [...]. Aristocracy is distinguished by the ambition to make itself the elite of Europe. Its culture of hierarchy is intended to transcend time and space, not only the provincial and national space, but also Europe, in truth the world."[9] Before the war of 1914, at a time when "money flowed freely, [...] the high social spheres of Europe formed an internationale of friendship, a freemasonry of elegance that found itself, that sought itself out, that united together. These societies belonged to one single almighty confraternity, of "the world", wrote a historiographer of the grande bourgeoisie at the middle of the century.[10] The methods have changed, but the cosmopolitan dimension is more alive than ever.

Today the countess de Quesnay, while making allusion to these international networks, acknowledges that "there is an international mafia that may not be visible to the naked eye, but that exists." One can wonder at this reference to an organization whose reputation leaves something wanting. It is probable that its author saw a good analogy between the internationale of high society and this tight network of complicities that unite families in a secret organization in the defense of common interests.

Through the family and the network of useful relationships, nobles and the grand bourgeois have at their disposal a cosmopolitan capital whose dimensions are cultural, economic and social. It is legitimate to distinguish this form of capital in the dimension where it produces its effects in a particular field, of which it is the product as well, that is, in international relations. Enrolling one's person, one's family and one's relationships to play at the planetary level places a lot at stake, even is these relationships don't cover all nations. To be present in these international networks, at the highest level of wealth and power, is to accumulate symbolic capital, by the social prestige granted today to the geographical extension of relations and alliances, and cultural capital, by the specific knowledge that this global basis presupposes and permits linguistic knowledge first of all, but also knowledge of art and literature, history and ethnography. All forms of capital of which the conversion into econc capital, that is into profits, is always possible.[11]

High society benefits from this rare privilege of being at home abroad. Not everywhere, of course, but there are always places that are reserved for them and where they are certain to recover the sense of being among their own kind that, in their country of origin, is one of the constants of their way of life. Luxury contributes to this affirmation of the internationalization of the dominant classes. Chic neighborhoods, luxury stores and luxury hotels offer a life-support system that does not leave much room for surprises but which allows one, in the same way as the Clubs in the big cities, to find a shelter from the vicissitudes of ordinary life.

THE ROLE OF LUXURY HOTELS

The feeling of being at home wherever one goes is enhanced by the uniformity of the way of life of the privileged classes, supported by international hotels which, since César Ritz, founder of the eponymous hotel on the Place Vendôme, have developed highly refined techniques for looking after a clientele that is no less refined. Establishments of this rank keep up-to-date a document recording all applicable information concerning their clientele. This clientele, which is limited, is composed mostly of regulars. So much so that the "the concierge of the golden keys" already knows the customers announced by his reservation book. For, rarely does one present himself in this type of establishment without having a reservation.[12] All is ready to receive the regular visitor, or even the customer who has already stayed once or twice in the hotel. The "cardex" is the document that permits a welcome so personalized that the customer knows he was expected and so that he can have the feeling of being at home. Yellow roses will be set on the table of his room, because it is known that he likes these flowers, and the refrigerator will contain the type of champagne that he prefers. At breakfast, he will be served eggs cooked precisely to his taste. To the extent possible, one will have reserved for him a room or a suite on the floor that he is accustomed to. Luxury hotels are thus an extension of the wealthy family heritage. These families are not treated like anonymous clients in the more ordinary hotels where everyone more or less has to accept the style and the service as it is given.[13] By contrast, luxury hotels endeavor to match their customers' expectations, by personalizing their welcome as much as possible, so that each can live at the hotel as at a supplementary residence, an additional real estate heritage that one only possesses intermittently but that can be listed as one of the places that make up the real heritage of great families.

There are even some families whose luxury hotels are their main residence. Since 1953 Mrs. Yvonne Embiricos, widow of a very rich Greek shipowner, has as her main residence a suite at the Hôtel de Paris in Monte-Carlo. According to Roger-Louis Bianchini, Mrs. Embiricos' grandfather Sir Basil Zaharoff, a "gun merchant who was one of the richest men in the world, frequented the Hôtel de Paris from the end of the last century until his death in 1921."[14] Her husband's family has inhabited the Hôtel de Paris for two generations. "When we came to the States," Mme Embiricos, now 80 years old, explains, "my husband had three cousins at the Hôtel de Paris. I think they were the most important clients, because there were three big yachts in the harbor." Mrs. Embiricos sees the essential advantages of life in the luxury hotel. Service is guaranteed without one having to concern oneself with managing the staff. She and her husband have owned homes, but they always ended up by preferring the hotel. "When we arrived at he start of the war, in 1940, in California, I fell in love with one house and my husband with another. So he bought them both, one by the sea, for he loved the sea, and the other for me in Beverly Hills. But all the time he kept saying, "You know, that's going to be trouble for you. I don't know if it will work, because we've never lived in a house, only in hotels. Just before moving into the house in Beverly Hills, America went to war and all the domestics, since they were Asians, were put in concentration camps. So I heard 'I told you so!' It was a whole house, it required at least five domestics. Then he said, 'We'll just stay at the hotel,' and he was quite happy!"

Certainly an extremely expensive approach, considering the category of establishments where these wealthy households elect to reside, but one that protects against all domestic worries. Mrs. Embiricos mentions the example of one of her compatriots, Mr. Haji-Ioannou, who continues this tradition since he occupies today, for his professional activities, the offices that belonged to Onassis at the Hôtel de Paris in Monte-Carlo. He gave a dinner recently for a hundred people in this establishment—that is, in a way, at home—without having to worry about the logistics of the event. If this manner of organizing one's daily existence, which does not exclude the possibility of owning residences here and there, is especially a fact of life for the grand bourgeoisie of international business, of necessity very mobile, it also concerns other people such as the Prince de Polignac. He resides in the other luxury hotel in Monte-Carlo, The Hermitage, which neighbors with the one where Mrs. Embiricos, of whom he is an old-friend, stays. The Prince de Polignac is Honorary President of the *Société des bains de mer*, which owns these two luxury hotels and the casino nearby. In Jules de Polignac, he has a common ancestor with Prince Rainier. The address of the Hermitage figures at the top of the list among those mentioned in the Bottin Mondain by Prince Louis de Polignac, but it is followed by a domain in the Morbihan and an apartment in the VIIth arrondissement of Paris.

Thus it seems justifiable to consider that the patrimony of rich families, at least the patrimony of enjoyment, includes also such collective locations as the luxury hotels, and clubs, which, without being privately owned are reserved for their use alone and in which familiarity is as great as that found at the family château. Literature and memoirs have set forth the extent to which such places serve as important supports to family memory and group memory.[15]

In France and abroad, when they are not received as house guests among friends, such wealthy families descend upon luxury hotels on the Riviera (such as Eden Roc at Cap d'Antibes), in Deauville, in Gstaad or in Marrakech. The presence of this type of establishment is an integral part of chic locations. At Marrakech, one may conjecture that the aristocratic families and the international grand bourgeoisie would be fewer in number if an establishment like the Mamounia had not been there over the years, concentrating a part of international society in a haven of peace and luxury. A contrario, the closing of the luxury hotels along the Champs-Élysées, of which had been three, is concomitant with a certain degradation of the avenue.[16] The rates of these establishments are elevated, but there are also the symbolic barriers which prohibit entry by those who would not be able to face the test of passing serenely in front of the reception desk, where the trained staff seem to require clients to be capable of showing themselves up to the situation. The clientele is, or at least was, up until recent times, socially highly homogeneous. These hotels are, like the clubs, exclusive places for an exclusive clientele—havens of security and calm, where everything comforts you with the sensation of being in your own place and deserving the attentions that surround you.

The Palace-Hotel at Gstaad was half empty on July 20, 1993, because it is at Christmas that one must be here—and if possible at Saint-Moritz for the second half of February.

The concierge of the Palace-Hotel has been greeting his guests for twenty years. "He knows all the customers," according to the director of the establishment, "and it pleases them to be recognized, because it is as if they were in their own homes." As in the other deluxe hotels, the great houses of luxury have introduced showcases, such as those of Van Cleef et Arpels, in the elevator cabins, which contributes to creating an out-of-the-ordinary climate. Especially since the staff can sell the jewelry on display.

But the Palace-Hotel has a strong personality. A few steps from the station, which it dominates, it is a strange looking building with its architecture in the style of a Bavarian castle, especially when the snow makes the horizons seem more distant. The suites that occupy the corners of the building have small salons or bathrooms arranged in the turrets.

These aerial spaces, open on all sides on the top floor, the tub marrying the curvature of the turret, give the feeling of have at hand these forested and rocky immensities where ibex graze.

When the season is at its peak, that is between Christmas and New Year's Day, customers go down to dinner in long gown or in tuxedo. That delights M. de Mazerand, who appreciated the worldly charm that Deauville had in earlier days. Gstaad and Saint-Moritz appear him today to be veritable reserves of sophistication and the fortune that must accompany it. In February, at the Palace-Hotel of Saint-Moritz, a place of supreme elegance according to M.de Mazerand, "all the jewelers of the world are there. One sees all the jewels from so near... The lake is frozen. From the hotel, you look out on polo games or horse races [on the lake]; it is fairy-like. Some customers even have themselves taken to the summit by their helicopter to enjoy the pleasures of the coming down on skis." Very disappointed by Deauville, one will come back here. Mr.De Mazerand considers Switzerland to be one of the last places that guarantee "being among one's own kind in the refined elegance of the grand people of this world."

Gstaad benefits from a severe town-planning regimentation that forbids all construction that is not in the style of the country, that is, a wooden chalet decorated with sculpted friezes and floral or geometric painted designs. These chalets, extremely vast, are in a state of perfect maintenance. Their luxury is not easily discerned. Discreet, in the midst of vegetation, they shelter nevertheless well-known personalities, from show business or the arts and letters. But amongst the residents whose names are less famous, industrialists and bankers are numerous. Julie Andrews is one of the current owners and she donates to the city the holiday lighting at year's end. Marshal Montgomery lived not far away. As well the Kandinskys, whose chalet was named Esmeralda. Elisabeth Taylor is still there, and she sometimes gets together with Charles Trenet, a regular at the Palace-Hotel. Shipowners, bankers, big landowners, industrialists complete this social universe. A luxury hotel would not be planted just anywhere, of course: it has to be isolated, and then to be in a splendid landscape. But, when it is constructed in a given locality, the latter could not entirely ordinary. Chic places are highly sensitive to their environment. The collective heritage of the high classes, in holiday resorts, would not accommodate massive invasions by crowds of package tour vacationers.[17]

SCHOOLS OF COSMOPOLITANISM

The internationalization of the great families' heritage comes with a specific culture, in any case with a "cosmopolitanization" of the culture that is characteristic of the grande bourgeoisie and the nobility. The heritage of these international families is also a factor in the accumulation of cultural capital. This is already very much appreciable in the practice of foreign languages. Even if under the pressure of school competition other social strata today very attentive to providing their children with precocious and efficient learning in this domain, the dominant classes benefit from a certain advantage. The idea of hiring English or German nannies, even Spanish, according to the family's traditions and interests, dates from the 19th century and is still carried on today. Véronique de Montremy, grand-daughter of Mauricede Wendel and daughter of Berthildede Wendel, was raised by an English nurse after the Second World War. Her two girls, today schooled at Saint-Louis-de-Gonzague, "speak English very ver well because they had nannies since they were born. They learned English as a mother tongue. It is an enormous advantage, but that has its price." These families do not turn to the traditional foreign language programs managed by specialized organizations. In addition to nannies, one can always stay abroad with family members or friends of the family. Internationalization starts very early with language learning under the best of conditions. That is a part of the human capital, the cultural capital that is acquired definitively and without much difficulty. The conventions of international heritage enable one continuously to maintain precocious training. Travel and contacts with foreigners are ordinary events. So that it is entirely natural that Véronique de Montremy studied at Harvard, in the United States, or that Michel d'Arcangues is a graduate of Hamilton College in New York State. Designing one's life on the global scale is crystallized in the very nature of the heritage that has a pronounced international character.

Swiss Schools

The private establishments of higher education are another manifestation of the international character of the upper classes. By this we mean private schools and not religious schools: at a certain social level one makes an abstraction of these differences. Éva Thomassin is descended from an Argentine family that had a large fortune. She spent part of her life in France and has resided there for several years. She frequented these international establishments. In 1937 "finishing school was fashionable. The very rich girls went there." The Anglomania of the French upper classes was mirrored by the Francophilia of the grand families of Latin America, or at less their taste for things from Europe. "We came to Paris to buy our wedding gowns, Limoges china, a piece of jewelry, and then left."

But high level schools are a Swiss specialty, even though some exist in France, such as the École des Roches close to Verneuil-sur-Avre. Thus Éva Thomassin joined the school of Le Manoir in Lausanne in December, 1937, and she remained there for two years.

"It was an enormous three-story chalet with a big garden and tennis courts. I occupied the room that the sister of the Albanian king had just vacated." Besides scholastic and linguistic training, "girls also came to learn to live among each other. It was important to be well dressed." These girls belonged to high society. "There was no question of anyone being there who was not from the families of the grand bourgeoisie, and some from royal families. It was unbelievably expensive! Me, it is my grandmother who offered me this stay. It was something she could permit herself because my family were multi-millionaires."

Like all big Swiss colleges, The Manor went to the mountains in the winter so that girls, some of whom came from countries where there was never any snow, could practice skiing. "We also went swimming, because we had our private beach [the establishment was at the side of Lake Geneva]. We crossed the Avenue d'Ouchy, went down a small path and arrived at the beach."

All the investments of which these girls were the beneficiaries were not destined to give them a profession. Many of them never worked, or only to manage their family's social capital—which is in any case a heavy task. It is exactly on this point—and even more so as the social capital of these families is international, that The Manor plays a useful role. The reason for this school's existence was certainly to cultivate cosmopolitan capital, in its cultural but also its social dimension. For this reason the school was not, and could not be, religious. "There were some Jewish girls. Everyone went to the church that corresponded to her. I went to the Catholic church. I always met King Alphonse[13] in exile, on Sundays, at the church of Lausanne. Rodica, the daughter of a Romanian minister, went to the Orthodox Church." And so cosmopolitan capital, in order to be accumulated in the best society, must to be founded on tolerance for differences linguistic but also cultural and confessional.

The father of Thomassin Éva had himself been schooled in a big international college in Switzerland, Le Rosey, situated at Rolle, not far from Lausanne, also on the shores of Lake Geneva. The establishment, which still exists, was founded in 1880, as the promotional brochure of this "school for life" specifies. "Le Rosey accepts, without distinction of race, religion or language, children coming from over forty nations." The tuition fees are steep: 47,700 Swiss francs for one year, in 1993, about 200,000 French francs. Room and board are included, but one must add the travel costs between the college and the parental home, pocket money, etc. However, the winter months spent at Gstaad, in the college's chalet, are included.

Le Rosey offers the picture of a multilingual microsociety where one comes to know oneself better in order to understand oneself better, and to understand oneself better in order to like oneself better. And these international friendships are one of the most precious possessions acquirement at the Rosey," affirms the brochure. Isn't it one of the greatest luxuries, to be at home while abroad, with foreigners? Pupils, as a result of this cosmopolitanism, converse among themselves in English, the new Latin of modern times. In a certain social universe, it is simply unthinkable to not speak this language. Conversations during dinners comfortably pass, in any case, from French to English and Spanish, as a function of the present guests' nationalities, and the topics of conversation.

But this cosmopolitanism doesn't mean Americanization, the loss of national cultural references, superficial modernism. By their layout, the buildings of Le Rosey recall a château and its dependencies. They are scattered in the midst of agricultural, cultivated lands. Orchards, fields, vegetable gardens and greenhouses encircle the college, whose surrounding wall is not even enclosed. Pupils live, as at Le Fraisse, in the middle of fields and hundred-year-old trees and can follow the agricultural work to the rhythm of the seasons. The venerable ivy-covered façades and the old tables of stone attest the age of the place. The sports facilities are implanted here and there. The swimming pool bordering on a wheat field, tennis courts, the archery range are indispensable complements of a healthy education. It is actually a question of upbringing, as for all establishments of this type. There again it is remarkable that the family delegates so much to its institutions. It all happens as if this delegation was at rt just the great confidence that this milieu has in itself. Children can be entrusted to a group of one's equals. Being among one's own kind, considering the exceptional quality of the milieu, should be sufficient to assure the quality of the teaching, the contacts, acquisitions of all sorts. As if the group was more important than the home environment, or as if, at bottom, one was dealing with one big family.

The Association of the Ancient Rosarians (AIAR) is charged with multiplying the international capital so accumulated. "The international friendships woven during years of study are an inestimable capital: everywhere in the world there is an ancient Rosarian ready to welcome and to help another."[18]

The College of Sion at Sâo Paulo

These establishments also have satellite educational institutions in countries of the South where the national bourgeoisie feels a great attraction for the culture of old Europe. Children and grandchildren of Count Cahen d'Anvers "have been educated entirely in Argentina, in the English prep schools." The French College of Oiseaux and the Swiss College of Sion have establishments in Brazil. Drosila Vasconcelos was able to take courses from the College of Sion at Sâo Paulo. In Brazil, too, the pupils benefited from having several places of instruction according to the season. During the hottest months, January and February, the college functioned on a farm situated at Petropolis, a chic resort above Rio de Janeiro. The centers of interest during these two months were the swimming pool and the barnyard, which gave them the opportunity to take care of the animals. The remainder of the year, at Sâo Paulo, the college offered, in addition to a minimal amount of school-type training, a systematic initiation to the European, or more precisely international, grand-bourgeois life style. In the realistic decor of a living room, Drosila Vasconcelos learned the art of conversation and the techniques of the body that permit one under any circumstance to preserve a dignified and noble bearing. Another room of the estaishment put the pupils in the decor of a dining room worthy of a grand home. The vast table, under its imposing chandelier, served as the practice field for the difficult art of table setting and planning a seating chart. Having succeeded at this production, the pupils go on to mimic a society dinner and must show themselves capable of subtly managing the progress of this social ceremony. The training concerned materials and means as well, every schoolgirl having to be able to discern crystal from glass at the first glance and to distinguish Limoges china from Bavarian.

Sion schoolgirls, whether educated in Switzerland or in Brazil, benefit from the international network organized throughout the world by the original establishment. It is quite normal, and even advisable, that a student from Sâo Paulo goes to pay a visit to her Parisian counterparts during a stay in France. Such practices aim to broaden the network of relationships, to extend the web of friendships and loyalties. The 1995-1996 catalogue of the high school Notre-Dame-de-Sion in Paris emphasizes that "by its tradition and by welcoming in its residence girls from various countries, Notre-Dame-de-Sion College has always favored opening up to the world at large, and more especially to Europe, while accentuating cultures in their diversity and their complementarity." At a certain level, social capital can only be international. And so Drosila Vasconcelos, to pursue her higher studies in Paris, will find without difficulty employment as a young lady companion for a couple of elderly people in the XVIth precinct. The young ladies of the College of Sion present all the required qualities to hold this trustworthy station in the best society, wherever they may be in the world.

The École des Roches

One finds in France, as well, this type of establishment where the international dimension is at the very foundation of their reasons for existing. Count Cahen d'Anvers, Parisian banker and businessman, and his friend Guy Sch/ler, descendant of one of the oldest families of Bordeaux wine merchants, did their secondary studies together at the Collège de Normandie, at Clères, in Seine-Maritime. The establishment became extinct, and its students then continued their education at the École des Roches at Verneuil-on-Avre, about hundred kilometers to the west of Paris. Conceived on the British college model, in particular Harow on the Hill, their early afternoons are dedicated alternately to sports or to physical work in the 60 hectares of the park of the school. Everything is put to work, for the tuition fees and board that reach 5,000 to 8,000 francs per month (depending on the class) to promote, "better than an education—an upbringing, an international culture!" according to the director. The school thus takes in about 20% pupils who are not French-speaking, and everyone is offered the chance to prepare an English foreign language diploma recognized by the University of Cambridge. Former pupils then can count on the association of the alumni of the École des Roches et de Normandie (AERN), whose 1800 members occupy eminent social positions throughout the world. "The College of Normandy," remembers Guy Sch*ler, was a school where one met South Americans, such as the Saavedras brothers, Moro, some Americans, like the one that became Colonel Ridgway Knight and who was ambassador of the United States, Henry Hide, chief of the OSS, Robert Guestier Goëlet; Englishmen and Frenchmen who were all, in turn, brilliant. Jean Goujon, a test pilot, was killed on active duty, General Jean-Louis de Rougemont... Of course I stayed in touch with Count Cahen d'Anvers, but also with a friend who became a general, another ambassador to the United States, others who were aircraft pilots..." At the former College of Normandy as well as at the École des Roches, a large place is reserved for sports, tennis, rugby, soccer, aviation... and for the development of individual responsibility. "There were no fences. No gates. It was in open countryside. It was designed," concludes Guy Sch*ler, "to shape men who would have responsibilities later in life."[19] It is still that way: les Roches is open to the four winds, as is the college of Le Rosey, and no enclosure separates its buildings, scattered in the vast park, from the remainder of the world. Paradoxically, these establishments, frequented by children from surroundings which one can suppose, a priori, to be the most closed—as they have grounds to fear for their security—are very open on the outside. Which is not unreminiscent of the traditional journey of initiation, of adventure far away, at the end of adolescence, as a formative experience, a rite of passage that permits one to take on adult responsibilities thenceforth. As, for example, for Count Cahen d'Anvers, that long roving journey in the United States which he filled with various forms of employment, including that of a cowboy, which was facilitated by his perfect bilingualism and his practice of horsemanship at Les Roches. The pupils' spirit of initiative and perseverance and their ability to be self-directed are the basis of the creation of the École des Roches as a "new school" in 1899.

As for the international recruitment of the school, the Editorial in the 1994 directory of Les Roches points out that "to be able to meet select people from 60 countries, representing 225 different professions, that's an asset—put it to good use!" Of about 1800 alumni, who performed their studies at the beginning of the century (for the eldest), and who are enrolled in this association, more than 350 live abroad. Either they are natives of one of the 60 countries in question, or they are of French nationality living abroad more or less permanently.

At the École des Roches, foreign languages are learned by the immersion method, as described by M. Dollfus, an alumnus, today delegated by the general management for implementing new, experimental pedagogical methods.[20] Courses are given exclusively in the language being taught. The teachers organize days during which the students have to speak only in English or in Spanish, including during the meal, and among themselves during leisure and during rest times. Of course exchange visits organized with establishments of the same quality, dispersed throughout the world, round out the excellent language education.

After receiving his two baccalaureate degrees from the Collège de Normandie (which merged later with the École des Roches), Count Cahen d'Anvers left for the United States. He returned with a diploma from Harvard Business School, only to leave again almost at once to take charge of the management of an immense property of 448,000 hectares in Paraguay. He thus began a career whose international character was hardly niable and which also supported the practice of sports whose features were not without profit in the management of the international capital of relationships of which college had been one of the points of departure. So it was that Count Cahen d'Anvers played a role in the world of polo, cosmopolitan sport that it is. He also took part in major hunts, such as grouse in Scotland and Spain, and large game in Germany, Austria and Africa.

The college Saint-Martin-de-France, Pontoise, is very similar in its recruitment and in its workings to the École des Roches. This college has 5th and 6th grade classes which work in close liaison with the British school of Hawtreys, with three semesters' stay in England divided over two years.

Alexandre and Philippe-Emmanuel de Fontmichel, twenty-one and eighteen years old, respectively, perfected their English and their Spanish during one-year stays at boarding schools in Scotland and in Madrid. "From the CM2," recalls Alexandre, today licensed to practice law at Assas, "we left for Scotland; we spent a whole year there. Then we returned for a trimester during the 5th level; in the 4th and the 3rd, we left for a boarding school in Madrid for one year. In Scotland it was a typical boarding school, private, but it was not at all a great chic international school. We were the only French, they accepted only one French student by promotion." The result is obvious: the two brothers speak English and Spanish fluently. Philippe-Emmanuel, educated at the *1st economic and social at Franklin*, a Jesuit school, also known by the name of Saint-Louis-de-Gonzague,[21] is learning Arabic as the third language, which he is going to try to present for his baccalaureat exam. "It is a very hard language," he says, "compared to English and Spanish, but it is quite important because in a few years I think that it will be necessary to speak Arabic, it will be a necessity." Beyond language training, Alexandre adds, "is the opening to other civilizations, because, when one knows a language, one can discover everything that goes along with it, that is to say the culture, the Hispanic, the Scottish civilization, culture in general."

The cosmopolitan capital of the upper classes is an essential part of their heritage, both individual and collective. Initiated very early, with precocious foreign language study, then consolidated by educational establishments that cultivate this specific skill—a decisive asset in the social struggles for power and renown—this part of the heritage of the dominant classes is sustained by the various institutions, including clubs, by the casual, friendly networks, and by networks of family alliances.

This cosmopolitan heritage is consubstantial to power and dominant social standing. It is valuable in itself and for itself. But it is also a powerful factor in the accumulation of cultural capital and thereby is a mark of distinction. Especially since this cultural capital is one of the elements of a patrimonial capital where all forms of capital reciprocally add value to each other. There is a certain interdependence between this international social capital, the forms of cultural capital that it generates and the international character of economic capital. The internationalization of the economy and correspondingly, of family heritages, is not recent. But the fact that they relate one to the other probably corresponds to the primary role of the foreigner's importance in the life of business. Elites are cosmopolitan because their interests are. The art market is international, with Christie's and Sotheby's in London and in New York. It would be absurd and risky for the social elites to limit their networkquote s useful relationships to the national level. Wealth management today goes beyond national limits. A big private bank like the Bank Paribas, in reorganizing its services, indicates that the tendency is to amplify this international dimension.[22] For two years the bank reorganized its "professions" on the global scale. "Everyone who practices the same profession," explains Pierre de Leusse, "in whatever country he practices, belongs henceforth to one grouping, is managed by the same men, has the same objectives and the same working accounts." That is the case with institutional and private management, retained as one of the four strategic professions on which rests the development of the establishment. "So that we are 1,100 in the world to exercise that profession on the account of Bank Paribas and its subsidiaries." Indeed, our interlocutor adds that, consistent with requirements of confidentiality, every account is known only in the country where it is opened, and only by the administrator or the administrative team to which it is confided in that country. But the counselors in every country will have the same formation, that is the same knowledge of markets and the same technical expertise in management. Thus the entity "wealth management profession" no longer has a national basis, but is well and truly structured at the international level, taking its existence, from the economic point of view, from one single world where problems cannot be examined and solutions cannot be applied in any valid manner without taking into account the whole ensemble of ramifications as they relate to other national arenas.

Cultures, networks of relationships and the management of family heritage cannot escape this international logic. Making a fortune and preserving it require a type of openness to the world. There are others - in the scientific sphere, or in politics, for example - but the *international* of power and wealth, the oldest in the world, has both formal and informal structures that multiply on a global scale the powers and skills of the elites, who are profoundly united by their concern for the proper management of their future.

Notes

1. Gala, n' 32, 20 to 26 January 1994
2. L'Éventail, n'7, September 1986
4. See Dans les beaux quartiers, op. cit., p. 193 to 252, for the names of the clubs.
5. Xavier PÉRISSÊ and Dominique DUNGLAS, La Privilégiature, Paris, RMC Édition, 1988, p. 272.
6. Op. cit., p. 9
7. It would not be very useful to count them because the under-estimation is considerable. Interviews showed that, in certain cases, one shows only a part of their homes on the worldly list, under the declared motive of modesty.
8. Michel CRESSOLE, "Blue Blood without Borders», Liberation, 7 April 1989.
9. Claude-Isabelle BRELOT, "Les Anticipations européenne de la noblesse francaise (1880-1914)", a presentation to the international symposium, *Ancienne et Nouvelles Aristocraties, de1880 a/ nos jours*, under the direction of Didier Lancien, Toulouse, 21-24 September 1994. A directory like the Gotha was international. Taking up that tradition, the Bottin Mondaincompany plans to produce the Bottin Mondain of Russian *Society* in 1996.
10. Gabriel-Louis PRINGUÉ, 30 Ans de dîners en ville, Paris, Édition Revue Adam, 1948, p. 40.
11. On cosmopolitanism and the social significance of such a relationshpi with the world, see for example Jean-Louis de FAUCIGNY-LUCINGE, Un gentilhomme cosmopolite, Paris, Perrin, 1990. See also Eric MENSION-RIGAU, Aristocrates et grands bourgeois, Paris, Plon, 1994, particularly Chapter VI, "Les usages au miroir de l'Europe", p. 299-357. Anne-Catherine WAGNER gave a very good analysis of cosmopolitan capital in "Point de vue local, point de vue international: une enquête auprès de la bourgeoisie d'affaires étrangère en France", Journal des anthropologues, n' 53-54-55, Spring 1994, p. 49-57, and in "Les riches: une identité internationale", Alternatives économiques, n' 25 (hors série), 3' trimestre 1995, p. 31-33.
12. These notations should be nuanced for the present, none too promising time, for a number of the big luxury hotels that must face a serious crisis. This has given rise to practices once unimaginable, such as the offer of "forfeits" (package rates) for several-day stays, which are a discreet means of lowering rates. Or again the possibility of discussing the price of rooms and suites, of "bargaining". As a consequence, more often than before, unknown customers are presenting themselves, who can afford the hotels due to the special offers, and who don't always reserve in advance—which has become an option because occupancy rates are low. This information was collected from directors of prestigious establishments at Deauville, at

Enghien-les-Bains and in Switzerland.

13. Marc Augé attributes the status of "non-places" to the interchangeable rooms of the big international hotel chains (see Non-Lieux, op. cit.), because they seem so impersonal to him. In the luxury hotels, in any event, the personalization of service palliates this risk.

14. Roger-Louis BIANCHINI, Monaco. Une affaire qui tourne, Paris, Le Seuil, coll. « Points-Actuel », 1992, p. 197.

15. As for the luxury hotels one may cite the one at Balbec, the Grand-Hôtel dear to the narrator of À la recherche du temps perdu, Paris, Gallimard, coll. « Bibliothèque de la Pléiade », 1954, I, p. 662 and following. On Clubs, see for example the recollections of Jean de BEAUMONT, who was president of the Cercle de l'Union Interalliée, Au hasard de la chance, Paris, Julliard, 1987.

16. The Élysée-Palace opened in 1898 and closed in1920, replaced by Crédit Commercial de France. The Astoria, where the present day Drugstore Publicis stands, lived for fifty years, from 1907 to 1957. The Claridge, put in service at the end of the first World War, closed in 1977. See Quartiers bourgeois, quartiers d'affaires, op. cit., "Les palaces", pp. 70-74.

17. See for example the description of the competition for space during the summer by Bertand POIROT-DELPECH dans L'Été 36, Paris, Gallimard, coll. "Folio", n" 1705, 1986.

18. From the presentation package of the college of Le Rosey.

19. Guy Schyler was also an army air pilot and a member of the U.S. Air Force, during the Second World War.

20. A former industrialist, M. Dollfus is licensed and holds an advanced degree in philosophy, is licensed to practice law, and holds an advanced degree in political economy. He was successively a trial lawyer in Paris, a medical doctor specializing in endocrinology, President and General Manager of the Institut français de développement économique (French Institute for Economic Development), and at this moment, Advisor to Jean Monnet at the time of the creation of the European Economic Community. Then he was an advisor for major corporations such as the Compagnie générale des wagons-lits in Alsthom.

21. On this establishment, see the study by Jean-Pierre FAGUER, "Les effets d'une 'éducation totale' - Un ollège jésuite, 1960 ", Actes de la recherche en sciences sociales, n' 86-87, March 1991. Also see Beatrix LE WITA, " Culture bourgeoise et éducation jésuite ", a talk given at an international colloquium "Anciennes et Nouvelles Aristocraties, de 1880 à nos jours," directed by Didier Lancien, Toulouse, 21-24 September 1994.

22. This international dimension has been present since the origin of the bank. It was founded in 1872 by bankers from various countries of Europe, including the Bischoffsheims, of German origin. It so happens that one of daughters of Raphaël Nathan Bischoffsheim married a Cahen d'Anvers, who participated in founding the Banque de Paris and des Pays-Bas. Raphaël de Bauer (1843-1916), director of the Maison Bischoffsheim in Brussels since 1870, married the daughter of Samuel Cahen d'Anvers, in 1867, called Lambert, correspondent of the Rothschilds in the same city. On the history of the Banque Paribas, see Éric BUSSIÊRE, Paribas,1872- 1872-1992, Europe and the World, Paris, Mercator Funds, 1992.

CHAPTER IV

Ceremonies, Fashionable Gatherings and Rituals

THE FAMILY AT THE HEART OF THE NETWORK

Successful transmission of the economic heritage presupposes that the transmission of the other forms of heritage—made up of the cultural capital, educational capital, social capital and symbolic capital—was also realized. Transmission requires having heirs who are capable and prepared to receive what the previous generations accumulated, with all the prestige attached to the name of a lineage and the density of networks into which this one is interjected. Also "the great have large families," writes Pierre Bourdieu, for whom this would be "a general anthropological law." "They have a specific interest in maintaining relations with their extended family and, through these relations, a particular way of concentrating capital. In other words, in spite of all the divisive forces at work on families, they remain one of the places where the different types of capital are accumulated, conserved and reproduced."[1] The family is at the center of the network of relationships that—through the numerous and varied social rituals that give the group existence—allows the accumulation and transmission. This goes from family ceremonies, whose magnificence clearly is not devoid of social significance, to the periodic grand gatherings that punctuate society life.

Social capital is built with support from the family. But social endogamy, which may be regional as is shown in the case of the grand bourgeoisie of Bordeaux, strictly limits the extension of the family network. The field of socially useful families, with whom it is reasonable to consider establishing ties through marriage, is narrow. However, during the last decades, considerable evolution has taken place. If, in the region of Bordeaux, characterized by the ongoing activities of viticulture and forestry, matrimonial alliances are still those of heritages, in other regions, and notably in Île-de-France, what is important is to marry someone of the same social group. Patrimonies have become financial and thus fluid, so that there is no longer any geographic constraint, only economic and sociological constraints. It is not so much the number of connections but their social quality and their extreme complexity that gives the family network, among the grand bourgeoisie, an importance that is social and symbolic—and decisive.

Members of good society from Bordeaux constantly reiterate how closed a world is this society.[2] "At dinners we attend," emphasizes Emmanuel Touton, one of the big brokers of the area, "90% of the people are always the same. For vacation, we go all of 70 kilometers away [to the shores of the Arcachon]. To marry into this group is fatal." Consequently, "If you are from Bordeaux," concludes Christel Baseden, "everyone is your cousin!" And her own case seems to confirm that statement.[3] Her aunt married Éric Schÿler, descendant of one of the great families of wine merchants, the de Chartrons, and brother of Guy Schÿler.[4] Christel Baseden herself married the grandson of Antoinette de Vibraye, Mme Clifford Baseden, descendant of the owners of Cheverny. Her cousin, Corinne de Secondat de Montesquieu, whose father is proprietor of the Château de Fougères at La Brède, married her brother-in-law, Patrick Baseden.

The family network branches out far beyond the limits of kin. But this extension depends nonetheless on family life. Thus France de Cerval, like Christel Baseden a descendant of a family of proprietors of forest land in the Landes, whose brother Henri de Cerval is Master of the Hunt in Gironde,[5] was godmother at her confirmation. Violaine Cruse, whose patronymic is as evocative of the grand epoch of the Chartrons as of the Schÿlers, has held the role, less official but quite significant, of *copine de soirée*. Emmanuel Touton and Pierre Lawton, whose mother Micheline Banzet was first married to Hubert Cruse, prior to remarrying with Hugues Lawton after the demise of her first husband, were her *chevaliers servants*: the geographic and social unity is very tight here since all these names revolve around Bordeaux and its wine market. We could go on: Virginie Calvet, whose family is firmly entrenched in the wine industry in Bordeaux, married Emmanuel Touton and lives across from Ariane Cruse, in the very fashionable, as well as very discreet, district of the Jardin Public. "When the families of Bordeaux marry among themselves, it shows," remarks Christel Baseden. "The ring is superb, and the parents are really happy. For example, the Calvets, who married the de Denis. Ah, well, they have superb lives, extraordinary lives, because the fortunes are associated. Friends of my generation all took over the top story of their houses at the time of their marriage, then they went down to the better floors after the first child came. That all snowballs, it creates a general sense of well-being in the family, and everyone is happy."

Clearly, the family network among high society in Bordeaux is very tight. Of course it extends "pseudopods" in various, and not minor, directions: the Cruse family is in this way closely linked with the Peugeot family. Violaine is the daughter of Henri-François Cruse and of Guillemette Peugeot, who thus has Jean Cruse as a father-in-law. Guillemette Cruse is the daughter of Rodolphe Peugeot and the sister-in-law of Alain Banzet (one of the former managers of the Groupe Peugeot, now deceased) and of Liliane Seydoux, who is the sister of Jacques and the cousin of Jérôme and Nicolas Seydoux, all families belonging to the great dynasties of Protestant high society. Pierre Lawton's half-brother, Jean-Paul Cruse, lets it be known that his uncle Alain Banzet, Micheline Banzet's brother, "lived his whole life at the Peugeots'. He was both the son of a Peugeot who is my maternal grandmother, and he also married a Peugeot [Monique Peugeot]." Finally, note that a daughter of Alain Banzet married a Cruse. Carine Cruse, Édouard Lawton's daughter, married Thierry Peugeot. France Cruse, daughter of Herman Cruse, married Christian Vernes, from the Protestant banking family. The complexity of such networks is endless. Whether the ties are of kinship or friendship, there is a very significant level of mutual acquaintance and relatedness. Now, these relationships are also based on business: nearly all the families mentioned are in contact with each other as a result of the business activities from which they draw their revenue. The patrimonies of these families reflect the alliances nurtured and the nature of the accumulation realized as a result. In the Landes, we know from the novel by François Mauriac *Thérèse Desqueyroux* that the assessment of property values entered into marriage planning in a fairly explicit way. "Bernard Desqueyroux inherited from his father, in Argelouse, a house neighboring with the Larroques [...]. Did he dream much more of Thérèse? The whole country would have married them, their properties seemed made to be combined, and the wise young man was, on this point, in agreement with the whole country."[6]

The networks are only overlapped insofar as the list of potential partners; the families with whom it is thinkable to ally oneself is extremely limited. The milieu of the grand bourgeoisie of Bordeaux rarely goes beyond its own borders, and when it does, it is perhaps, as with the Peugeots, in order to nurture strong ties that are already in place, with a new link. "The scope of the social capital that an individual can mobilize," writes Luc Boltanski, "depends not only on his family origins, but also on the social breadth that he commands individually (which in itself is a function, at least in most cases, of the social capital accumulated by the family) upon which in its turn the extent of his network of relationships depends, multiplied by the social breadth of each of the members of his extended family and, to a lesser degree, of each member of his social network."[7] One can see that the density of the social network would be, in Bordeaux, an exponential factor of the social capital, and a powerful support to be mobilized in case of need.

Elsewhere, as well, ties among the big families are multiple. The Seillières, the Demachys, the Wendels and the Schneiders share industrial and financial interests, reinforced by a system of kinship that, in a way, parallels the network of economic relations. "Throughout the years," writes Ernest-Antoine Seillière, "family ties have been nurtured. Of the two daughters of Charles Demachy one, Hélène, married Léon Seillière, the other, Germaine, Ernest Seillière, future member of the Académie Française. The second son of these latter, Jean, married Renée Wendel. For his part, Jean Schneider, son of Eugène and brother of Charles, married Françoise de Curel, descendant of François-Ignace Wendel, founder of Creusot."[8] Ernest-Antoine Seillière, an alumnus of the École Nationale d'Administration and Finance Inspector, manages the financial companies of the Wendel family, of which he is a member through his mother. He celebrated his fiftieth birthday at the Grévin museum and his 387 guests were the living incarnation of a remarkable social capital. Gabriel Milési noticed among them the presence of Michel David-Weill (Banque Lazard), André Bettencourt (the former Minister, whose wife Liliane Bettencourt, née Schueller, is the heiress of the founder of L'Oréal, and as of now holds the largest French fortune), Philippe Bouriez (Groupe Cora-Revillon), Jean-François Lemoine (a landowner in the South-West of France), Édouard de Ribes (Groupe Rivaud, son-in-law of Jean de Beaumont, President of the Cercle de l'Union Interalliée, and himself Vice-President of the cercle), Guy and David de Rothschild, Jean-Pierre Soisson (a former Minister), Pierre-Christian Taittinger (Mayor of the XVIth arrondissement, head of the wine-producing e, and hôtelier, including the Crillon and the Campanile chains).[9] Thus the family plays a considerable role in business leadership. That is indispensable in the transmission of the patrimony of relationships.[10]

And even today, the system of alliances is so intermingled that as soon as a person's name is mentioned, at a cocktail party or a dinner, the guests immediately outline who the relatives are and throw themselves, with great skill, into elaborating the family tree. It is so important to know who is who, that is to say, what is the network of relationships one is talking about. People are so aware of the importance of the stakes of this family and social life that they intensely cultivate an extended network of friends. This amounts to a considerable social task which, in the end, melds the individual into the indissoluble family and sociological group.

Generally speaking, godfathers and godmothers are selected from the heart of the family group, with the aim (among other objectives) to reinforce the intergenerational ties. 'An uncle is good,' one might hear, 'but uncle and at the same time godparent is even better.' A priest who is related to the family will be invited to perform the newborn's baptism. A large family allows for a diversity of emotional ties and therefore a certain euphemization of the "generational conflicts" and the "adolescent crises."

Family life is linked to certain places, some of which are emblematic. It may be the Parisian house, built by an ancestor, like the one on the Champ-de-March, which was built by the maternal grandmother of Catherine de Persuy, granddaughter of a rich oil baron. "My mother," she says, "lived all her life in this building. When I was born—I am thirty-six years old now—my grandmother had her own apartment and each of her three children had his. It was a pretty exceptional ambiance, we could go for a walk in the house, we used to go to see our grandmother everyday." Wealth seems to allow, and maybe to require, the cohabitation of generations, a family structure that has become rare, including at least a part of the grand bourgeoisie. One of the privileges associated with these vast homes is the option of living in this inter-generational cohabitation as a choice and not an intolerable constraint. The parallel life of generations, who have numerous opportunities to meet due to their spacial proximity, is an element that organizes the transmission of traditions and knowledge, relations and possessions.

It remains that, when one reaches old age, in these surroundings also, retreat seems to become the rule; but under conditions that remain exceptional. When the burden of an apartment becomes too heavy "past a certain age," says Catherine de Persuy, "in my father's family, they go to live in a hotel where everything is taken care of. My paternal great-grand-parents finished their life in a hotel. Their three daughters, too."

Family meals are opportunities to take the measure of the available social capital, that is, the size of the network of family or extra-family relations. There is no sector of social activity where the family has no "correspondents", whether in business, the army, culture, the church. This display of the capital that is fundamentally social, fundamentally linked to the family, helps teach the future heir to see himself and to conceive himself as one link of a lineage, one stitch of a net, of a family network that spreads in this way through the past and the present, and projects itself into the future. The family is not an entity in itself, it is a veritable social construct that requires the accumulation and the management of this particular form of social capital that is the family capital.

The best districts themselves encourage the maintenance of social and family relations. Whereas the other social categories are dispersed in the urban space, the extreme spacial concentration of elites encourages their meetings, impromptu or deliberate. It is in such neighborhoods that one bumps into each other in the bakery, whiles one also frequents the same club, with all that that means in terms of spacial proximity and things in common. The neighbor is also a cousin, or a schoolmate from the École des Roches. In the best neighborhoods of Paris people go to visit on foot. To drop in for tea, or for an aperitif, without having to make appointment, that too is a privilege in an agglomeration where the least meeting requires recourse to the Filofax (appointment book) and long deferrals. Rallies and clubs, by their spacial dimension, take their place within these parameters proper to the higher classes who, at least in the very large cities, can live on a few square kilometers because the immense majority of urban territory matters so little to them, or at least is of little use socially.[12]

This concentration explains the ideological homogeneity as it is unveiled through electoral results. On May 7, 1995, Jacques Chirac collected 83.2% of the votes in the XVIth arrondissement and 85.9% in Neuilly. This marking of territory is both a social and a family affair: all one's kinship also lives in the narrow circle of the useful part of the city, that is, a few well delimited districts.[13] One understands the utility of the *Bottin Mondain*: all the relevant population is listed there.

THE NOMINAL HERITAGE AND ITS LISTS

The limits of the field for possible alliances are not as imprecise as the uninitiated might think. The existence of the *Bottin Mondain*, and, before that, of its famous predecessors such as the *Almanac of Gotha*, created in 1763, or of works with a more regional focus such as the *Book of Families of the North* or the *All-Lyons Directory*, demonstrates it clearly enough.[14] The *Book of Families of the North* presents itself indeed, according to Bruno Duriez, "as a compilation of genealogies [...] of which pairs of ancestors were generally born in the first half of the 19th century. It is the social standing of these ancestors that determines whether all their descendants belong in the social group of 'the Great Families'."[15] The milieu that is socially useful is thus defined by lists and indexes as numerous as they are redundant: social lists, alumni directories from prestigious schools, club membership directories, more casual lists such as those from automobile rallies. To appear in these indexes is as crucial, from a social point of view, as for a prep school student to make it onto the admission list for a top university. To make it onto the lists is a struggle, and the results of this struggle are grounds for hope or despair. These lists of names, without other refinements, are for internal consumption. Family names in these ancient surroundings are known and condense unto themselves all the forms of capital accrued by the family. The name identifies and denotes everything that lends renown and prestige to a family.

The *Bottin Mondain* and *Who's Who* are the best known of the directories that present a census of the social élite. However, the conditions for inclusion differ.[16] "Inclusion in the former is at the initiative of the person or the household that wishes to be listed, but it requires more than simply paying the fee (in the form of a subscription to the work). It assumes that the person in question has recommendations from two people already included therein, which is not unlike the sponsorship rule that is in place at all the great clubs in Paris. In 1995, the *Bottin Mondain* contained 42,500 listings that group families by "household", a total of some 200,000 individuals, of which 145,000 are babies."[17] Inclusion in *Who's Who*, by contrast, is at the initiative of its editors. They are the sovereign decision-makers, deciding which individuals they will include there, on the basis of social standing and renown. Also, *Who's Who* is not an index of great families, but a biographical dictionary of personalities, containing political leaders of leftist parties, included the PCF, as well as captains of industry, dignitaries of the Church or the army, or again members of the Institute. An eclecticism, therefore, that offers no guarantee as to the social respectability of the people listed.

It is not at all that way with the lists that preside in the organization of rallies or with the membership directories of the great clubs. Reflections of selections and exclusions linked to the process of induction, these lists and directories provide all the guarantees of a rigorous choice, without complacency. To be included there is the equivalent of having a patent of social excellence—a strong patent envied by those that, too near this world not to feel concerned about the consecration that finding one's name included there would constitute, yet too far to be represented among the elect.

It is not at all indifferent that, on these lists of names, aristocrats cohabit with the bourgeoisie. And that the noble names are put first, whether in the denomination of rallies that happily carry the name of a very ancient family (rallies being designated by the names of founding mothers or other influentials), or in the induction of names of members during the controlling processes of a club. Thus, whereas 90% of members of the Cercle du Bois de Boulogne are not members of the nobility, 8 of its 11 successive presidents since 1867 carried a noble title, including the five that have held office since 1941, the current president being Count de Gouvion Saint-Cyr. One finds the same phenomenon in other clubs with a preponderance of bourgeois members, such as the Cercle de l'Union Interalliée with Count Jean de Beaumont. In other words, the great families of the bourgeoisie find, in mixing in the company of aristocratic names, in using these family names charged with references to the past, a kind of compenn for the formal triviality of their own names. By putting forward the emblematic names of the aristocracy, the bourgeoisie uses some of the symbolic capital conveyed by a "big" name that, by its very form, manifests several centuries of prestigious ancestors. The name, by itself or, if it is lacking in fame, then in proximity to big names, thus plays a decisive role in the accumulation and the transmission of social capital. "The result of this work of accumulating and maintaining social capital is the greater as this capital is greater," writes P. Bourdieu, "the pinnacle being represented by those who hold inherited social capital, symbolized by a big name, who don't have to make the acquaintance of 'all known (cf. "I knew him well"), to an extent transforms all circumstantial relations into lasting

NAME	Address	NAME	Address
Amaury de Cherisey	1st ardts	Christels de Nervo	16th
Isabelle de Chezelles	6th	Noëlles de Aboville	16th
Alessandra Serey	6th	Carlos de Cordoba	16th
Elvire Letourneur	6th	Carines de Vregille	16th
Geoffroy de Verdun	6th	Alexander de Soye	16th
Dorothée Bacot	7th	Alix O'Neills	16th
Marie-Aimée d'Hotelans	7th	Sophie de Labarre	16th
Laurent de Castelbajac	7th	Marie-Astrid Tarneaud	16th
Moirent de Samucewicz	7th	Florence de Gamay	16th
Marie-Astrid d'Harambure	7th	Thomas de Lussac	16th
Thibaut de Ladoucette	7th	Frederico Vecchioli	16th
Elvire de Rochefort	7th	Anne de Buffevent	16th
Anne-Sophie Gilbert	7th	Guillaume de Bartillat	16th
Clêmence Maze-Sencier	7th	Ghislain d'Auvigny	16th
Emmanuel Maze Sencier	7th	Albane de Broglie	16th
Philippe de Miribel	7th	Christian Ledoux	16th
Agathe de Baurepaire-Louvagny	7th	Marie-Laure de Bueil	16th
Diane Hervé-Gruyer	7th	Frédérique de Bueil	16th
Patrick d'Hérouville	7th	François-Laurent de Beauregard	17the
Elisabeth de Montmorin	7th	Anne-Laure Morel d'Arleux	17the
Alexandra de Gontaut-Biron	8th	Claire de Bussv	17th
Laurent Bremond	8th	SYbille de Changy	17th
Diane de Poncheville	8th	Frédéric Henriot	Neuilly
Julien Schoenlaub	8th	Catherine Henriot	Neuilly
Patrice Bênilan	8th	Eric Cosserat	Neuilly
Eléonore de Montesquiou Fezensac	15th	Laetitia Gérard	Neuilly
Thibaut de Diesbach	16th	Laurent de Pontevès	Neuilly
Alexandrine de Roquette-Buisson	16th	Maximilien Tieleman	Neuilly
Marie-Gabriella de Roquette-Buisson	16th	Maguelonne de Buchet	Boulogne
Astrid Villeroy de Galhau	16th	Eleonore de la Tour du Pin	Boulogne
Hortense de Labriffe	16th	Pierre-Hemi de Villeplée	Boulogne
Bénédicte Henry	16th	Stéphane Huygues Despointes	La Celle St

100

Marie-Laure Papin	16th	Laurence des Rotours	Versailles
Charles-Edouard de Lacretelle	16th	Cécile Pastré	Lisses
Guy-Patrick de Broglie	16th	Chrystèle Brossette	Ste Foy
Ida de Poncins	16th	Madeleine de Ginestet	Htes-Pyr.
Etienne de Poncins	16th	Hugues de Robien	Amiens
Guenola de Saint-Pierre	16th	Marie-Aimée de Laguiche	Dijon
Thierry de Vulpillières	16th	Camille Francez	Besançon
Lucie de Prémont	16th	Irène Léon-Dufour	Aisne
Jean-Baptiste de Proyart	16th	Aurélie de Chezelles	Londres
Aurélie de Virieu	16th	Constance de Suzannet	Londres
Ombeline de Clermont-Tonnerre	16th	Jean-Edwin Rhea	USA

This list was established from the society pages of *L'Éventail*. It is not, therefore, exhaustive. It includes, in addition, some members of the O'Neill rally that had a party together with the Bretesche-Broglie-Montmorin rally.

were reported, in the form of a photo gallery of of the guests; the names of the young people photographed, and the parents who were responsible for the party constituted the captions of the photos. This means of publishing the list stays confidential, considering the public of such a magazine. The only significance it has is the presentation of a milieu in itself, as a display of the group in action. Belonging to the "grand" world isn't proclaimed from the rooftops. A sect without proselytism: it is certainly important to be in it, but it is sufficient that this membership is recognized by the insiders alone. Discretion is the rule, knowing very well what one is. Nothing would be more vulgar than being ostentatious of an affiliation that owes nothing to recognition by the profane. The guest book, which guests must fill in at the request of their hosts, demonstrates to what point the name lists can be important and serve to draw contours of the group, to specify the limits of the network that can be mobilized.

Other lists have the same function: they have a strong symbolic value, such as the "Social List" (it is titled thus explicitly in the work) of the *Bottin Mondain*, distributed commercially certainly, but in a limited way all the same. Directories of major clubs, well, those are confidential, for internal use, distributed in principle to the membership alone. For those who are not members of the seraglio, procuring a copy is not easy—when it is not downright impossible. These lists enhance a name through proximity with other names that are famous, or simply spectacular names in their form (double or triple family names with the particles denoting nobility, and the titles that accompany them).

So the grand council of the Interallied Union presided over by Count Jean de Beaumont, whose father created this club in 1917, includes a number of individuals of the first class, in very diverse domains, mingling the big names of the nobility tied to land or to business with the bourgeois family names from industry, finance and politics. The business community is largely dominant and it is not astonishing that the former president of the CNPF, François Ceyrac, appears there. However, it is the whole category of the dominant classes that is represented there, in its various modes. To belong to such a club is to enroll oneself in a network of relations covering all the domains of social activity at the highest level. It is a particularly typical form of accumulation of social capital, and affiliations to other clubs can multiply the effects.[22] Some members of the grand council of the Interallied Union are also present at the Jockey Club, at the Travellers, the Automotive Club, the Bois de Boulogne Club, the Polo in Paris. According to specific activities, they frequent the Saint-Cloud Golf Club, the Yacht Club of France, the House of Hunt and Nature, or again the Club of Deauville.

In these directories, the simultaneous presence of parents, ancestors, children, cousins and collateral relatives displays the "family" capital owned by those families which, because they merit representation in these listings, appear there several times. One has thus, in the *Bottin Mondain*, an accumulation of homonyms that puts a value on the extent of the family network. In the Jockey Club directory one can count 13 La Rochefoucaulds, 7 Broglies, 12 Dampierres, 6 Polignacs... Lists and directories delimit an "exceptional" space within the social space, to which the specific fractions of geographical space correspond, as shown by the addresses of the people cited.

A name's effect never appears more clearly than in the case of the aristocracy. As a general rule the family name, by its very form (with the almost systematic presence of the particle 'de', 'La'), and because it often comes with a title, expresses the exceptional character of the person. Even when the particle is absent, which does not prejudge the authenticity of membership in the nobility, the frequent citation of the title fills this lacuna. Also, the name, sometimes the title that comes with it, is sufficient to establish the person's social excellence. That is why these two elements are subject to such finicky vigilance: the presumption of nobility must be founded. The nobility stays alert to denounce usurpations of names and titles, in truth to call attention to family names that can pretend at most to the appearance of nobility, even in the absence of any fraudulent intentions on the part of those families whose name is decorated with a particle without their belonging to the aristocracy and without their dming of making any such pretense. Laxity would not be tolerated, on the grounds of depreciating the specific heritage that the name constitutes.

The Tribe

With a tight network of relations, with a true unity of location (that of ththe "beau quartiers" of Paris and the private resorts), the nobility and the grand bourgeoisie evoke the sense of a tribe. The way Michel Panoff and Michel Perrin define the term ("a politically and socially homogeneous and autonomous group occupying its own territory"[23]) reinforces the analogy with high society. Certainly, there is a deliberate will, on the part of the privileged classes, to control their living space. We have seen the intensity of the exchanges and their socially exclusive character. However, the analogy quickly reaches its limit in a major fact: the grand families become part of the dominant relationships that imply direct relations with the dominated social groups. Thus one may suppose that the notion of "tribe" is readily used to designate the aristocracy and the grand bourgeoisie, according to a logic that is ironic and at the same time envious: the tribe is marked with the seal of archaism, but at the same time it is impossible to become a part of it if one was not born into it. So that this "tribe", the tribe of the upper classes, has the singular characteristic of being distinguished by the privileges it enjoys.

One of the most visible can be seen in the locations where good society lives. Whether in Paris, Bordeaux or in other large regional metropolises, the grand bourgeoisie understands perfectly well how to control its residential neighborhoods. First of all, with their financial resources, they can live any place that looks good to them. Also they adhere to the rule of keeping among themselves, one of the means of assuring the conditions most favoring a successful transmission of the various forms of patrimony. But territorial control cannot be absolute because space, insofar as economic assets are susceptible to being bought or sold, is subject to the laws of the market. The aristocracy's and the bourgeoisie's taste for preserved land, sheltered from common development, property belonging to country clubs or to golf clubs, for example, is based on this fundamental principle of the impossibility of perfect control over the environment of daily life. But this control can, on the other hand, be attained through vng a free option, which is still the best means of ensuring that one will not have to mingle with just anyone. Territorial vigilance must be augmented therefore by social practices that, while calling for private use of certain spaces where access is subordinated to criteria other than material convenience, exclude symbolically and, especially, practically those that are at the margins of the group. Given these considerations one may understand the upper classes' taste for resort locations that do not always present truly exceptional characteristics. Only the one, truly essential characteristic—the assurance of being, if not absolutely, then at least sufficiently, among one's own kind.

Summer at Arcachon

The Arcachon Basin is representative of these exceptional locations. It constitutes an extension, still preserved, of the bourgeois districts of Bordeaux which all of polite society visits. On weekends and vacations, numerous families whose fortunes are tied to commerce, wine growing, or timber in the Landes come to the Basin. Certainly, the shores of this immense body of water are not uniform, and their diversity reflects sometimes the subtle distinctions deep inside the grand bourgeoisie itself. The basin also includes some more popular areas that derive their revenues from fishing, oyster farming, or even tourism. Nonetheless, in spite of these variations, Arcachon, Le Moulleau, Le Pyla and Cap-Ferret, where villas surrounded by vast parks exude a sweet and discreet perfume of well-being, are places where the grand-bourgeois lifestyle exists in crystalline form. Emmanuel Touton, a wine broker, gladly leaves his office in the Chartrons district for Cap-Ferret, where his grandmother's house can be found, orPyla, where his wife, the daughter of the big wine trader Jean Calvet, has a villa. Shared between these two emblematic places, he is more aware than most of their similarities and their differences. "There is a certain rivalry between the two sides of the Arcachon basin. There are those who reside at Arcachon, at Moulleau or Pyla, and those who are at Cap-Ferret. It is a friendly rivalry, but the Ferret-capiens hate to go to the other side and the Arcachonnaises and the Pyladaises don't like to go to the other part either." This opposition has more to do with a fairly different urbanization than with any specific social characteristic.

Arcachon, like Deauville or Biarritz, is a beach resort created during the Second Empire. The banker Émile Pereire, a native of Bordeaux, was the first to take an interest in the Basin. He acquired several hectares of forest and undertook to create from scratch a whole town with a grand atmosphere, whose purpose was to be, at the beginning, to allow people with respiratory ailments to regain their health. "In this forest, purchased in part by the Compagnie des chemins de fer [the railroad company of which he was president], and in part by himself; he had chalets built with people suffering from 'illnesses of the chest' in mind. That was in 1862; success was immediate. 'Winter City' then passed into the hands of individuals."[24] Napoleon III was recruited to contribute to launching the success of the Arcachon basin, whose air, both salt and balsamic, was considered ideal for treating respiratory insufficiencies. First in 1859, when he came with the Empress Eugénie and the imperial prince, and a second time in 1863, when Émile Pereire presented the Winter City to him.

Winter City, situated on the Arcachon heights, on the wooded dunes, still offers an exceptional architectural ensemble today. The city was conceived as an urban park. It winds along by sinuous alleys, whose curves were intended to break the winds from the sea, between Swiss chalets, Norman villas, Gothic manors and pavilions of Moorish inspiration. This diversity winds up giving a charm and a unity to the whole: the eclecticism of architectural forms characteristic of vacation places, sea resorts and seaside towns at the

Table 5. The grand council of the Cercle de l'Union Interalliée (Interallied Union Club)

NAMES	PROFESSIONS, RESPONSIBILITIES
Comte Jean de Beaumont	Corporate director. Member and Vice President (1970-1974) of the International Olympic Committee.
Édouard Bonnefous	President of the Senate Finance Commission. Former State Minister. Chancellor of the Institut de France (Académie des sciences morales et politiques).
François Ceyrac	Corporate director. President (1972-1981) of CNPF. Economic and social policy advisor.
Olivier Giscard d'Estaing	Corporate director. Former deputy (1968-1973). President of Groupement International de Coopération économique et Commerciale (GICEC).
Edmond Marchegay	PDG d'Air Paris (1968-1974). Corporate director.
Comte de Ribes	Banker. Corporate director.
Comte Arnold de Waresquiel	Head of an agricultural estate. Vice-president of the General Council on the Mouth of the Rhône (1957). Vice-president of the Hospital Works of the Order of the Knights of Malta.
Claude Bertrand	Director-adjunct of the Banque Louis Dreyfus.
Prince Karim Aga Khan	Imam of the Ismailite Moslems.
Prince Rainier III	Sovereign Prince of Monaco.
Édouard Balladur	Former Prime Minister. Former Economic Minister.
Bernard Baudelot	Avocat à la cour de Paris. Ancien bâtonnier (1971-1973).
Général de Boissieu	General of the Army (CR). Former Chief of Staff of the Army. Former Grand Chancellor of the Legion of Honor (1975-1981).
Jean-Pierre Bouyssonnie	President, then Honorary President of Thomson CSF. President of Thomson-Brandt. Corporate director.
Prince Gabriel de Broglie	Former President of the CNCL. State Advisor. Director General of Radio-France. President (1979-198 1) of the National Audio-Visual Institute.
Comte de Brossin de Méré	Commerce executive, Beghin-Say Company.
John Crawford	President of the American Chambre of Commerce in France. Member of the Council of the International Chamber of Commerce.
Étienne Dailly	Head of an agricultural estate. Corporate director. Vice president of the Senate. President of the General Concil of Seine-et-Marne. Vice-president of the Radical-Socialist Party.

105

Michel David-Weill	Banker. President of Groupe Lazard. Corporate Director (BSN Gervais-Danone, Fiat Crédit Corporation, etc.). Member of the arts council of the Union of Natinoal Museums. Member of the Institute (Academy of the Arts).
Jacques Dreyer	Auditor. Honorary President of the auditing firm Streco-Durando.
Jacques de Fouchier	Banker. Honorary President of the finance company Paribas. Inspector of Finances.
Comte Bruno de Galbert	Vice-president of the Steeplechase Society of France. Leutenant-colonel (CR).
Jean-Louis Gavoty	?
Philippe Guérin	?
Robert Husson	President of the French Insurance Union. Corporate Director.
Jean de Lachomette	Former Senator. Vice-president director general of Éts Hotchkiss-Brand (1957-1966). Director of Thomson-Brandt (1966-1980). President of the French delegation to the International Hunt Council.
Roger Lebon	Corporate Director. President of the Paris Banking Union.
Jacques Maillet	Director General of SNECMA. P-DG of Intertechnique. Corporate Diretor.
Jean Matteoli	Former President of the French Coal Board. Former Labor Minister. Deputy to the Mayor of Paris.
Count Olivier d'Ormesson	Head of an agricultural company. Regional Counselor of Ile-de-France (1976-1980). Mayor of Ormesson-sur-Marne. European Deputy. Councillor General du Val-de-Marne.
Jean-Bernard Raimond	Ambassador of France, Former Foreign Business Minister (1986-1988).
Baron Edmond de Rothschild Banker.	President of the Benjamin and Edmond de Rothschild Bank S.A., Geneva. Corporate Director.
Pierre-Christian Taittinger	Former Pres. of the Municipal Council of Paris. Vice-president of the Senate. Secretary of State. Adjunct to the Mayor of Paris.
Silvestre Tandeau de Marsac	First Secretary of the Law Practicum Conference.

SOURCES: *Directory* of the Cercle de l'Union Interalliée, *Bottin Mondain* and *Who's Who*.

July 14 thus marks one of the prime moments of the summer reunions of a population where nearly everybody knows each other—because people come to the basin throughout the year. In winter or the off-season people meet on the square by the church Saint-Seurin de Bordeaux, at the exit from the Dominican Mass, and make a date for tea in

Cap-Ferret or Moulleau. In any case, on a given Sunday in October, everyone is in weekend garb: cotton jackets for youngsters, evidence of target practice or hunting; a silk foulard for the gentlemen, rather than ties, and corduroy trousers; skirts with Scottish motifs for the ladies. But villas fill up especially during the summer season, which allows for gathering in the branches of the family that now live far from the region. A walk on the beach is then an occasion for multiple stops, for exchanged greetings, for the uninterrupted demonstration of the unity of the group. Neighbors from Chartrons or the Jardin Public seem to take an intense pleasure in running into each other again, in swimsuits by the shore of this calm bit of ocean. It is true that, quite often, this neighborliness which is as m wintry as summery, goes on throughout several generations. Christel Baseden spends her vacations in one of apartments fitted out by her grandmother in the enormous family villa des Genêts. This was constructed on the initiative her great-grandmother, Blanche Prôme, née Bordes, whose father was one of the big shipowners of Bordeaux. Her grandmother, Countess Arthur de La Taille-Tétrinville, taking action with the changing times (which had become less favorable to the big permanent gatherings of the extended family), had the immense family villa, situated at the side of the basin with "its feet in the water," as the real estate brokers say, restructured into eight independent apartments for each of her eight children. "We are not there for nothing," said one of her daughters, "that is a gift from the gods! Today we are independent. Me, I just look after my children and grandchildren. But it is marvelous to be with my brothers and sisters, who become uncles and aunts, first cousins for the following generation. One celebrates his fortieth birthday, another his fiftieth, it is marvelous! Thanks to this house, the family hasn't split up." For that to be possible for another generation requires that the habit be formed while very young. Even though these ways of doing things may become dull, there is still always something there and in the present case the independence granted to the households by restructuring the villa encouraged maintaining this tradition of a joint vacation. "We were always in the habit of spending our vacations together," concludes this aunt of Christel Baseden positively. "By necessity we are not among those people who go to hotels, who travel and have very dispersed lives in the summer. We leave our home to come to Arcachon. It is also a way of complying with tradition." This does not preclude other forms of leisure and vacations. But it offers the advantage of a heightened level of acquaintance. Christel Baseden met her future husband on the beach, her future in-laws having a villa one hundred meters from her grandmother's. Descendants of the latter's sister still occupy the neighboring villa des Genêts and a breach has been opened to permit free transit between the two gardens. On the beach Christel Baseden greets many bathers, among them the Seillière family of Laborde. "They are Parisian, but they have been coming here for generations. They have an enormous house that overlooks the church, the villa Saint-Arnaud."

This permanence of habits and the quality of the available leisure are elements that structure memory. What must it be like, to have childhood experiences of summer vacations in such conditions; in what ways and to what extent must these experiences contribute to the structuring of habits? Jean-Paul Cruse, the journalist's, grandparents "purchased at Moulleau, from the Gervais family (the cream cheese ones), a big Basque style house." It is a constant in this kind of milieu to mention the former owners of villas or apartments that one buys: as if real estate possessions themselves should have a pedigree.[26] The acquired asset owes part of its symbolic, and probably market, value to the renown of those who occupied it. "In this villa, I used to meet all my cousins on my mother's side," continues Jean-Paul Cruse. "I went there all the time when I lived in Bordeaux. A big part of summer vacation. That is where I learned to sail. Around the age of fourteen, fifteen years, we would bicycle to Arcachon. Which means that all my memories, all my good memories of childhood and adolescence, are actually more of Arcachon than Bordeaux or Paris." And still today again, for his vacations, Jean-Paul Cruse returns to this family house where the memory of his young years lives.

So therefore there is something of the tribe in these social and regional microcosms. But the commonly accepted definition of the tribe bestows upon it an archaic status—it would come somewhere after gangs, before chieftains and organized states.[27] Also, in keeping with the analogy of the tribe, one risks implying a stigmatism by assigning the bourgeoisie to a less developed stage of civilization. The use of the term 'tribe' suggests, among other problems, rejecting to an obsolete past a social group that, actually, while recording its domination in tradition, continues to this day to accumulate all forms of capital with great efficiency. And that is how it is with social capital, too, which all forms of sociability, including those that may appear the most outdated to the uninitiated, contribute to maintaining and expanding.

THE EFFICACY OF SOCIETY EVENTS

Dominant groups, certainly, but also minorities, the nobility and the haute bourgeoisie gladly serve as the object of sarcasm and irony from the dominated groups, far more numerous, who find in this laughing derision a sort of symbolic yet mystified redress. Because, in underestimating the power of those who do have power, in laughing or smiling at their characteristics that seem different, one only underestimates that which constitutes their social strength. Thus one plays against his/her own camp by encouraging the reproduction of hierarchies and inequalities. That is the case with forms of courtesy and the linguistic practices of the high classes that draw smiles and provoke the sneers of those whom these acts separate from positions that may be envied and that are, in any case, out of reach. Kissing the hand; a certain language both refined yet blunt, an accent peculiar to the better districts; the rules of courtesy; a discreet but constant elegance, including in the most unexpected places, as in the fort when riding to the hounds, holding one's body both straight yet supple: all these signs and many others are all affirmations of social standing, proclamations of membership in the dominant classes.

These modes of being, apparently rigid and codified, are opposite to the demonstration of values founded on what is "natural" or "relaxed," for example in the education of children where laissez-faire seems to prevail. These are the ways preferred by the classes of middling intellectual means. Without doubt one must see, in this system of opposition, one of the grounds of the real phobia that the very idea of riding to hounds may provoke, a practice often considered in these urban intellectual surroundings as a holdover from the *Ancien Regime*. This way of rejecting other people's world as an anachronism is, however scarcely, compatible with the sociological approach for which all social forms still in use are held to be contemporary.

Corresponding to every specific form of heritage there are forms of organization and rituals, ceremonies and social manners whose reason for being may be found in the requisite conditions for the accumulation and the transmission of these heritages.

Social Events

Thus, under conditions *a priori* rather unexpected in such surroundings, through learned societies or through preservation committees, the privileged inhabitants of the *beaux quartiers* of Paris have always tried to defend their real estate heritage, menaced by the covetous appetites of merchants and business. Luxury trades defend the signature style of the good address, so dearly acquired, by employing the social form of prestigious "open-door" evenings.[28] Champagne flows in rivers then, buffets beckon: be it for the evening of Vintages, organized by the Committee of Montaigne Avenue, that brings together the big couturiers, audiovisual firms and the Plaza-Athénée, for the open-door evening of the Committee Vendôme for which the majority of expenses is covered by jewelers and whose name is better known in London, New York, Tokyo, at Abu Dhabi or, recently, in Moscow, than in Aubervilliers. The ostentatious lavishness of luxury establishments benefits their customers, delighted not so much by the charity as by the pleasure of being together.

Economic capital can serve as the basis for highly symbolic displays, oriented not so much outwardly as toward the group itself. In these displays peculiar to the beautiful districts of Paris, or to luxury establishments who take up residence there, the public is very severely restricted, by the invitation system and by that social self-censure that is so efficient that it makes everyone keep to his place—there is hardly a teacher or a carpenter who would hazard Place Vendôme or Avenue Montaigne to take advantage of the occasion, even though entry is absolutely free. These social ceremonies are above all celebrations of the group itself, functions coming at regular intervals that permit those moral reassurances that all esoteric rituals provide.

There are, however, other opportunities where the economic heritage, in putting itself on stage, reinforces the symbolism of domination. This is the case in the equestrian universe. Racing stables are one of the most hierarchical possessions. Owning them, which may represent income producing capital, is as often owning symbolic capital where the cost is greater than the profitability. But the advantages, from the point of view of affirming one's social standing, are considerable. The world of horse racing, to an unparalleled degree, involves popular classes of the public, which form the majority of the spectators at a grand prix. The grands prix, like the one from Diane to Chantilly, or the one at Deauville that closes the resort season at the end of the month of August, are the occasion for an exceptional display of power and wealth. Then the group displays itself in all the magnificence of the luxurious feminine toilettes, in the aristocratic rigor of the masculine performance. At Deauville, the popular folk can admire everyone and, as a bonus, attend the rustic lunch of those happy elected, which sometimes gives one the pleasure of seeing a recognizable face.

These society ceremonies may be on the occasion of cultural events, art exhibitions, openings of performances, music festival ... The symbolic gains are most elevated in circumstances that mingle the cultural capital and the social capital with the charity, when luxury and demonstrations of charity join together. This was once the case of the Circus Molier, a circus for society people, whose profits went to charity and mobilized good society in theaters as well as at the track. Whether it is to benefit unhappy childhood, the Red Cross, Rwanda or AIDS victims, the wealthy families gladly make a spectacle on occasion of these big collective impetuses of organized charity. Such demonstrations have high visibility: the national press and the local press cover the event, the specialized magazines, *Gala* and *Point de vue*, grant significant space to the largest events. The Red Cross Ball in Monaco, which the royal family attends, has been a society event of the first caliber for 46 years. The ticket price was 6,000 francs in 1994. But, "although tickets are very dear, obtaining them is not a question of money. The difficulty, the only real difficulty, is to be accepted. To choose the 1000 elected from among the 3000 requests that flow in every year despite refusals of the previous year, the SBM [the Society of Sea Resorts, owner of luxury hotels and the casino] named a selection committee. There again an order of priority has been established: fidelity, celebrity, notability, are the principle criteria."[29]

There are various causes to be supported. Thus, in the fall of 1991, the big jeweler Paolo Bulgari gave a sumptuous reception at the orangerie of the castle of Versailles to help the Worldwide Fund for Nature.

In Deauville, Saturday, August 28, 1993, the traditional Racing Gala, sponsored by Mercedes-Benz, organized as a benefit for hospital establishments for jockeys, amplified the social melting-pot that takes place every evening at the casino. Every guest of this banquet, enhanced by a floor show, acquitted himself of the sum of 1,400 francs. A few dozen idlers wait for vehicles dropping off their share of tuxes and long gowns in front of the perimeter of the establishment, which is more illuminated and resplendent than ever. Among the spectators, some come on purpose and others are taken by surprise, having had the innocent intention of spending the evening at the slot machines. Participants in the official reception, like stars at the entrance of the palace of the Cannes festival, must therefore face the attentive looks of an improvised honor guard that watches them climbing the staircase that goes around twice, decorated for the occasion with voluminous floral arrangements of which one, including fruits, is rongly influenced by the theme of the horn of plenty.

The atmosphere is relaxed, good natured. This show of wealth goes over well—no doubt because this evening one is in the presence of a charitable event. This guaranty of charity permits putting on a show of social domination without that being seen as aggressive. The benefit is double, since one makes evident the dominant position that one occupies in society, while legitimizing this position by the social preoccupations that are the official purpose of the evening. Young jockeys on the steps hold the places that would otherwise be occupied by the Guards of the Republic. In a certain way the beneficiaries of the evening are there and attest to its merit.

The climate is not tense and one feels no animosity from those who come to contemplate the toilettes and the lifestyles that will never be accessible to them. This type of fascination, at least apparently, is ornamented by the hope, sometimes fulfilled, of seeing a known face, an established fortune, a local personality or television star. The spectacle is worth the pain and no one dreams of breaking this kind of enchantment of suddenly feeling so near to the inaccessible. So it all takes place in a relative confusion and an amused mess. While participants in the official reception sip champagne, amateurs at the slot machines find they cannot enter the rooms. They amuse themselves by enjoying the spectacle from behind the green plants that have been placed momentarily to bar entry. Then, the last guests having arrived, all participants go into the Grand Salon of Ambassadors where the Gala takes place. Moved away by the casino staff, the green plants in their pots must then permit the migration of the crowd oidlers that has grown and is waiting to go to the slot machines. A complex maneuver, not understood by some, takes place when a sudden mixture of traffic and of types of people intermingle for an instant before each finds his own place.

The Meaning of Society Events

Cultural and charity events, promotional events for luxury goods, the practice of hunting, golf or boating, etc.: opportunities to exercise one's social aptitude, for those who have any, are numerous. Society life is made up of infinite variations on the same plot, that of obligatory rituals and networks of mutual acquaintance with the people who belong to "high society." The structure imposed on grand bourgeois life by social events is almost daily, if we include dinners and afternoon teas. Such a superfluity of receptions, such an abundance of ceremonies where rituals are repeated that have no place in other people's lives, has given the term "society events" a pejorative value. These forms of accumulating and managing social capital are ill-accepted by those who owe everything to their educational capital. To understand the importance of it, we must consider these techniques in their social context. One can then admit that the formalism of society events is actually structural, with regard to the reality of the group. The latter integrates an obligatory integration into the system of relations that encompasses all fields of social activity, an integration without which one's membership in the leading class is never complete and remains uncertain. One can apply to society life what Norbert Elias wrote about life at court, by the way: "One has a tendency to judge men of another time or another society by taking the values of his own time as criteria, to select from the infinity of facts those which, in the light of one's own estimation, seem to bear a particular importance. But with this approach it is impossible to discern the interdependences of the men whose behavior one wants to understand. One detaches them from the inter-relationships that they maintained with others, one inserts them in a heteronomous manner into contexts that are not theirs and that are determined by the scale of values of the researcher and his own times.[30] Transposing this temporal distance into social distance, one can apply this analysis to the difficulties of researchers in social sciences. They are always at risk, without realizing it, of demonstrating a devastating class ethnocentrism towards the populations that they study and, in the present case, of taking for a radical social critique what is only the alienated reflection of the confused perception of those in the dominated position. This attitude prevents one from seeing, for example, in such antiquated practices as the kissing of a hand, all the social benefits that are procured by mastering these practices. Because as much as etiquette remains incomprehensible for members of the intellectual middle stratum, and even seems somewhat ridiculous as so many irrational old crazes, that is how much it speaks to inside even if only as a reliable sign of recognition among members of the same minority. It is in this manner, writes Elias again, that one can understand etiquette: it has no need of being explaed by advantages. Through etiquette, the society of the court conducts its own self-representation, each distinguishing himself from the other, all together distinguishing themselves from the people foreign to the group, each one and all together managing the proof of the absolute value of their existence.[31]

From the outside, the perception of society life readily directs commiseration or irony towards those who appear unable to evade the liabilities that it implies. But let's not forget that the social agents who manage their social capital this way have been produced by their family and by society in such a way as to have both the material and cultural means, and the taste, for it. There is a pleasure specific to the habitude when the practice is the realization of the constitutional predisposition that composes it. There is always pleasure in being that which one is. Also, the courtier in his day and the grand bourgeois today do not see it as "a chore, as a limit on their liberty, the necessity of adapting oneself to the canons of Society. Masculine attire (considered prim by teachers or technicians who wear jeans these days) goes without saying, and that which others consider "relaxed" is on the contrary perceived as slackness or bad taste, which one would not permit oneself—which one could only experience as a debasement, a degradation, far from claiming it as a liberation, a conquest of his "self-actualization." There again one may transpose the writings of N. Elias: "The social and worldly life at the court and in court society was invested with a double purpose. It was, on the one hand, the equivalent of our private life, it assured to these men and women relaxation, pleasures, entertainment. At the same time it fulfilled the role of our professional life; it was the direct instrument of self protection and of getting promoted, for the men at court, the milieu where their rise and fall would be decided."[32]

No doubt we should take care to make the distinction—court society and today's society life are analogous but not identical. The absence of a monarch, the loss of the nobility's exclusive rights, what is at stake with these customs and practices, many parameters have changed. N. Elias affirms that the "representative of the professional middle class [...] receives fewer private visits and cannot receive as many as can the aristocrat. The latter dedicates far more time to social life."[33] But that is valid only for the period that he studied. Today, on the contrary, one of features of society life is to mingle nobility and middle class. The degree of social success and integration into the leadership class can even be improved as a result of the degree of integration into the society world. A consequence of the disappearance of court society was this relative "trivialization" of society concerns that are no longer the monopoly of the aristocrat alone. This was one of the signs of the fusion of the elites, which is still going on today.

As a result, participation in society life is one of the most discreet but also the most effective principles of division that separate the most dominant classes from all other social groups, including the newly rich and top executives in management or business who do not belong to this universe by birth. This involvement in the universe of society life is all the more clearly an indicator of real involvement in the most central spheres of power and domination since the importance of symbolic capital and social capital goes equally with the more imperious necessity of using the most sophisticated forms for managing, transmitting and reproducing them. When social standing is defined mainly by one's professional position—which is never the case in the dominant spheres, where the person cannot be reduced to a social standing defined in a uni-dimensional way—then social capital, indispensable to executive positions, can in large part be independent of working in interpersonal management, from person to person, and is reconstituted on a professional basis when there is, for example, a change of employer. This is what N. Elias seems to suggest in writing that "there, where the foundations of social existence are essentially financial or professional, the social standing of every individual can be replaced with a relative ease."[34] In every social group people turn to a wealth of relationships, but its extent varies greatly and, as a consequence, so do the requirements for managing it. Social capital is, in the grand families, a fully-fledged form of capital that even has its own "professionals." A grand bourgeois or a noble who is financially ruined (whether male or female) can change occupations and specialize in managing the social capital of the group. And so one finds specialists at the worldwide hunting organization. Such a young woman will be solicited to draw up the invitation lists for a dinner party. In every fashionable town, Deauville, Biarritz, Monte-Carlo, there is always someone who can make introductions to all the local families of consequence.

In the high spheres of society, they understand how important everything is that contributes to preparing the new generations to take their turn in this essential work of managing the social capital. The preparation is apparently successful, when you may hear Alexander de Fontmichel, a law student, affirm that "business law, in itself, does not really exist. You have to have a lot of relationships in order to do business. Law without relationships is not enough." Specific types of knowledge are an essential part of any good upbringing and educational establishments themselves, as we have seen, are not above including training in such social techniques as part of their pedagogical program. During childhood and adolescence, youngsters are submitted simultaneously to the involuntary inculcations of their milieu, by example and by habit, and to deliberate inculcations, trainings, consciously oriented toward the techniques that they will have to put to use once they become adult. Christel Baseden's recollections suggest the first kind of inculcation: "I was invited everywhere, at the time there were extraordinary parties, long gowns and castles that would sweep you off your feet! It was always in dream houses with very pretty pieces of furniture. "The Bordeaux region, with its narrow circle of grand bourgeoisie where everyone knows everyone, is conducive to this training, which is carried out without any difficulty in the private hotels of the Jardin Public or Xavier Arnozan Court, in the villas of the Arcachon basin, at winter sports resorts in the Pyrenees and in châteaux of the Médoc and the Sauternais.

But these sweet trainings are supported by the much more deliberate educational activities such as rallies. There, one learns the pleasure of being among one's own kind, and the conditions that permit one to taste this pleasure. These gatherings of young people, hand-picked, have the objective of allowing each one, without risk of making a mistake, to recognize his counterpart in all foreseeable social situations and to choose, knowing the underlying reason, his partners for friendly, loving or conjugal relationships. At the same time, what one could call a club mentality is developed, that disposition that makes you feel that you are never so comfortable as when you are with your peers and equally that they, themselves, won't tire of your company. Fundamentally, it is about instilling solidarities that, while making you feel that others in your group are your neighbors, are one of the strongest symbolic foundations of an unparalleled class-consciousness.

Notes

1. Pierre BOURDIEU, *Raisons pratiques*, Paris, Le Seuil, 1994, p. 196.
2. Blandine Grosjean and Yves Harté gave us precious assistance in making the acquaintance of the great families of Bordeaux.
3. Note the spelling of "Christel": Cyril Grange, in his studies on given names, has noted that in high society great liberties are taken in spelling. As though it were necessary to give an ordinary first name, used to a greater or lesser extent depending on the exact social group but present in all of them, an individual style, a form of distinction, in the same way that one must manage the maintenance of one's body, which in itself is also scarcely distinctive, as a way of expressing one's individuality.
4. The Chartrons' district, north of the Place des Quinconces, is home to the grand families of the wine industry, big business, and finance. The wine merchants' cellars occupied the ground floors of their houses.
5. Henri de Cerval is responsible for the hunt of Poussignac, which goes after roebuck in the forest of Les Landes. It is a passion shared broadly in the high society of the South-west of France but it is also a popular sport. See: Michel PINÇON and Monique PINÇON-CHARLOT, *La Chasse à Courre. Ses rites et ses enjeux*, Paris, "Petite Bibliothèque Payot", 1996.
6. François MAURIAC, *Thérèse Desqueyroux*, Paris, Grasset, 1927 (Re-published by "le Livre de Poche", 1994, p. 25-26).
7. Luc BOLTANSKI, "L'espace positionnel. Multiplicité des positions institutionnelles et habitus de classe," *Revue française de sociologie, 14* (1) 1973, p. 3-26.
8. Ernest-Antoine SEILLIÈRE, "La saga industrielle et financière de trois familles lorraines: les Schneider, les Wendel, les Seillière", dans *Les Schneider, Le Creusot. Une famille, une entreprise, une ville (1836-1960)*, Paris, Fayard/ Réunion des musées nationaux/Écomusée de la communauté Le Creusot-Montceau-les-Mines, 1995.

9. See Gabriel MILÉSI, *Les Nouvelles 200 Familles. Les dynasties de l'argent, du pouvoir financier et économique*, Paris, Belfond, 1990, p. 260. This is only a small example of the people who were assembled together that night.

10. On the transmission of enterprises, see Pierre-Paul ZALIO, "Échec industriel et réussite sociale, le cas du capitalisme familial marseillais. L'industrie marseillaise des corps gras à travers la trajectoire sociale d'un groupe familial de la bourgeoisie," *Entreprise et histoire*, June 1995. The study concerns the Rastoin family.

11. On the alliances among families composing the various élites, see Emmanuel BEAU DE LOMÉNIE, *Les Responsabilités des dynasties bourgeoises* Paris, Denoël, 1943 à 1973 (5 volumes covering the period from 1799-1945).

12. When Maigret must conduct an investigation in the Faubourg Saint-Germain, Georges Simenon notes that he "didn't go far. One never had to go far in this business. One could have said that for all those that were involved in it, from near or from afar, Paris was reduced to a few aristocratic streets." Georges Simenon, *Maigret et les vieillards*, Paris, Les Presses de la Cité, coll. "Tout Simenon," 10, 1990, p. 669.

13. Monographs have the advantage of showing the role of the urban space in the formation and the reproduction of a newborn bourgeoisie, thanks to all the networks of inter-connectedness and to all the matrimonial alliances. See Olivier MARTIN, *Familles de la bourgeoisie blésoise. 1765-1964. Le rôle d'une ville moyenne dans un processus de mobilités personnelles*, EHESS thesis, 1994.

14. On this question of names, one may read our article "Le nom de la lignée comme garantie de l'excellence sociale" ("The name of the lineage as a guarantee of social excellence"), *Ethnologie française*, 1990-1 January-March, volume 20, p. 91-97.

15. Bruno DURIEZ, "La bourgeoisie répertoriée: le *Livre des familles du Nord* ", *Ethnologie française*, 1990-1, January-March, tome 20, p. 71-84. On the *Tout-Lyon Annuaire* (Directory of all Lyon) , one may ready Yves GRAFMEYER's work, *Quand le Tout Lyon se compte*, Lyon, Presses universitaires de Lyon, coll. "Transversales", 1992.

16. On the *Bottin Mondain*, see Cyril GRANGE, "La 'liste mondaine'. Analyse d'histoire sociale et quantitative du *Bottin Mondain*", *Ethnologie française*, 1990-1, January-March, tome 20, p. 83-90, as well as "Le Bottin Mondain, l'annuaire chic", *Alternatives économiques*, No. 25, 3rd trimester 1995 (an occasional publication: "Les Riches"), p. 36-37, and *Les Gens du Bottin Mondain: Y être c'est en être*, Paris, Fayard, 1996. On *Who's Who*, see Olgierd LEWANDOWSKI, "Différenciation et mécanismes d'intégration de la classe dirigeante. L'image sociale de l'élite d'après le *Who's who in France*," *Revue française de sociologie*, 15 (1) 1974.

17. Their dates of birth are given, which is a considerable aid to the mothers in planning their rallies. The various addresses are always given in full, complete with telephone number. For it is of utmost importance in the management of social capital that one be accessible to others from one's own background. Telephone numbers will be given in the *Bottin Mondain* even when the user is unlisted in the general telephone directory!

18. Pierre BOURDIEU, "Le capital social, notes provisoires", *Actes de la recherche en sciences sociales*, January 31, 1980, p. 2-3.

19. Jack GOODY, La Raison graphique, Paris, Midnight, coll,. "Le commun", 1979, p. 150-15 1.

20. On rallies, see our work Dans les beaux quartiers, op. cit., pp 147-192.

21. *L'Éventail* went out of print in 1992. Its first number, whose concept borrowed closely from a publication by the same name in Belgium, was published in January, 1986. *Point de vue* took up the formula of an illustrated social chronicle, but the weekly publication seems to waver between being a tear-off calendar of the royalty, for the cottage-dwellers to dream over, and a pocket calendar for use within Society.

22. See our work, In the beautiful districts, op. cit., p. 193-252.

23. Michel PANOFF and Michel PERRIN, *Dictionnaire de l'ethnologie*, Paris, Payot, coll. "Petite

Bibliothèque scientifique," 1973, p. 259.

24. Éliane KELLERS, Arcachons, villas et personnalités. Le temps retrouvé, Éditions Équinoxe, p. 10.

25. Roger MARTIN, "Arcachon, ville impériale", Nouveaux Cahiers du Second Empire, 29. The Moorish Casino was destroyed by fire in 1977. The Chinese buffet at the station had a shorter lifespan, having been demolished in 1882.

26. This is also true for art works and art objects, and old books, whose provenance is generally mentioned in auction catalogues.

27. That, for example, is the concept developed by Marshall SHALINS in Âge de pierre, âge d'abondance, Paris, Gallimard, coll. "Bibliothèque des Sciences humaines", 1976.

28. On these displays, see our work Quartiers bourgeois, quartiers d'affaires, op. cit., p. 264-268. On the notion of "Designer real estate", ibid., p. 8-10.

29. Roger-Louis BIANCHINI, Monaco. Une affaire qui tourne, op. cit., p. 196-197.

30. Norbert ELIAS, La Société de cour, op. cit., p. 236.

31. Ibid., p. 97.

32. Ibid., p. 32.

33. Ibid., p. 38.

34. Ibid., p. 84.

CHAPTER V

WEALTH AND CULTURE

Families of the aristocracy and the grand bourgeoisie, particularly those who have occupied their position for several generations, can accumulate all forms of capital and be as well endowed with cultural capital as with economic capital. But by this same association, it becomes a delicate matter to distinguish between the different forms of capital. Cultural capital seems to change its nature and to be a different species from the one that secures the social position of the dominated fractions of the dominant classes, that is, to those classes who owe everything to their educational and cultural capital. In the old families of the nobility or the grand bourgeoisie, culture becomes a material and economic element of the heritage, with its art objects and its antique furniture. Their possession does not go without a certain knowledge. This knowledge and these objects being of an everyday order, it becomes difficult even to maintain the classic distinction between the two meanings of the word "culture," which may be read as "erudite" culture or as "anthropological" culture.

SCHOLARLY CULTURE AND ANTHROPOLOGICAL CULTURE

The notion of culture incorporates two different meanings. "Knowledgeable" or "cultivated" culture refers to the production and the consumption of work conceived and distributed in a relatively autonomous field, the cultural field. This culture is therefore the product of specialized agents, of cultural producers whose profession is to feed a specific market and to assure the diffusion and the transmission of adequate knowledge. Intellectuals, scientists, artists and teachers form the bulk of the corps of these producers and distributors of culture. Pierre Bourdieu's works show that the appropriation of these cultural possessions was far from being distributed equitably and that it depended on the academic training and the available cultural capital in family milieu.[1]

It is different with the anthropological meaning of the notion of culture. There can be no question of inequalities in its distribution since, by definition, such a culture is the organized system of practices, of lifestyles, in a society or in a social group. In the first sense, the existence of a working man's culture does not come about on its own. Bourdieu challenges the very idea that the dominated groups could have a "cultivated" culture of their own. They can possess at most some scraps of this culture, have a deformed access to it, distorted by the failure to master cultural principles. But then, in the anthropological sense, one can affirm the existence of a working class culture (or aristocratic, or bourgeois...), whose foundations rest on the conditions of existence and on the social position occupied. Food, clothing, relations between the sexes: by multiple aspects the groups distinguish themselves from each other and affirm their identity through their lifestyle. The relationship to worldly cultan enter into this anthropological culture as an element of the lifestyle, but in ways that vary widely depending on the social group in question.

To such an extent that in the case of the dominant fractions of the dominant classes, this distinction between the two accepted meanings of the term "culture" seems to become muddled. It becomes difficult to make the distinction between "cultivated" culture and daily life. Not that the grand bourgeois or aristocrats are creators of cultural works, or even that they always demonstrate a high degree of cultivation. But they maintain familiar relationships with cultural possessions because these possessions are elements of their daily life. Cultural knowledge is unexceptional. Integrated into daily life, it constitutes a part of the anthropological culture of the group.

House-Museums

Privately held stylish pieces of furniture, objects and works of art, old books, make up part of the familiar universe. These are the trivial and priceless decors of lives outside of the ordinary. For other social groups, works of culture are held in an environment that tends to isolate the works from their "natural" environment, that of their origin. Among the wealthy families, cultural possessions seem to escape the museum effect that pulls the work out of its context. As Hans Haacke puts it, "the most widespread practice remains that of decontextualizing objects, a bit like the presentation of a rare butterfly collection."[2] Grand-bourgeois apartments, with their antique furniture, their carpets and their tapestries, their art objects, a profusion of paintings, and portraits of ancestors, are museums and at the same time the setting for ordinary life within which the family exists. So much so that some homes have been bequeathed "as is" to show the presented art works "in their juice", as the auction catalogues say—that is, with all the effects of family life that is more "natural" to them than the cold rooms of an exhibition hall. Thus there are, in Paris, the Nissim de Camondo and Jacquemart-André museums. This is also the case with the château de Champs-sur-Marne that used to belong to the family Cahen d'Anvers. Of course one finds similar examples abroad. In London at the end of the 19th century, Sir Richard Wallace bequeathed his immense mansion to the state, together with precious furniture, art objects and an exceptional collection of pictures that belonged in the house.

Villa Ephrussi de Rothschild at Saint-Jean-Cap-Ferrat, now open to the public, has preserved, in accordance with the wishes of its legatee Mrs. Maurice Ephrussi (born Baroness Charlotte Béatrix de Rothschild) the ambiance of a private home. This house, built between 1905 and 1912 "on the narrowest portion of the isthmus of the headland of Cap Ferrat, [...] dominates the harbor of Villefranche on one hand, on the other the bay of Beaulieu, commanding a brilliant view that extends from the Cape of Antibes to Bordighera and the Italian coast. The mountain there blends into the sea, the sharp perfume of the scrubland of Provence and the marine air blend into the refined emanations of villa gardens that border the coast by the hundreds."[3] The villa was bequeathed in 1934 to the Academy of Fine Arts of the Institute of France, to become a museum. "The Villa Ephrussi de Rothschild," wrote Marcel Landowski, perpetual secretary of this academy, "like Hadrian's villa at Tivoli, which brings together the marvels of the world, is much in demand as a locale for artistic meetings. The collections put together by Béatrix de Rothschild and her spouse Maurice Ephrussi are encyclopedic. Just in itself the villa is a kind of Victoria and Albert Museum that combines furniture and tapestries, sculptures and objects of art, ancient and modern paintings. It is part of the very select club that unites the Wallace Collection in London, the Jacquemart-André Museum in Paris, the Frick Collection in New York."[4] The patio holds an ensemble of Renaissance and medieval art works including a painting by Carpaccio. A salon in the style of Louis XVI is decorated with panelings of the 18th century coming from the hotel Crillon, and with a carpet from the Savonnerie. The Louis XV salon is decorated with Gobelin tapestries and a Boucher painting. The house holds a collection of Sèvres and Vincennes china, of sketches and cartoons by Fragonard—in all, "close to 5,000 works of art," as the tourist brochure proudly emphasizes. Beyond the somewhat obvious enthusiasm of those who have the burden of setting a value on this bequest, even if such a home cannot leave one indifferent, it remains true that it is an example of this interweaving of art with fortune. It also presents a type of museum of the art of gardens, highly prized in high society; the park offers on 7 hectares, a garden in the French style, but also Spanish gardens, Florentine and Japanese, a lapidary garden and an exotic garden, etc.

Some kilometers from there, at Beaulieu-sur-Mer where it occupies the extremity of Pointe des Fourmis, the Kerylos Villa was built during the same period for Théodore Reinach. This fervid and wealthy hellenist was, by the way, related to the person who built the villa of Saint-Jean-Cap-Ferrat since, like him, Charlotte Béatrix de Rothschild had married a member of the Ephrussi family. The villa "presents itself," as is written in the brochure for the public visiting the house (likewise bequeathed to the Institute of France), as "a remarkable reproduction of ancient Greece, unique in the world, a striking picture of beauty. Even in Greece one cannot find a home as reminiscent of the existence of the ancient Hellenians of Pericles' century through a domestic setting and that which it includes: reproductions of artworks, furniture, fabrics, frescos, mosaics. Everything has been thought through, even how to disguise the elements of modern comfort: mirrors, electricity, the piano." Again, this is about an exceptional home, where each element has been conceived to integrate into this whole which must evoke ancient Greece: every piece of furniture has been designed especially, the woodwork, the flooring. Collections of pottery, Tanagra figurines, oil lamps, ceramics, and a library dedicated in Greece complete this evocation. Beyond the relative authenticity of certain aspects, it is in itself an original work. This house that used to be lived in has become, just as it was conceived and lived in, just as it was when it sheltered the family life and the society life, a museum, a setting of life thus immortalized. Coming to visit it, like the Villa Ephrussi and the other homes thus bequeathed, tourists legitimize the symbolic capital crystallized with the help of the stamp "Institute of France." This institution, in sacralizing under the form of a museum these exceptional homes, and in opening them to the public at large, contributes to reinforce the symbolism of violence that associates good taste and cultivation with wealth, and makes those who enjoy these circumstances seem to be quality people. Likewise, those châteaux that are open to the public, whether or not they are still private property, achieve the alchemy that transforms the everyday circumstances of privileged families into an eternity of art, and that founds the belief in the excellence of those who would have chosen to shelter their existence in such settings.

Other homes, such as the abbey of Vaux-de-Cernay, in the Yvelines, which belonged to the Rothschilds, have been purchased and refurbished by hotel chains, and are therefore open to the public while preserving a large part of the original decoration and furnishings. One of these chains, the "Hôtels particuliers" ("Private Mansions"), is "concerned" to provide its guests with "exceptional places." This hotel group, controlled by Philippe and Gérard Savry, intends to bring to life "the soul of the stones, the spirit of a place, timeless values of reflection, of escape." The group has purchased several castles, transformed into luxury hotels. At the Vaux-de-Cernay, the rooms still preserve the character the Rothschilds gave them. The 19th century plumbing has not been changed in the bathrooms. There is no television in the rooms. The whole ensemble retains a rustic enough aspect to add value to the places and respects the amenities in which the former owners lived. Visitors to bequeathed homes and customers of these "private" hotels can live for a time in the atmosphere and the decor of the great families of legendary wealth. Which does not come about without involving some of the effects of symbolic domination, in which it is quite difficult to distinguish between the symbolic power of cultural capital vs. economic capital. This is so true that, in these house-museums, the perceived symbolic violence is the product of the show of wealth, and the legitimacy that it derives from the cultural contents in which it is clad.

Scholarly culture contributes to defining the anthropological culture of great families. This integration of cultural production into the grand-bourgeois universe only reinforces itself. Indeed, under the pressure of the competition of pretenders, children of the grand-bourgeoisie owe it to themselves to achieve brilliant university degrees. So that "Currently," writes Pierre Bourdieu, "an increasingly large fraction of employers, the world over, comes from the best schools. Those who dominate the economic world, the captains of industry and trade, without being great intellectuals, are not at all the narrow-minded bourgeoises of the 19th century. In the 19th century, artists, Baudelaire, Flaubert, could be opposed to the bourgeois, as to beotiens, stupid Philistines. Today the bosses are often refined people, at least as far as social strategies of manipulation, and also in the domain of art, which, even when it is the product of heretical ruptures and real symbolic revolutions, can enter without problems into the bourgeois art of living."[5]

Books and Reading

These general considerations on the place of culture in the grand-bourgeois lifestyle merit some discussion of nuances and detail—particularly on the place reserved for books and reading. The book is certainly present by dint of the widespread practice of bibliophilia or the existence in the family heritage of a library to which every generation brings its contribution. But the company of collected texts, and of books in general, varies greatly. Weak readers and great readers may occur within the same families or in the same salons. The trouble is that reading is one of the most solitary cultural practices in existence. Thus it is not a very social activity. However, the relationship of the grand bourgeoisie to culture is above all social: cultural activities are among the forms of socializing proper to the group. The decoration and furnishing of homes, by contributing to preparing sites for social gatherings such as drawing rooms or guest rooms or houses, introduces culture into this aspect of grand-bourgeois life. Bibliophilia makes sense in this context. Reading is not the most central cultural form in a social group more inclined t activities that permit them to affirm their existence and to maintain their networks. By contrast, groups less favored with economic capital but well endowed in cultural and educational capital will value reading above all, one of the cultural practices most accessible from a material standpoint.

In the effort to appraise cultural practices within their proper contexts and to construct a space for the configuration of the possible practices, one must guard against the tendency to establish hierarchies, to allow a class ethnocentrism to take over. That would tend to reduce culture to the book, that is to say, to a product that is widely available to those having a good cultural and educational capital, without benefiting from the economic capital that would enable them to appropriate cultural products on a more than symbolic basis. One must also watch out for the tendency to assign a hierarchy to the array of possible readings, the subject matter, styles, and authors, according to the readings associated with the researcher's social universe. Such a tendency to establish hierarchies can only lead more or less to a euphemistic contempt for the indigenous hierarchies. One will also notice that a researcher is, in principle, a professional reader, the same as college and university professors. Thus it isonly in comparison to the actions of these specialists that we must size up those of nobles or grand bourgeois, whose principal activities are elsewhere, particularly in business. One finds this same viewpoint in the development of studies such as the one on "cultural practices of the French" conducted from 1973 to 1989 by the Département des études et de la prospective du ministère de la Culture et de la Communication[6]—it basically gives priority to the symbolic consumption of cultural works in their possession.

These nuances aside, it remains true that, given the quality of their life's setting, children of the nobility and the grand bourgeoisie benefit from an atmosphere where elements of scholarly culture are abundantly present. They end up maintaining a familiar and intimate relationship with scholarly and legitimate culture, as with their native language. This familiarity permits an immediate identification of styles, of epochs, of artists, and transforms the family training into tastes experienced and often perceived as innate. Incorporated as good manners and refined language, culture, both scholarly and anthropological, becomes an essential element of social rank, with the transformation of the most social acquisitions into differences of nature.

GROWING UP IN A MUSEUM

References to an exceptional life setting abound in the volumes of memoires that describe like a menu the daily existence of the nobility and the grand bourgeoisie, as well as in the interviews taken with families close to these milieux. This material proximity with works of art, their integration into the domestic universe, has a profound effect on the relationship one has with cultural products. Part of the cultural difference inherent to the dominant classes must be found in the unequal opportunity to acquire such pieces for inclusion in the decor of daily life. "The fact that for members of the dominated fraction [of the dominant classes]," writes Pierre Bourdieu, "and in particular for teachers, a work of art is exclusively (or mainly) an object of symbolic appropriation—that is, acquisition in the name of knowledge and ostentation in the name of discourse—whereas the dominant fraction are in a position to materially appropriate the objects in question, or their equal, and integrate them into the set of luxury possessions which one "owns" and "enjoys," without needing to show in any other way the excitement that they procure and the taste to which they testify—this contributes to encouraging two fundamentally different relationships to the work of art [...]. The conjunction of the material appropriation and the symbolic appropriation gives the ownership of luxury possessions [...] a legitimacy that [makes] it the symbol *par excellence* of excellence itself."[7]

The description of a close relative's apartment by the heiress of one of the oldest families of the French nobility, Victoire de Montesquiou, daughter of the duke de Montesquiou Fezensac, is characteristic of the fantastic memories that a privileged environment can generate in a childhood that is no less so. "We always ate lunch at her home, at 44 Gabriel Avenue," she writes. "In this apartment, looking out on the market and on the Puppet Theater, there was only beauty: the walls of the grand salon and the furniture upholstered in Gobelins tapestries with a rose background, based on designs by Barcher. On the tables, the marquetry dressers, Meissen figurines mounted on bronze sat next to busts by Rodin, most of which represented Granny Fenaille, my great-grandmother. Pictures by Fragonard and Boucher, Debucourt engravings, gave this whole ensemble a perfect estheticism of irresistible poetry."[8] Family portraits are given the place of honor in these private galleries. "My grandmother did look like the painting that Foujita made of her," remembers Victoire de Montesquiou. Whether their subject is family members, a place that was dear to them such as one of the ancestral castles, or a favorite passtime such as hunting, pictures are often integrated into the family context. They represent a part of the saga of the lineage.

These life settings are at the origin of childhood memories that depart from the ordinary. "I lived an exceptional childhood, stupefying," says Monique de Rothschild. "Anyway, I often wonder if this is not a daydream, I have so much difficulty sometimes

127

believing that I lived that childhood. I grew up at the Abbey des Vaux-de-Cernay, a fabulous property that belonged to my grandfather. For me it is a fairytale, a legend. It was astonishing by any consideration—with eighty horses in the stables, with spring water from the fontaine Saint-Thibault that was bottled and labeled there. It was a magical property. Even the smell, that mixture of stone and wood." Monique de Rothschild passed her childhood, until the age of seven, in the milieu of the dentelated stonework of Gothic rooms and the vestiges of a Cistercian abbey from the 12th century, under the stone ogive arches that held collections of art from the Middle Ages and the Renaissance, sculptures from the 15th and 16th centuries, Orfèvre porcelain, and tapestries.[9]

The Château of Arcangues, close to Biarritz, contains numerous works of art. The vast reception room, where Michel d' Arcangues welcomes his visitors in front of a painting by Renoir, is illuminated by a glass roof, like the one at Ferrières. This immense "hall" goes up two stories. The first floor is marked by a corbelled gallery that overhangs the ground floor on all four sides. This gallery is occupied by the library that holds 15,000 volumes. These ample spaces are filled with the family's mementos, photographs, paintings, objects of art, in a profusion that makes one forget the majesty of the scene and gives them a warm intimacy. It is quite difficult to separate what is "culture" and what is "the family" in such a universe. Passionate about literature and cinema, Michel d'Arcangues' grandfather and father published several volumes of poetry, memoires and critical essays. They welcomed in their house many artists and writers whose autographed photos, letters, and dedicated works fill several shop windows of a salon adjoining the main hall. Maurice Ravel, Stravinsky, Hemingway, Cocteau, but also Churchill and de Gaulle, along with many others, honored Arcangues with their presence. Traces of their passage fill with a very family flavor the private museum that iangues: culture, here, is life itself.

In the same way, at the heart of the old city of Grasse, the private mansion where the family de Fontmichel lives, artistic and historic culture mingles with daily life. This house has been in the family since 1774. It offers a succession of salons "decorated with canvases executed in Frankfurt in the house where Goethe was born, at the request of the count de Theas Thorenc [the first owner of this home] who found himself there in the capacity of representative of Louis XV in 1759." A classified historic monument in some of its parts, this building is mentioned in the regional guides.[10]

Count Hervé de Fontmichel, a former pupil of the Institute of Political Studies of Paris, is descended from a family whose nobility was acquired through service in the 18th century. They had the special characteristic of combining "relatively significant financial means with a very high cultural level," scholarship having always been esteemed among them. To the educational capital is added the fact that the men of this family "all contracted marriages with intelligent, brilliant, diverse women, and the fact that they were all extremely musical." To corroborate these statements, Hervé de Fontmichel recalls that one of his ancestors was chosen, on the founding of the École normale supérieure, in 1794, to be one of the two literary young persons of the département of the Alps-Maritime to take part in the first promotion of the new and prestigious establishment. "He was a Latin poet [...]. My great-grandfather received the Grand Prix de Rome for musical composition in 1822, but he was at the same time also a historian." In his law offices, which occupy the top floor of the imposing building, Master de Fontmichel works at a desk behind which Chateaubriand used to sit. It belonged to one of the writer's mistresses, the Marquise de Custine, and was produced "by the Parisian cabinetmaker Gaudreaux, under Louis XV. My father was a big reader of Chateaubriand and of all historians of the 19th century." The furnishings themselves have their pedigrees and their functions are eclipsed by the quality of the historic recollections and the evocation of ancestors. The furniture is thus a material support of the cultural transmission and the family identity.

At the age of twenty, a law student, Alexander, one of M. de Fontmichel's sons, affirms that in "growing up surrounded by beautiful things, one can only appreciate them thereafter. We have very cultivated parents who never told us: 'This picture is pretty because it is very expensive,' but who always explained to us the origins of pictures, who spoke to us of painters and the way each of them painted. We were thus taught to enjoy beautiful things for what they are and not for what they might be worth if one sold them. And to admire the beautiful for its beauty is pleasant, because that permits one to see the beauty of things without immediately seeing the patrimonial aspect."

Cultural Holdings and Knowledge about Them

Real estate holdings, luxury articles such as high style furniture, the arts of the table, old books, major jewelry, sculptures and paintings are on a par with a specialized language and a culture that permit one to understand and to appreciate the technical skill that went into their realization. Members of these families also participate in sales at auctions, at antiquarians or art galleries with the ease that expertise and learning give. These areas of knowledge, both technical and cultural, linked to luxury articles and to art objects, are transmitted within the family by the subtle familiarization from which those who grow up in real museums benefit. These scholarly trainings come at first in the setting of daily life and owe a part of their efficacy to the fact that the family identity itself is also transmitted through them.

The techniques and knowledge thus acquired enable one to learn those of the painter, the goldsmith and the cabinetmaker and to appreciate the finished work, the quality of the art object. The wealth of the vocabulary associated with these objects and its current use, in salesrooms and magazines about art and decoration, testify to the extent that the grand bourgeoisie has absorbed this culture. "There are domains," writes Claude Duneton, "where the French lose all notion of abstraction and haughty detachment, where they become suddenly serious, concrete, finicky even, in their need to designate things with a fierce thoroughness. What domain? That is what is surprising! The technical domain that is part of the conversation and preoccupation of the higher spheres of the society!"[11] The examples given concern jewelry and the equine world. These vocabularies and knowledge are shared with practitioners, craftsmen, breeders and trainers. The world of art, architecture and the art of gardens could have provided other lexicons, whose use surpasses the professionals' as a concern for enlightened amateurs, among which noble and bourgeois family members are numerous.

All this technical culture is marked with the seal of tradition, which preserves it from the threat of obsolescence. In the traditional techniques of high jewelry, it is important to replicate ancestral motifs. This traditional knowledge may concern domains as varied as oenology or horse breeding (the term "trader-breeder" is used equally in the domain of wine, by the way). Knowledge of art history and the evolution of its techniques is highly prized. This knowledge is in deep homology with the idea of lineage.

Certain things, as time goes by, improve and become more refined. But especially, the more the time passes, more the produced object and the activity itself enjoy enhanced prestige. Thus this is the opposite of electronics and data processing where time quickly renders materials and technologies obsolete—where the criterion of speed is essential, which hardly makes sense in luxury craftsmanship and still less in artistic production.

Growing up in a museum, undergoing one's first training there, within a cultural and artistic heritage, contributes to forming the eye, as they say in the art market. So much so that an expert's title in the sphere of art requires no diploma, which was also the case, up until 1973, for appraisers themselves.[12] It is not astonishing under these conditions that expert appraisers come from elevated social origins. "For a long time, the post of appraiser has been available to a relatively restricted number of families. Given the elevated cost of acquiring such an office, these were acquired traditionally by the bourgeoisie 'of the office' or, more extensively, by the bourgeoisie of the legal profession."[13] However, fortune is not sufficient, and minimal artistic and cultural credentials were necessary, lest the office be discredited. This expertise is acquired from the youngest age by being in the company of works at home, at grandparents and the family's other members, at the family's friends, in all this grand bourgeois residential universe where a significant portion of the national cultural patrimony lives a semi-clandestine life. The successful incorporation of such expertise, acquired through familiarity, is seen as and appears to be a personal gift, an innate quality of the person.

Today the auctioneer's position requires at least a license to practice law and a DEUG (two-year university degree, roughly equivalent to a Master's Degree) in art history (or a DEUG in law and a license in art history), rounded out by two years of traineeship as a student intern, after an entrance exam and sanctioned at the end by a professional exam. This new regulation seems to have been adopted due to difficulties that have occurred within the profession, the positions transmitted on the basis of heritage not always having been fulfilled in a satisfactory way. But that has not changed the social characteristics for the recruitment of auctioneers, a large preponderance of whom continue to come from good families. The importance of having an artistic and cultivated upbringing, mastering social relations in the grand-bourgeois universe, and adequate manners remain the decisive elements for effective recruitment. Even if, as Alain Quemin notes, "One may see in this common social origin the weight associated the acquisition of such a position," and even if "the professional practice of being an auctioneer means having to put up with 'work' that requires mastering the rules of the bourgeois social game and requires being part of good social networks," training one's 'eye' through a childhood immersed in fine art objects and artworks is decisive. "The orientation of the children of the bourgeoisie toward the profession of art auctioneer can be explained as well by the type of social expertise that is used in this professional capacity."[14] One such colleague of Jacques Tajan recalls having "always lived in houses that had lovely things. My ancestors," he adds, "had close relationships with the famous art merchants." In fact, as in the world of banking, we have a profound social homogeneity between the art business, the universe of auctions, and the grand bourgeoisie. The professionals and their clients belong to the same world, speak the same language, have the same manners and the same tastes—to such an extent that the vocation to be an art auctioneer is still present among the young people of this milieu. Philippe-Emmanuel de Fontmichel has this career in mind, "because this profession involves commerce, law, the social sciences, culture and art."

But heirs sometimes exhibit a certain coyness in recognizing the effects of such an environment on the formation of taste and sensitivity. Like Thierry de Valréal, an expert on modern paintings, proprietor of an art gallery, who refuses to admit that having been a child in a grand noble family could have contributed to the formation of his taste for beautiful objects. Just seconds after having affirmed that he was not predestined in any way to assume these professional occupations, as his "family is not involved in that at all," he implicitly acknowledges having grown up in an extraordinary environment. "I had the luck, through my family, of being amid beautiful things," he says. But that is said in order to add that when it comes to beautiful things, "you see them without actually seeing them, since you are inside. You don't pay attention." The reason for this denial, which is quite frequent, is no doubt the difficulty of clearly perceiving the effects and influences which are all the more decisive for beinerceptible. But furthermore, by limiting the influence acknowledged to the social milieu to that which could be considered as relating to acquired knowledge, the role of the innate is preserved, the intrinsic quality of the person. With this denial, we leave open the possibility of explaining it as a talent, which is perceived as more valuable than that which applies to heritages and socially determined transmissions. Or more precisely, one encloses social excellence within the logic of an inherited gift, a family talent. It is the whole lineage that is exceptional.

This domain of cultivated taste, of intimate familiarity with styles and objects, is one of the most revealing of class because it goes back to primordial experiences, foundations of the individual identities as much as the social ones. Internalizing the incorporation of knowledge organized in this way transforms the acquired capacities of judgment into innate qualities. It is understandable that this ease—or its opposite, this maladroitness—in mastering cultural assets would be at the foundation of those nameless ways we judge people, recognizing them and accepting them, or despising and rejecting them. These social judgments are used to separate the wheat from the chaff, inside the wealthy families themselves, to distinguish the *nouveaux riches* from the old families by their relative ease in mastering periods, styles and schools. One can make a fortune without having inherited such specific knowledge. Having recourse to specialists, and handing oneself over, culturally, like a patient constrained to hand himself over the knowledge of the head of a medical clinic, reveals the cultural misery of these parvenus that betray themselves as such when, at the antique galleries, their confusion places them at the mercy of the professionals. These are then solicited to help the wealthy neophytes orient themselves in this maze where only long practice permits one to move with ease. The sums at stake are significant but for the newcomer on this market of art and antiques what counts is to not commit a blunder and to buy only what has an incontestable cultural legitimacy, and therefore a real symbolic value. "These newcomers, who have a lot of money but as yet little experience with objects of art, naturally will be going to take advice and to buy at the big antiquarians," notes Christiane de Nicolay-Mazery, who works in her cousin's practice, Raymond de Nicolay, considered to be the auction director of families of the aristocracy. "It is only after buying for a long time at the big antiquarians that the recently wealthy risk frequenting auction galleries where one must make up one's mind quickly and by oneself, even though one may have gotten advice beforehand."

The Art of Living and Works of Art

In any case, commerce in art objects and antiques takes on the social forms characteristic of this interlacing of socializing, culture and business proper to high society. Mrs. Girardet is an antiques dealer on the heights of St. Maxim, oppposite the port of St. Tropez which can be seen across the gulf from her place. She maintains close relations with all the old families of the region. "I have purchased things from big families from around here," she says, "when they needed money, notably at the time of a succession." Using plans drafted by her son, an architect, she built a villa every part of which is suffused with light, very modern but perfectly melded into the hill. She lives there in the middle of her pieces of furniture, pictures, vases, and statuary of baked clay, her collection of black figurines and objects made of straw marquetry.[14] The villa is the display case in which are presented the marvels that she offers for sale to the wealthy guests whom she receives for dinner. They visit the house and Mrs. Girardet counsels the most hesitant in the purchase of such and such piece. "The newly rich families," she says, "buy pretty things at very high prices, as if they are trying to acquire legitimacy at any price by appropriating some antique furniture that belonged to the great old families." These expenses are difficult to distinguish from those that demonstrate financial strength too overtly for their meaning to be reduced to functionality alone. Thus, in a region where roads are often crowded, these families readily take a helicopter to get around, for example for going to spend the evening at Monte Carlo when one resides at St. Tropez. Purchasing a piece of furniture, a table, a secretary, or some armchairs, for considerable sums, enters into the same sumptuous logic. It is necessary to prove—and to prove to oneself—that everything is accessible. It has little in common with the passion of the well-informed and erudite collector, even if cultural disinterestedness would, there as well, deplete the meaning of a practice.

At this level of fortune one takes several opinions gladly, and if the antiquarian always has his word to say, Mrs. Girardet must count on the rivalry of the decorator who jets down especially from Paris to accompany his customers, who often more or less blindly follow his dictates. "It is he who makes the law."

One of the features of high society is to transform everything into something cultural, to make every domain of human activity a pretext for collecting and for apparently disinterested knowledge. That is how it is with wine and oenology. Wine is in perfect harmony with the idea of lineage not only because it improves with age—at least up to a point—but also because the vinestock, like horses and hunting dogs, are the object of incessant care, of knowledgeable crossbreeding and careful husbandry in every respect. A grapevine is a product mastered over time by observing tests and mistakes in research in the interest of improving the lineage. It is not, therefore, inconsistent that there might be prestigious wine sales in famous places. On November 22, 1993 in the salons of the Hotel George V, Master Tajan distributed some 3000 bottles from the cellar of the house of Countess Josée de Chambrun. Vintages of the first order, such as Yquems 1900 and

133

Château-Ladore 1875, of "beautiful and aristocratic provenance," could not fail to attract collectors who take into account the label, the outward appearance of the bottle, and the wine—even though the latter, at more than a century old, is no longer drinkable. However, one may also dream of drinking an exceptional wine. "Among amateurs," one of the collaborators in this study declares to visitors at the exposition, "there is also a taste for a certain hedonism. To drink a grand cru bordeaux, such as 1945, with one's friends is indeed an exceptional moment."

Every aspect of daily life is therefore transfigured, transformed into a cultural element, the distinction between the cultural and the anthropological no longer being meaningful. As if good taste, distinction, quality and the sophistication of credentials weighs in at every instant to legitimize and reinforce the position of the dominant. The last suit purchased comes from Chanel, the watch given to an adoescent for his eighteeenth birthday is signed Cartier, and the meringue cake is a masterpiece of Lenôtre. The label contributes to sanctifying objects from the quotidian and changes their status: consumer items, simple necessary supports to ordinary practices of ordinary life, become objects worthy of museums, of parades of styles from the culinary sections of big newspapers, of home decorating and architecture magazines. Art infiltrates the daily life of those who can make their daily life into an art of living.

The Arts of Celebration

This art of living is the basis for commissions that are placed, and indirectly causes the existence of certain sectors of the production of artworks. The art of portraiture, and animal and hunting arts, are examples. These forms of art, caused by the bourgeoisie itself, are even more interwoven with the daily existence of these families.

Before the advent of the photograph, noble and grand bourgeois families used plastic artists to immortalize their features. These artists sometimes belong to the family itself, like the Duchess de Doudeauville, wife of Stanislas de la Rochefoucauld, who painted portraits of her relatives. These were auctioned in 1989 at the Drouot Hotel. It is not rare that famous artists contribute to maintaining the family memory. The gallery of ancestral portraits perpetuates its memory while increasing the family's symbolic capital, as the family name thus enters into the history of art. Examples abound. Two small daughters of the family Cahen d'Anvers are captured in blue and pink by August Renoir. Foujita was almost an official painter of good society and did several portraits of the Countess de Noailles. When they are of ordinary characters, the names of a painter's models are generally omitted from the title of the picture. That is not the case when known personalities are involved, whose names continue to represent in catalogs and museum guides after the works leave the family's heritage. So it is, in the home of the painter Hébert (1817-1908) on the Rue du Cherche-Midi in the VIth arrondissment of Paris, which has been converted into a museum. Here one may contemplate portraits of high society women next to those of servants. Thus the portrait of "Agnès de Pourtalès, Marquise de Loys-Chandieu" keeps company with one of a "pensive young laundress."   The passion for hunting on horseback has called forth within the realm of animal art a whole sector of production which legitimizes a practice that is, in turn, magnified by its artistic celebration. Artistic depictions of hunting maintain and nourish the passion of hunters, who see in these works a kind of consecration. What is prized first of all is the perfect knowledge of the animals, of their morphology, of their attitudes. The desired precision requires, as does the hunt, an eternal attentiveness and patience in the concern for finesse and care for detail. The watercolors of Baron Karl Reille are just such excellent evocations of various hunting episodes. This occasional painting, whose production has by no means ceased, evokes the emotions of hunting, and numerous are the hunters, among those who have the means for it, who adorn their homes with this type of work. In this way, hunting art is illustrative art where strictly plastic invention is at the service of the encha relationship of hunters to nature, the forest and the animals. The art must give account of these emotions, grasp their foundations, and do it in the only way possible, with the realism appropriate to the arts of celebration.

These artistic forms intimately blend the plastic works into the daily life of families, their memory, their passions. An equivalent of hunting art is found in the traditions of maritime painters and artists. The Marine Museum created by Roland de La Poype in the Antibes constitutes one of attractions of Marineland, which he founded. A descendant of Admiral de La Poype de Ventrieux, he inherited already remarkable collections that he developed thereafter. Numerous models retrace the evolution of the different methods of navigation, with oars, under sail or under power, from antiquity to our days. Many objects, both curious and refined, evoke the sea in all her aspects and the distant journeys that she suggests. Tortoise shell opium pipes are side by side with canes made of shark vertebrae, and inlaid mother of pearl and scrimshaw jewelry. Many pictures evoke the naval battles and long distance journeys. A tapestry from the 16th century represents a whale-hunting scene. Marineland offers attrctions linked to sea and to exotic countries with its spectacles of killer whales and dolphins and a tropical jungle of butterflies. The whole forms an enterprise of 85 permanent salaried employees (appreciably more in peak season) on the 5 hectares at the ports of Antibes and Biot, and hosts some 800,000 visitors per annum. Roland de La Poype, owner of the ensemble, built his fortune on technological innovations linked to plastic materials and packaging. And so business and culture are combined, and this museum of the sea permits us to take the measure of the riches that can be accumulated in a family setting.

Cultural Complicities

The private museum that constitutes the home of a great family is used for certain practices whose educational orientation is sometimes deliberate. One depends on this constant presence of remarkable works charged with history and culture to develop taste and knowledge. Here again, interviews and memoirs abound in testimonies of a childhood where the living environment is a pretext for lessons on literature, history and art history.

Countess Jean dePange describes the family house, property of her grandparents, thus: "Magnificent furniture and art objects from [grandfather's] collection filled the house. The ground floor, especially, was a real museum." Then she shows how the elements of this museum entered into her education. "The armchairs and sofas of the grand salons were covered with tapestries, no doubt very beautiful, that represented fables or scenes from mythology. My grandmother invented a following game between the pieces of furniture, from one armchair to another, while chanting: 'Let's walk through the forest/While the wolf is away!' But, while making a path through the furniture, she gave me explanations of the characters and animals from ancient myths. She knew the histories of these Greek and Roman gods perfectly." Through this family heritage, the academic culture enters there into the domestic sphere, curls up there like a cat on a sofa, and purrs, completely at its ease. Familiar animal, it is an everyday companion, it is alive and warm, comforting by its constant presence that assures the continuity between the domestic and the public, between the family culture and that of museums, of performance halls, of educational establishments. Culture is not an individual's expertise, acquired by a deliberately pro-active attitude directed toward the establishments that specialize in its diffusion, but a manner of being, a way of living, an element of the habitus like courtesy, respect for ancestors and traditions, and a taste for being among one's peers.

Familiarity with culture also depends on financial ease. Véronique de Montremy remembers the bookstore at the corner of the Avenue Marceau "where Papa had opened for us an absolutely unlimited account, which was brilliant because the director of the bookstore adored everything that was foreign literature. Every Saturday afternoon we spent at least an hour discussing foreign books. Because Papa was nevertheless very centered on the 19th and 20th centuries of France, so that it is thanks to this lady, a sort of intellectual mentor, that we read a lot of foreign literature." Her maternal grandmother made it possible for her to attend the Bayreuth Festival as a reward for passing the baccalaureat exam. "So I went to Bayreuth for my graduation. Culture was integrated into our life indeed."

School can take the place of the family milieu—but it depends on which school, of course. Éva Thomassin, as we have seen, daughter of a rich family originally from Argentina, boarder at a Lausanne school frequented by royal children and heirs of great international fortunes, shows that these exceptional private schools replicate this relationship of complicity with the cultural universe. "We took a trip to Italy, from Milan to Naples; all of Italy—visiting museums. I will never forget that trip! The marvelous trains of that era, the paintings I saw in museums. We must have been very, very well escorted, to have succeeded in getting us to like Fra Angelicos at that point... Unforgettable! to the point that when I see a picture today, I immediately recognize it. The other day I said: Ah! that is a Filippo Lippi. You don't forget these things." This cultural training always has as a social dimension: it is a question of mastering the culture necessary to efficiently manage the social capital. "They prepared us to go into a salon and know how to converse intelligently, in a cultivated manner." In any case, what characterizes the schools favored by the big families resides in the complementary fashion with which they assure the transmission of all forms of capital: academic, cultural, and also social, symbolic and even physical, by the importance granted to the body and sports. In sum, a complete education for a complete person.

Academic culture is a fundamental element of the implicit pedagogy implemented by the upper classes. The cultural rally, the first stage of those rallies that bring together exclusively, through the use of closed invitation lists, the adolescents who belong to the same world, is one of the social forms of familiarization with works of culture. Indeed, it is not insignificant that in this group of young persons descended from good families, visits to châteaux, churches and performances are made in a group manner. The rally created by Count Henri de Burton started with a set of cultural visits, including Chantilly. "We went to Mass in the village church, whose stained glass windows are very beautiful. The vicar was forewarned to have us visit the church." Then the castle of Chantilly. "For that," continues M. de Burton, "I had called a friend who is a member of the Institute of the Academy of Fine Arts, who put me in contact with the administration of Chantilly. We had our picnic. In the aristocracy one does things simply. We ate the picnic in the tennis courts. We made sure the children were aware that that was a privilege of which they must be cognizant." So simplicity does not exclude favorable treatment that would not be granted to just anyone: not everyone who wants to may picnic in a room of a historic monument. And thus the young persons learn that they are not just anyone.

They also learn it by escaping the anonymity of the average tourist. The vicar expects them and brings them to visit the church, the administration of the château welcomes them and grants them what it refuses to others. Visits are thus the opportunity to try out the social capital which one has at his disposal by dint of his parents and which he will inherit. The rally included some embassies. "The children visited the embassy of England on their own, but the ambassador—I have a lot of friends who are ambassadors— invited the parents to take tea." At the Château de Breteuil, "We were received by Mr. and Mrs. de Breteuil. They are friends. We picnicked at the foot of the orangerie." In their memories, the youngsters will no longer be able to dissociate the pleasure of the acquired familiarity with a work of culture from the feeling that the unusual conditions that allowed them to reach to this work were due solely to the quality of their family. So culture is not separated from social life: on the contrary, it is an aspect thereof that cannot be disassociated and may culminate with theatrical premières, art exhibitions and other conferences. What is inculcated is an extreme familiarity with culture that surpasses that which the parents can transmit: it is the social familiarity of an elite in its whole with the cultural past, the national and international heritage. As Fernand de Saint-Simon wrote à propos of another rally, "Society, that's fine; culture, that's better; but the two together— that's the best of all."[19]

A WELL ESTABLISHED CULTURE

The familiarity maintained with cultural works, the knowledge accumulated in their regard, their presence in the family universe and in the everyday environment lead to security and serenity in the relationships between enlightened amateurs and things of art. In part, because the works and the objects often are within the scope of a known art, certified, ratified by historians. But above all because, on the basis of collective methods of appropriation, as the pretexts or support for intense socializing, cultural manifestations give art its roots at the heart of the social identity of the group.

However, this inculcation of the scholarly relationship to scholarly culture finds frequently enough a certain limit in the "classic," or at least the established, character of the culture thus transmitted. The families considered here are old families, whose dominant positions and grand fortunes are ancient. However, the older these families are, the richer the heritage may be in objects and works of art, but the farther this heritage may be distanced from modern or contemporary forms of art. Thierry de Valréal explains that the old families of the nobility of the legal profession, and Protestant bankers, allowed Impressionism and Fauvism to pass, and generally all of modern art (in the mind of appraisors, that is posterior to 1830). "We stayed with our old things, portraits of our grandmothers and landscapes, still in the spirit of the 18th or the beginning of the 19th century," he explains. "We weren't working. The rising industrial bourgeoisie, they brought in money. They constructed the beautiful houses in Paris, all the buildings by Haussmann, which then needed to be decorated. And what did they buy? Things that were made to the taste of the day. One looked at them and said to oneself: Look at these nouveaux riches. And the new rich of that era, they bought the paintings that were being made at that moment. You will very rarely find in the aristocratic families any pictures by Renoir, Picasso, or Monet and Manet. Very few. Whereas for people who were in industry, or banking, finance, everything that exploded at the end of the 19th, they went to buy what was being made, the contemporary painters. Although there are some who, poor luck, bought kitsch that is not worth anything today—even though they paid fortunes for them. But they were also buying canvases by Cézanne that were hard to sell, a Gauguin, a Lautrec, or painters like that. All these new rich bought what was being made at the time."

So the children of the oldest families are not always the best positioned to be initiated and sensitized to the living art. What they have before their eyes makes them closer to the classic works, of more ancient times, times when a great part of the heritage was accumulated. "As for myself, when I went into this profession," admits Thierry de Valréal, "I was brought up on traditional painting: the 18th-19th centuries. I recognize that when I went into the art market, I looked at a picture by Braque, Picasso, I looked at that and I said to myself: 'but what are these smudges?' Because I was not mature, I was not ready." Véronique de Montremy, daughter of Berthilde de Wendel, whose family fortune was established in the 18th century, relates that for her maternal grandparents, "The idea of buying a Picasso would never have crossed their minds. They bought the 18th! And they stopped at 1789, the date at which aesthetics disappeared". On the paternal side, where, to keep a sense of proportion, the fortune is less significant, "There was a very pronounced aesthetic taste. My great-grandmother traveled systematically in Italy. She built and furnished a private hotel on the Avenue Marceau. My grandfather, he had responsibilities in the national museums. He liked everything that was Gothic, trunks, golden statuaries, tapestries, but also Louis XV furniture. It was still the aesthetics of the old regime." One sees the same disposition among contemporary young people. "Me," confesses Alexander de Fontmichel, "I am a little old-fashioned in my artistic tastes. I am not very fond of modern painting." His brother, Philippe-Emmanuel, confesses that when he sees "modern pictures made in a barbaric manner," he does not "see the point of them."

Norbert Elias, speaking of the court society, insisted on a homology between the classical culture and this society. "The artistic style to which one gave the name of 'classicism'," he writes, "takes its origin from this same mindset. What characterizes classicism is the same lucid and rational order of structures, the meticulous calculation of the effect and the prestige value of the whole, the absence of all spontaneous ornamentation, of all display of uncontrolled sensitivity."[20] Here we probably have one of the principles of the well-founded illusion that would have it that, in representations that the average or superior intellectual classes (that is to say, those who owe the essence of their social standing to their cultural and academic capital) make about the moneyed classes, they are not really aware of living culture and are at best merely familiar with established culture. That belittles the patronage and the participation in the art market of the culturally most active families of the grand bourgeoisie.

The case of the d'Arcangues family is very illuminating from this point of view. The estate of René Tassin de Montaigu, dispersed by Master Jacques Tajan during a sale in the salons of the Hotel George V on June 13, 1995, was primarily dedicated to contemporary art, with works signed by Arman, Klein, Mathieu, Christo, Chaissac, Delaunay.

Furthermore, a classic heritage and culture offer a good basis for rapid training and an opening on the more contemporary forms. Particularly since the more or less imperative necessity to work and/or to pass by the Caudin Forks of school selection transforms one's relationship to culture. Today, Thierry de Valréal works as an expert in modern paintings with one of the biggest Parisian appraisal studios, with insurance companies, and for the Paris court of appeals.

It is still true, most often, that in the old families the formation of taste is first classic. One could give other examples in the domains of literature or music, from the contents of library shelves, or from the selections chosen by family members who are musicians when they wish to play in domestic settings. But is not this, also, the most prestigious way to seek access to the most contemporary forms—with all the culture that is implicitly required to access those works that are apparently most distant from academic tradition?

The Private Appropriation of Public Cultural Possessions

The public means for diffusing cultural works have been developed quite a bit since the beginning of the 20th century: museums, performance halls, theaters and cinemas, libraries. Access to these facilities is available to a wide public. Yet the nobility and the grand bourgeoisie make up a countertrend and exhibit a clear propensity to preserve as private as possible a character to their approach to the works thus socialized. There was a time when the great families, who assured the subsistence of artists and writers, were able to convene them at their homes and to organize spectacles or concerts there, or to enhance their table with the presence of famous authors. But this private form of appropriating the living culture could also take a less domestic turn. Thus, until 1914, one had his own box at the opera, a box whose annual rental was one of the privileges of society.[21] The "box leases," as they were called, were practically the equivalent of ownership: recipients had the freedom to decorate the space to their taste and could receive family and friends there in their own way. Culture and socializing were closely intermingled.

Although these old ways of appropriating public cultural possessions are in regression nowadays, they are still very much present. The great families do not escape the general movement toward socializing cultural consumption, but they preserve a number of features that recall earlier periods. A characteristic publication of this milieu, the *Bottin Mondain*, dedicates sixty pages of its 1995 edition to convenient information on museums and to theater and concert halls; fifty pages present detailed floor plans with each room numbered. This work positions itself as the indispensable practical directory for families of good society; the presence of a category so well supplied makes quite evident their privileged relationship with the world of spectacle and how this cultural life overlaps with family life and forms of socializing in this milieu.

It has become difficult to get seats for a performance at the opera, and boxes rentals on an annual basis has disappeared. But members of the big Parisian club have provided themselves with a service, a tourist agency that also takes charge of organizing certain cultural pursuits. Members of the Jockey Club, the Cercle de l'Union Interalliée, the Automobile Club of France, the Cercle du Bois de Boulogne, the Polo de Paris, can call this agency that is always in a position to obtain the requested places. But that's nothing. Intercercles Voyages also organizes private ways of appropriating the public cultural assets: "In France and abroad," according to the person in charge of the agency, "after the scheduled visiting hours, we have such and such museum stay open and we make a private visit. Then we have a dinner in the museum with the curator. That, of course, is a closed event. The museum is ours." Intercercles Voyages must always show the members of the clubs from which it sprang "that they are not treated like other people." That irresistibly evokes the cultural outings of the rallys.

In other words, if the power of the public sector in the distribution of cultural goods has become considerable, the old and wealthy families maintain all the same a special relationship with these goods and they appreciate above all the forms of appropriation which enable them to escape from the mob and the common fate. It is not just a preoccupation with comfort. Chic exhibitions and premières are the occasion of memorable crowds. But they take place among one's own kind: one does not leave the universe of one's peers and the indiscriminate mixing is only physical and not social. These private visits to public places, accompanied by a cocktail party or a dinner, are occasions to manage that form of capital which is essential to these mediums, social capital. Culture as an element of the way of life constitutes one of the group's identifying principles. Cultural capital and social capital, inextricably linked, are mutually reinforcing. The activity of cultural organizations like the

AROP (Association for heiends of the Opera of Paris), chaired by the Countess Guy de Brantes, exemplifies this point. The members of this association recently attended a representation of Lucia di Lammermoor de Donizetti. After the spectacle, the guests gathered for a dinner party which had the honor of being reported in the February 14, 1995 issue of *Point de vue*. Thus, participation in a cultural activity coincides with a social ceremony which, like any ceremony, also serves to consolidate the belief in the social excellence of the group. The cultural life of high society thus forms part of the implicit, not deliberate, strategies which give certainty again to those whose faith might be wavering as to the legitimacy of their privileges and, for all of them, to consolidate that self-assurance without which it would be useless to try to establish social supremacy.

The great families are also present in the process of socializing the cultural assets through the system of gifts, donations and bequests to museums. "The name Rothschild, alone, occurs some 20 times in the list of the 2,700 donors to the Louvre. Names which, in addition, are not listed as having given a few pieces but for the most part an impressive series of gifts."[22] Michel David-Weill, whose personal fortune was estimated at between 4.5 and 4.8 billion francs, and his professional fortune at 8.5 billion,[23] President of the Lazard group and member of the advisory council of the Cercle de l'Union Interalliée, grandson of David David-Weill, regent of the Bank of France in 1936, belongs to a family whose members "count among more munificent donors to the museums of France." Michel David-Weill is "a member of the Institute, President of the *Conseil européen du mécénat*, a member of the board of the Union of the National Museums of France, as well as of the Council of Museums in the United States."[24]

Having a better understanding of the relationship to culture of the families that accumulate all the forms of wealth allows another view of that of the other social categories. For cultural and artistic assets, when they are combined with the knowledge and competence that go with them, produce considerable profits, whose influence in the relationships of domination and in the process of social reproduction are generally underestimated by the cultural intermediaries and more generally by the average intellectual sectors.

Social Ceremonies and Cultural Ceremonies

This collective management of the relationship with the cultural universe can be seen in certain ceremonies where the group thus constituted celebrates at the same time its own existence and its privileged ties with culture. So it is on the occasion of "open door" evenings organized in the high places of the art and antiquities market, the Triangle rive droite (Right Bank Triangle) and the Carré rive gauche (Left Bank Square). These two names denote associations which gather, in the first instance, some 80 galleries located on Avenue Matignon, rue de Miromesnil, and rue de Penthièvre, i.e. in the district of the Élysée, and in the second instance, approximately 130 antique dealers whose shops are located in the square delimited by the quai Voltaire, la rue du Bac, la rue de l'Université and la rue des Saints-Pères, between the Museum d'Orsay and the Beaux-Arts academy.[25]

The gallery owners and the antique dealers of these districts organize open-door days every year. The expression can be taken literally—the doors of these shops, which conceal treasures, are usually closed and one must ring the bell in order to enter, which is very dissuasive for those who are merely curious. According to the President of the Triangle rive droit, these days are primarily an occasion to hold a collective exhibition and thus to draw the most people possible. The galleries of the Triangle show a great eclecticism, going from Dresser to Dubuffet, from Michel Henry to Poliakoff; but with a majority of galleries dedicated to contemporary art. The antique dealers of the Carré rive gauche present furniture of various epochs and styles, objets d'art and furnishings, antique paintings, works from the Far East ... All these objects are worthy of the greatest museums.

South of the quai Voltaire, between la rue du Bac and la rue des Saints-Pères, this district of upscale antique dealers is close to the Beaux-Arts academy. Therefore some of the members of the elegant crowd squeezing itself on the sidewalks and in the boutiques at the time of the inaugural evening of the "five days of the extraordinary object," have something of the artist about them, a knowing negligence in their dress, showing that they are there for the beauty of the things and not for fashionable vanity. The double-breasted suit is still very much present, but a red cravat, a Panama elegantly removed upon entry into a shop—all of these are details which, by marking a certain detachment with regard to the accepted canons of elegance, are enough to show that one is not here in the honest but hard-working company of the vulgar business executives. It is true that, even with a comfortable remuneration package, mighty few of these latter would even propose to buy a pair of 17th century seats at 80,000 francs a piece, or the Jan Bruegel painting offered for nearly 7 million francs. Whereas usually the shops are closed and open only when a customer rings, on this day they appear as accessible to all comers as any grocery in the neighborhood. And yet the social barriers remain: the only people who enter into these vaults of good taste, cultivated and expensive, are those who can feel at their ease and with naturalness obtain information about the price of the displayed objects, and grasp the proffered goblet of champagne like a self-explanatory thing and not like an unhoped-for miracle.

At this time, of course, the champagne was flowing in rivers to honour all these beautiful people of every nationality which was squeezed into the shops for wealth is, by definition, international. But, like the Place Vendôme in December, at the time of the major jewelers' open-door days, the people who come here belong to the narrow circle of great fortunes. So it is not astonishing that they know each other and greet each other: "So, are you going to the salon, are you going to the party?"

On such occasions, the temporary adequacy of the attendance and of the urban setting appears almost perfect. And we must see in the quality of such an accord the reason behind the convivial aspect of all these faces, relaxed in spite of the late hour, in these manners that remain gracious in spite of the multitude. There is no doubt that the men and women who are there have the assurance of being very much in the right place, champagne glass in hand, giving themselves without restraint to the pleasures of conversation in good company.

It is a social ceremony, a celebration solemn and at the same time festive, that one seems to be attending. Fortune and culture go well together. The works being offered are like the housing of this excellent company. The guests are the privileged customers of these shops, and the goods that they contain are theirs, if not individually, at least collectively.

THE CONCEPT OF PATRIMONIAL CAPITAL

The concept of patrimonial capital indicates this overlap of the various forms of capital which appear specific to the dominant classes, and which mixes economic capital, symbolic capital, cultural capital and social capital. Any objet d'art supports all of these various dimensions. The book is a source of knowledge, therefore of cultural capital, but it is also a collector's item, a calligraphy manuscript, an original edition dedicated by a great author, or a hard cover book by a known artist. It may, then, reach a great monetary value: in 1995, the Tajan studio sold at auction, in the salons of the hotel George V, 26 "beautiful books in beautiful bindings," according to the catalogue. Their estimates reached 200,000 francs for an edition of *Paul et Virginie*, by Bernardin de Saint-Pierre, in two volumes, 60,000 francs for an edition of Prévert and Ribemont-Dessaignes' book devoted to Miro, bound, with 10 lithographies and many reproductions of the painter's works, or 500,000 francs for an edition of descriptions of animals taken from *l'Histoire Naturelle* by Buffon with an etching by Picasso for each one, the binding being by Paul Bonnet. An edition of *The Odyssey*, estimated at 250,000 francs, illustrates the sociability linked to this type of cultural goods since it is due to the Company of Bibliophiles of the Automobile Club of France, sociability in any event displayed by the character of social ritual that such a sale Signals.[26] Thus books can also provide a way of managing and accumulating social capital. In 1995, the library of the château of Esparrou, in the Eastern Pyrenees, which belongs to the Sauvy family (whose fortune was essentially based on wine and the wine trade) counted approximately one thousand volumes. Among them appear many works dedicated by the authors to François Sauvy (1862-1906). Founder of this library, he invited writers and painters to visit. Many of these books are bound according to the manner specific to Esparrou. Thus they come to form an integral part, including in their material presentation, of the patrimonial funds represented by the domain.[27]

The dominant classes have objets d'art, paintings, old books, furniture, residences which have a great economic value, but which cannot be reduced to this dimension. These cultural goods are also part of the family memory and the reputation of the name. This capital is patrimonial insofar as it is the material form of accumulation over several generations of the good fortune that made it possible for the family to be formed and maintained.

Escaping the Wear of Time

In that, the great families profit from a preferential treatment. For the other social groups, indeed, these traces and this sedimentation of the past can be registered only exceptionally in material traces. In general, accumulated goods lose their value over time and generations, and thus become obsolete—while the residences of the great families and what they contain reach the enviable status of historic buildings and works of art. The goods which form this patrimonial capital are in homology with the disposition specific to the families of the nobility and the bourgeoisie: they have a very clear propensity to record themselves in the long term, even in eternity. These families, which constituted themselves over long lineages, prefer goods which escape wear from time, for they are based on this time, in the succession of the generations, to ensure and legitimate their dominant position. The majority of the accumulated goods, château or private mansion, masterpieces or furniture, goldsmithery or jewellery, age so that not only their monetary value does not stop increasing, but also their symbolic value, due to increasing demand in specialized markets. The specific objects and spheres of knowledge which are related to them do not cease developing—they cannot become obsolete. Whereas, in the other social groups, family residences—having little historical significance—and furniture, being of poor quality, lose value over the course of time.

This exceptional bonus of what, for others, tends to be devaluated explains at least in part the paradox of the relative satisfaction felt by those lords of the manor constrained to open their residences to the public. The visitors, who certainly represent an intrusion into the family nest, also attest by their presence the quality of the place inhabited by the family and thus the quality of the family itself. The feeling of fulfilling a duty, a responsibility inherited with the château, dominates: it is a question of maintaining the inheritance which was received on deposit, of which one has to some extent the usufruct but whose true owners are all the members of the family, even the people of France, a portion of whose inheritance one would thus find in one's charge. Far from losing his identity through this opening to the public, the lord of the manor and his close relations ensure an inherited charge which consolidates their exceptional identity.

The "Monuments and Museums Management" service of the Institute of France is a collective organization thanks to which the great families can ensure the maintenance of the fragments of their patrimonial have that fallen into the public domain. It is thus with the villas Ephrussi de Rothschild and Kerylos, bequeathed to the Institute. The precursor in the matter was the duke of Aumale who made a gift of the domain of Chantilly to this same institution at the end of the last century, charging it with "preserving this domain, with the museum and the library which it contains, and placing them at the disposal of the public." The bonds between the great families and the academies which form the Institute are old and close. In her will on January 19, 1912, Mrs. Nélie Jacquemart, widow of M. Edmond Andre, bequeathed all of her possessions and her art collections to the Institute. It is the same for the Marmottan Museum and its collections of Impressionist works. The architect of the Villa Kerylos was a member of the Academy of the Fine Arts while its owner, Theodore Reinach, was a member of the Academy of writing and belles-lettres. The Institute is thus available to deal with the goods whose material and symbolic perenniality it will ensure: thanks to its intervention, the memory of wealthy individuals can be preserved in spite of the absence of natural heirs

Money and Culture

This overlap of the economic with the cultural and the symbolic—the emotional dimensions of this patrimony—accounts for the irrationality of some behaviors. For it is quite difficult in such a context to adopt the policy of an economic agent who would look to maximize his monetary profits. There are plenty of possible types of profit other than just economic profit. Certainly, for some, the works are reduced solely to their venal dimension. As Thierry de Valréal admits, art objects not being subject to the solidarity tax (social security) on wealth, some wealthy taxpayers may have chosen to invest in this domain to reduce their tax basis. Some even try to speculate on art works. "Last week I went to see someone at Neuilly," he says, "who deals in precious stones, and since precious stones are not doing well at all at the moment, hey well, he sold a little of his stock and he turned to paintings. There is no feeling. It is only about size and weight. And it is about money in the coffers, and then he resells it to you in six months. It is solely the lure of profit."

Certainly, as Raymonde Moulin has written, "In extreme cases, collector-speculators see paintings as the equivalent of a stock certificate." Nonetheless these businessmen, by getting involved with the art market, "ennoble their professional activities by giving them a game-like and apparently gratuitous aspect." The motivations of the speculator appear then in all their ambiguity. "Esthetic enjoyment does not exclude the possibility of gain, conspicuous consumption is not independent of rational calculation, the ennoblement conferred by art to those who possess it comes together with the prestige associated with capitalist activity itself."[28]

However, an art object is always also part of the patrimony, in the strictly economic sense of the term. The wealthy families hardly like to say it, nor even to think of it, but paintings, furniture, clocks, table-top objects, they all represent potentially considerable sums. It is therefore a reserve upon which it is always possible to draw, even though this possibility appears to be sacrilegious, highly unlikely until such time as necessity renders it ineluctable—or until it seems more reasonable to part with certain possessions in order to cope more comfortably with expenses such as getting one's children or grandchildren settled.

Failing to include art works in the basis of ISF taxation is justified by several considerations, relative to the art market, whether it is a question of protection, or of the difficulty of assigning a value to these unique possessions. From this point of view, patrimonial accounts themselves recoil at the delicate thought of inclusion in numeric estimates.[30] But, beyond incontestable technical reasons, this special treatment of art works situates them outside the field of the economy. Even in the case of succession (when they again become taxable), the possibility of a donation—that is to acquit a part of the duties by donating to the state some part of the goods concerned—maintains this status of exception. It means that the family is holder of a part of the national heritage. This arrangement encourages the denial of the venal significance of these possessions. Or at least there is an affirmation that something else is at play, of a value superior to all evaluation in monetary terms. In the movie by Marianne Lamour, already mentioned, the ex-wife of the Duke de La Rochefoucauld is asked why the family does not sell a high-priced painting in order to make some indispensable repairs to the castle. "We think of it very often," she answers, "but we will never do it. These paintings belong to François-Xavier [seven years old at the time of the filming, future heir of the title of Duke and of the castle] and after that they will belong to his son. We have to keep them. This painting," she says, motioning to a portrait, "represents Ernestine de La Rochefoucauld and it is attributed to David. Selling it would cover a whole summer in Greece on a yacht like Onassis', with forty stewar. But then, no, it will remain there."

Nonetheless, the art market sees some transactions carried out at astonishing levels. On December 15, 1993, in the salons of the Hotel George V, a sale of old paintings (15th to the beginning of the 19th centuries) took place, directed by Master Tajan. The lowest bid was 55,000 francs. But the prices were often much higher. There were 95 "lots" offered and each found a buyer. The total of the biddings reached 92 million francs. The purchasers having to cover 9.495 % of expenses, that makes approximately 100 million francs which were spent that evening to purchase paintings. The whole event lasted one and a half hours. The total reached owes a great deal to just one painting, a view of Venice by Canaletto. For this work, the bidding reached 66 million francs, before expenses.

Dispersion and Reconstitution of Patrimonies: Auctions

Public auctions sometimes make it possible for the families to reconstitute part of their patrimonial capital that was dispersed for various reasons. "When I go to Drouot—that happened to me again not long ago," says Thierry de Valréal, "I buy up forks and spoons with the Valréal coat of arms. It annoys me to see them slipping by. If I have money at the time, I buy them. What irritates me is that somebody sells them before warning the members of the family." The appraisers of course are particularly well placed to see any goods which would have belonged to the family going by in the sales. Thus François de Ricqlès buys all of his great uncle's porcelains when they are in a sale catalogue, "because they have a seal 'Collection Emile de Ricqlès'—it is a great porcelain collection."

The memory of the family from which the objects put on sale originate is therefore not lost. It is used to enhance the value of the items. Each time the source of an art object is known, it is mentioned in the sale catalogue because it is a factor in its evaluation. Pedigrees are mentioned in these catalogues, including for a piece of furniture, for example, and the former owners are as important (and sometimes more) as the creators themselves. The source forms part of the label, part of the quality of the work. In addition, the appraisers to do not hesitate to organize certain sales within the setting which had housed the objects and for which they had been gathered or created. Thus part of the collections of Hussein Pasha was sold in the auctions at the Sporting Club de Monte-Carlo and another part in the sumptuous villa of the former owner at St.-Jean-Cap-Ferrat, close to the villa Ephrussi de Rothschild. According to one of the people in charge of this sale, "the bidding was high because they were held in the actual villa of the pasha. They certainly would have been lower if they had taken place at Drouot. The magic of the locations enters into the definition of the price insofar as the purchasers have the impression of getting a piece of history, a past and a name linked to a fashionable figure of the Riviera in the Fifties."

The importance of the location where the sales proceed applies to a number of them and apparently the appraisers are aware well of it since, in Paris, they vary the location and sometimes leave Drouot for the Champs-Élysées theatre or the Hotel George V, when they want to give a particular splash to certain auctions. "There is a close bond," writes Alain Quemin, "between the quality of the objects sold and the place, but also between the characteristics of the goods and those of the inhabitants of the various districts, beautiful objects being spread about in beautiful neighborhoods."[31] Thus the premises depending on Drouot are themselves treated on a hierarchical basis, from Drouot-Montaigne to the Champs-Élysées theatre, located on the avenue of luxury which concentrates the big dressmakers today, to Drouot-North, in the XVIIIth arrondissement, including Drouot-Richelieu, whose renovated buildings are in the heart of the IXth arrondissement.

But the public sales are places where patrimonial capital is formed. It is an important source of purchases for professionals but also collectors and families, so that the universe of auction sales, when they are most prestigious, is of a great social homogeneity. The appraisers, the experts, the private individuals whether purchasing or selling, certain professional buyers—many belong to high society or are very close to it. That is not astonishing since one finds all and sundry at the same big clubs, the same dinners and the same receptions. "Social activities that go on outside of business hours always help me find merchandise to disseminate," writes Alain Quemin. That is part of the reason why auctioneers enjoy sports like golf, (...) which also puts them in contact with so many people (lawyers, attorneys...) and potential clients. The time they invest (...) in clubs and associations, or at dinners in town, stems from the same logic.[32]

There is certainly a relative homology between an appraiser, his social background, and his clientèle. Raymond de Nicolay's is regarded as one of most aristocratic there are. Furthermore, specifies Christiane de Nicolay-Mazery, "we only do the willing ones, not the legal ones; we do not work at all with ruined families." In another corner of this professional space, the customers of Master Jacques Tajan, according to one of his collaborators, consists rather of large industrialists, recently wealthy families. But there is a very great diversity within the profession, in particular as to the proportion of voluntary sales vs. legally prescribed auctions per each studio. We are interested here only in those auction houses specializing in sales of art.

These auction sales are the scene of exchanges where, ultimately, the same goods, while changing owners, do not leave the grand-bourgeois milieu. Appraisers and experts are one of the links of this collective body which manages, accumulates and redistributes the patrimonies. It all takes place as if these professionals had the responsibility of channeling the valuables, "*les belles choses*", those things that are worthy of the big antique dealers and the vast residences of the beautiful neighborhoods, toward their natural owners, those who have at the same time the material means and the cultural means to take on these goods materially and symbolically.

Works of art, when they belong to the same family for several generations, are indissolubly economic capital, cultural capital and symbolic capital. In other words, patrimonial capital. So much so that this patrimonial capital itself is given a label: one speaks of the Givenchy style or the Rothschild style to indicate the way in which the décor of these families' residences were conceived and arranged. In the Sixties Givenchy contributed to the rehabilitation of the Boulle style and it can associate the Regency style with linen-covered wing chairs and with contemporary sculpture. The Rothschild style would be characterized by a mixture of objects and furniture from the 18th century with objects and furniture in the style Napoleon III, very comfortable with their thick red silk cushions.

One can understand part of the special relationship these families maintain with the dominant culture, given this patrimonial capital whose role is important in maintaining their social position. The desire and the pleasure of culture are all the more sharp and present when they are felt as a passage to the act of the habitus many aspects of which relate to this patrimonial capital. For the families of the dominant classes, the cultural practices merge with the anthropological practices; cultural life is a principal aspect of the way of life and, in the cultural practices, satisfaction is all the greater since it is a way of being that which one is.

Art and Patrimony

The various forms of capital, thus melded into one, under the patrimonial species, are not easily dissociated. The large investment banks' centers for the management of patrimony know it, and they have integrated the cultural dimension into their management. Thus, the Bank Paribas manages the various elements of the patrimonies in an all-encompassing way, a specialized service having charge of art works. "This team," says Pierre de Leusse, "was formed in 1975. The same person, who comes from the School of the Louvre, directs it. The approach at the Bank Paribas was never an approach in terms of investment. It is rather a question of having a hub of competence available for our customers in case they need it. It is the same concept of an intermediary in transactions and an advisor all in one, which applies to the other services."

In addition the Bank Paribas cultivates relationships with its customers in particular through invitations "to cultural and artistic events organized under the aegis of the Paribas Foundation." Customers of the center for the management of patrimonies will thus receive invitations to premières of the Opera, to concerts of South American baroque music or the Isaïe quartet. Certain concerts are given in the orangerie of the Paribas headquarters, a magical space made up of a covered patio whose calm, in the midst of the hubbub of the Opera district, has something miraculous and gives that same feeling of escaping the common fate and reaching a space outside of the ordinary constraints that reigns in the salons of the great clubs, they likewise being situated at the tumultuous heart of the center-west of Paris. These particularly cherished customers receive, from time to time, art books published by the Paribas Foundation. One of the permanent activities of this foundation is to conceive and publish catalogues, like those of the museum of Limoges porcelain or the museum Nissim de Camondo, in Paris.

The formula "art and patrimony" has a certain success in the wealthy milieux in any case. *Intercercles* review has a heading with that title; articles there have covered the Nabis exhibition at the Grand Palais and a Gromaire exhibition, more confidential but more directly of interest to the patrimony since it was held in a gallery in the Faubourg Saint-Honoré.[33] It is under this name indicating the overlap of the economic and the cultural that the Crédit Municipal de Paris, formerly called Mont-de-Piété, created a branch of industry with the slogan: "Finance and art, that's everything." Various teams offer specialized services there, like financing works of art, legal and tax assistance, advice on investments and acquisitions, banking services, sales by auction, the restoration and transport of works, and conferences on art. But if this service has contributed to transforming the image of the Crédit Municipal, it is not clear that it was able to compete with the services of the large investment banks, for it seems to have had some problems. The advertisements abundantly published by the Crédit Municipal in the Jockey Club's *Le Courrier* or *Intercercles* magazine always emphasize how much the estate managers and the financiers appreciate the extent to which culture and wealth are interdependent.

One even could speak of a "patrimonial district" concerning le Marais or the Faubourg Saint-Germain. However, these districts, threatened at one time with degradation and urban degeneration, were created by and inhabited for a long time by high society. The high social and symbolic value of these districts were due to the solidarity of all the elements, including the historic, whose combined qualities made them exceptional districts. By an action of the State, with the intervention of André Malraux, they acquired the status of a protected area, which enabled them to preserve the collective quality of their habitat. To maintain the patrimonial value of a district thus assumes that a collective action will be put in motion, the only way to maintain or to restore the work of a social group in its urbanization of an entire district. This is still the case today for chic developments in the Paris area or the Riviera

Notes

1. See especially Pierre BOURDIEU and Jean-Claude PASSERON, Les Héritiers, les étudiants et la culture Paris, Minuit, coll. "Le Sens commun", 1964, and Pierre BOURDIEU, La Distinction. Critique sociale du jugement, Paris, Minuit, coll. " Le Sens commun " 1979.

2. Pierre BOURDIEU and Hans HAACKE, Libre-Échange, Paris, Seuil/Les Presses du réel, 1994, p. 102.

3. Jérôme COIGNARD, "Un palais sur la mer ", Beaux-Arts, special edition: " La villa Ephrussi de Rothschild," 1993, p. 7.

4. Marcel LANDOWSKI, " Avant-propos ", Beaux-Arts, op. cit., p. 4.

5. Pierre BOURDIEU and Hans HAACKE, Libre-Échange, op. cit., p. 49.

6. Olivier DONNAT and Dennis COGNEAU, Département des études et de la prospective, ministère de la Culture et de la Communication, Les Pratiques culturelles des Français (Department of Studies and Forecasting, Ministry of Culture and Communication, Cultural Practices of the French, 1973-1989, Paris, La Découverte - La Documentation française, 1990.

7. Pierre BOURDIEU, "Les fractions de la classe dominante et les modes d'appropriation de l'oeuvre d'art," Information sur les sciences sociales, 13-3, June 1974, p. 7-32.

8. Victoire de MONTESQUIOU, Je suis née un dimanche, Paris, J. -C. Lattès, 1990, p. 86. Avenue Gabriel, in the VIIIth precinct of Paris, connects the Place de la Concorde with Avenue Matignon and passes in front of the "grille du Coq" of the Élysée gardens. It is only built up on the north side and apartments look out, to the south, on the Champs-Elysées garden.

9. See François G. ROCHE, Les Rothschild à l'abbaye des Valley-of-Cernay, Paris, I.D.C. and, coll. "La vallée de Chevreuse en 1900," s.d.

10. Thus in the guide Alpes-M, Paris, Gallimard, 1994, p. 316.

11. Claude DUNETON, Parler croquant, Stock, 1973, p. 125.

12. "It is obvious that a good diploma has never made a good expert, since in this calling everything depends on the eye, on flair and experience," one will find written in a special edition of Connaissance des arts, dedicated to Drouot, published in May, 1988. On this theme, see Raymonde MOULIN and Alain QUEMIN, "La certification de la valeur de l'art," Annales, November-December 1993. The authors write that "an expert's title, in France, is not recognized nor protected, and the profession is not regulated. Anyone whatsoever can call himself an expert [...]. "The eye," "the look," "the sixth sense" nourish the anthology of subjects traditionally held by experienced general practitioners. The eye is over-valued as a gift of nature, the basis for the specialist's superiority over the layman. He claims this title as a surrogate for a diploma." (p. 1428).

13. Alain QUEMIN, Les Commissaires-Priseurs: analyse d'une profession et de son rôle dans les ventes aux enchères, doctoral thesis, Paris, EHESS, December 1994, p, 54. See also, by the same author, "Les commissaires-priseurs français: de la tradition à la modernité," Encyclopaedia universalis, vol Universalia 1994, p. 274-277.

14. Alain Quemin, Les Commissaires-priseurs. La mutation d'une profession, Paris, Anthropos, 1997, p. 244.

14. It is significant that the luxurious magazines dedicated to real estate and home furnishing devote long articles to homes that are, like Mrs. Girardet's, veritable museum display windows where the cultural and the everyday are mingled inextricably.

15. See La Peinture mondaine de 1870 à 1960, Paris, Édition Celia, 1993. In this book initiated by the Duchesse de Gramont and created by Patrick Chaleyssin and Thierry Vasseur, there is a portrait of the

Duchesse de Gramont by Trafford Klots, of the Vicomtess Charles de Noailles by Salvador Dali, and of the five de Ganay brothers by Sébastien de Ganay, the son of Victoire de Montesquiou.

16. Countess Jean of PANGE, *Comment j'ai vu 1900, op. cit.*, t. 1, p. 21. 17. Ibid., p. 65-66.

18. On this point, see our work *Dans les beaux quartiers, op. cit.*, p. 167-169.

19. Fernand de SAINT-SIMON, " Le rallye du Peloux ", *L'Éventail*, no. 4, November-December 1987.

20. Norbert ELIAS, *La Société de cour, op. cit.*, p. 109.

21. See our work *Dans les beaux quartiers*, op. cit., p. 79-80.

22. Louis BERGERON, *Les Rothschild et les autres... La gloire des banquiers*, Paris, Perrin, coll. " Histoire et fortunes", 1991, p. 140.

23. See *Le Nouvel Observateur*, "Les 200 Français les plus riches," No. 1257, 8 to December 14, 1988, and *Le Nouvel Économiste*, N ° 967, October 14, 1994 ("Fortunes professionnelles, les quatre cents").

24. Rene SÉDILLOT, *Les Deux Cents Familles*, Paris, Perrin, coll. "Vérités et légendes", 1988, p. 108.

25. See our work *Quartiers bourgeois, quartiers d'affaires, op. cit.*, p. 247-267.

26. The catalogue published by the studio of Master Tajan, appraiser, gives a precise and fairly technical description for each book. Thus for *The Odyssey*: "Homer, *The Odyssey* Translation by Victor Bérard, Paris, La Compagnie des Bibliophiles de l'Automobile Club de France, 1930-1933, volumes in-quarto, black morocco decorated with sequences of gilt lines intersecting in various compositions and extending onto the back and the second plate, each first plate decorated with embedded lacquer, crimped with a listel of colored morocco, repeating an illustration from the work: for Volume 1, Pallas armed with a lance and a shield; Mount Olympus overlooking the Aegean Sea in Volume II; the eagle messenger of Zeus perched on the roof of a palace in Volume III and the armies of Ulysses in Volume IV, the interior decorated with a gilded net and a cold-rolled metallic net, lining and fly-leaf of reps of golden yellow, pink, vermillion and dark red, gilded top, edging and back, case." (*Beaux Livres dans de riches reliure*, sale catalogue for Monday, March 27, 1995, Étude Tajan, 1995, No. 20 of the catalogue). However, part of this technical lexicon primarily relates to the professionals, and the competence of the families in this field varies.

27. This information is drawn from the inventory list drawn up by Jean-Baptiste RENDU, *Bibliothèque de l'Esparrou: alphabetical classification*, 90 pages

28. See Raymonde MOULIN, "Un type de collectionneur: le spéculateur", Revue française de sociologie, 5 (2), 1964, p. 161. See also Raymonde MOULIN, Le Marché de la peinture en France, Paris, Minuit, coll. "Le Sens commun", 1967.

29. The following goods are exempted from ISF tax: antiques more than one hundred years old (which includes old furniture); art objects and collectibles (carpets and tapestries, paintings, engravings, prints, postage stamps, mineralogical and paleontological collections, etc.); and vehicles of collection.

30. André BABEAU, *Le Patrimoine aujourd'hui*, Paris, Nathan, 1988, p. 60. Gold is also excluded but for another reason, namely the impossibility not of calculating but merely of counting, the quantities possessed.

31. Alain QUEMIN, "L'espace des objets. Expertises et enchères à Drouot Nord ", *Genèses*, No. 17, September 1994, p. 52-71.

32. Alain QUEMIN, "*Les Commissaires-priseurs* (Anthropos, op. cit.), p.244-245.

33. *Intercercles magazine*, No. 12, Autumn 1993.

CHAPTER VI

The Collectivization of Private Property: Chic Properties

"Private Property, No Trespassing": this sign decorates the lobby of bourgeois buildings, the gate to the private walkways in the 16th arrondissement, the porch of the private Parisian mansion and the seaside villa, and stops the tourist at the verge of the château's park; it seems to make the grand bourgeois and the aristocrat into determined individualists, since it is the goods of which they have reserved the use that is in question. At any rate, a fair reflection of the majority of the owners who, great or modest, appear to set great store by protecting the intimacy of the private sphere.

But the practical value and exchange value of the great families' real estate patrimony depends on the buildings and the population which, by their vicinity, form the architectural and social environment. The value of a building or a house depends on the physical and sociological characteristics of the space of which the building forms a part. This dependence seems more marked for the most prized assets whose value is due for a great part to the context that they enjoy. Thus, since there is a sort of spacial designer label, i.e. since a district enjoys a reputation related to the social quality of those who live there, it is necessary that the whole of the elements which constitute this district be "chic." That is as true for the architecture of the buildings and for the urban landscape as it is for the life style and the look of those who live there. This stamp of quality is not self-sustaining and the most highly valued spaces can be threatened with losing their hallmark, like so much old clothing sold at reduced prices after the tag authenticating them has been removed. To control the social and zoning qualities of a chic locale requires that individualism, paradoxically, so consubstantial with private real estate, be restrained in favor of collective modes of management—in fact, in favor of those same collective modes by which these patrimonies are formed.

In the case of a town whose development was planned from the beginning, as at Maisons-Laffitte, in Vésinet or in the parks of St. Tropez, the high society families participate at the institutional and legal level in the zoning ordinances and the details of town planning which are derived from them. Thus the families or their representatives control the means of managing these exceptional places. Social clout gives a considerable power over space, which is expressed sometimes by ad hoc institutions. These latter make it possible to supervise the urban processes and to intervene effectively, as is the case in a number of chic locations.

Indeed, the dominant classes invented the housing development in the 19th century, one of the first forms of concerted town planning. The patrimony thus made up is the family's, insofar as there remains the private property of a family, and collective for that part which is held in joint ownership and especially because each partner, given the draconian regulations of town planning, has a right to keep a watchful eye on the others. It is only at the beginning of the 20th century that the social reformers would implement similar procedures in favor of working labor with the implementation of garden apartments.[1] But before it came to the suburbs of the popular classes, efficient town planning, and a concern for landscaping and the environment, were expressed through achievements whose objective was far from being social.[2]

THE CREATION OF THE GREAT HOUSING DEVELOPMENTS OF THE BOURGEOISIE

The Park of Maisons-Laffitte

One of the first property developers was certainly the banker Jacques Laffitte who, faced with serious financial difficulties in 1830, resolved to parcel out most of the park of the château de Maisons of which he was proprietor. But the transaction was conceived under very original terms: a schedule of conditions defines strict rules of construction, "with a broadness of outlook and a requirement for severe rules which one may call, a century before the term was in use, town planning."[3] Of the 307 hectares of the park, 171 were sold in the form of individual lots while 136 remained under the collective ownership of the purchasers in the form of squares, public gardens, wooded areas and planted avenues. The latter, which excludes any passage that might be called a street (that term no doubt being considered too ordinary), cover 70 kilometers with broad green arteries.

Today this development, or rather "the Park," as it is customary to respectfully designate this urban development that is original in so many respects, covers 60% of the communal territory and incorporates 40% of the population of the township of Houses-Laffitte. The Park is still governed by the schedule of conditions worked out under the control of Jacques Laffitte in 1834.

One hundred sixty years later, sales contracts signed in the notary still reproduce its text—as if the new inhabitants, by taking possession of their house, were in the situation of those heirs "inherited" by their heritage, caught in the duty to maintain and pass on in their turn.

The plan of occupation of grounds (POS) is particularly restrictive in the Park "and does not allow," according to the mayor-adjunct in charge of economic affairs and the environment, "the creation, except very, very rare exceptions, of collectives; with the result that today, it is truly possible in the Park to build houses only for individual families." The 1834 schedule of conditions is published in the introductory report of the POS and all its constraints and encumbrances are still in force.

Laffitte the banker, in his will to create an exceptional habitat reserved to a social elite, had the foresight "to raise on each portion of land sold, a dwelling whose construction [should] be finished within one year from the day of the contract of sale and for a sum of 2,000 francs minimum." This is for the purpose of preventing precarious and temporary constructions from spoiling the landscape. Also to preserve the pastoral aspect of the Park, the property enclosures must be discrete. One cannot "fence oneself in on the side bordering the avenues, boulevards, squares and intersections, other than with hedges, shrubbery or waist-high walls." The residential character is absolute. In the Park, "factories, industry, and farming are prohibited." "No trades, no industry, in a word, no practice of any type that might harm either by noise, or by odor," is accepted.

J. Laffitte, in the advertising folders of the time, used the term of "colony", then very much in vogue, meaning thereby that he specifically intended to create a middle-class phalanstery. "All things considered," concludes G. Poisson, "he reconciled, with some elegance, his need to raise money, his preoccupation with esthetics and his desire to keep the illusion of a park that was intact and continued to belong to him."[4]

The New City of Vésinet

At Vésinet, we find this collective urbanization of a great domain under different conditions. The township, not far from Maisons-Laffitte, still in the residential agglomeration west of the Paris, was created in 1875 from a subdivision of the forest of Vésinet, divided at first between the three communities of Chatou, Pecq and Croissy. The current town conforms to the boundaries of the transaction as it was conceived in the 19th century.

Under the Second Empire, the Duke of Morny, half-brother of Napoleon III, was the instigator. He had the idea of effecting an exchange of Malmaison's 300 hectares of forest for Vésinet's 400 hectares of woods, to increase the property of the imperial house, but especially to recover from the banker charged with the transaction the sums that he had entrusted to him. To carry out the development Morny chooses a wealthy industrialist, Alphonse Pallu. "With his two-fold expertise as head of an enterprise and local administrator [he had been a mayor of his community in Auvergne, then general councillor], Pallu understood the importance of the work to be carried out by making Vésinet, well served by railroad, a model development, while trying to fulfill that eternal idea of mankind: to marry the city and nature. Pallu imagined doing with the woods of Vésinet what had been done for the park of François Mansart [at Maisons-Laffitte]: to transform it into a "colony," as they said at the time, a place of summer residence where rivers, ponds, lawns would surround dwellings scattered among the greenery."[5] As at Maisons-Laffitte, the patrimony of the well-to-do families falls under a collective unit, a true landscape which the interested parties look after jealously.

In addition, the concept of urban landscape was declared. The schedule of conditions, in 1858, provided for the prohibition of any industrial plant and of fences that might be likely to interrupt the view. Only authorized businesses, nurserymen and other gardeners were considered not to spoil the bucolic character of what was not yet a town. Vésinet was conceived as a gigantic English park, decorated with 5 lakes connected by rivers a total length of 4 kilometers. The private property of each purchaser had to fit in with this design from the start. "Count de Choulot's essential idea being to design and to even paint," he said, "a landscape ensemble where the colors, the vistas, the layouts of plantings would be composed in a harmonious whole into which the owners would be integrated and even controlled."[6] So that, as at Maisons-Laffitte, the private parties and the public parties must be based in "the same composition in order to safeguard the unity of the ensemble: a new and even revolutionary idea, at least in France, in this golden age of 'property' where every small domain, carefully enclosed, was designed and arranged in complete abstraction from the environment."[7]

For G. Poisson, as we have seen, it is a question of marrying the city and nature; for others, it is a return to nature, an idea that "developed and spread toward the end of the 18th century with a burning advocate in the person of Jean-Jacques Rousseau."[8] But one can also interpret this pastoral urbanization as the realization of the desire of a rising bourgeoisie to adopt an aristocratic way of life, at the same time marked with a multi-territoriality and blurring of the lines dividing the city and the countryside. The château embodies this Utopian mixture of the urban and the rural,[9] while the private mansion in the suburb of St. Germain strives to be the symbol of the countryside in the city.[10] Furthermore, it was a noble aesthete, the Count de Choulot, whom Alphonse Pallu asked to design the residential park of Vésinet. To carry out this project, Alphonse Pallu created a limited partnership. The company, owner of all the grounds, dealt directly with the purchasers of lots, without administrative intermediaries.

Other Experiences

It is also under the Second Empire that the grounds of the north of Neuilly were developed, which corresponded to the property of the duke of Orleans. "Napoleon III decided, in an abuse of his rights, to parcel out the immense park of Orleans which was between the street of Villiers, the Seine and the enclosure of Mr. Thiers. They make 700 lots out of the former royal property, served by 7 boulevards. More than a third of the current Neuilly is built on the site of the estate."[11] But there is still a list of conditions, always with the goal of safeguarding the qualities of the original space, providing for various constraints from the fences and the plantations of trees until the width of the ways. One of the principal characteristics of these lists of conditions is "the waste" of space that the rules impose. The size of the building lots, always high, the importance of public or collective spaces, the obligation of maintaining distance from the property boundaries, all these clauses organize an ostentatious expenditure of space which, while being transformed into symbolic capital, is one of the guarantees of maintaining the excellence of these spaces and thus maintaining, even increasing, their monetary value.

The 19the century saw other fashionable developments, such as the floriferous Hameau, at Billancourt (1840), and the park of the château at Chatou (1862).[12]. Considerably later, the development of part of the park of Sceaux in 1926 was a similar deal where the rigor of the town planning regulations guaranteed for everyone that the quality of the place would be maintained. With far fewer requirements, social reformers applied the principles of the development to improve the living conditions for working class families by creating garden cities like the one at Suresnes (1921-1947) and at Châtenay-Malabry in 1931. If certain ideas that governed the dealings of Vésinet or Maisons-Laffitte are repeated in the workings of the offices of HBM (French subsidized housing agency), the differences are considerable. They are visible in the relationship with space, much more generous in the bourgeois townships: the prodigality with which it is used is one of the most immediately readable symbolic markings. Power is power over space, and occupying a large space signifies as well the place one intends to occupy in social space.

Several conditions seem to be necessary for successful transmission of the bourgeois housing developments from generation to generation: a location in the west of the Paris area, a certain magnitude of scale, and mastery by the owners of legal and urban

Table 6. Pattern of the working population according to the socio-professional category

	Metropolitan Paris	Le Raincy	Maisons-Laffitte	Le Vésinet
Craftsmen and tradesmen	4.9	7.1	5.4	6.6
Heads of undertaking	1.0	2.1	2.0	4.6
Intermediate Professions	1.6	4.8	2.7	4.6
Cadres	11.9	14.3	24.2	26.3
Public Employees	6.5	7.3	6.0	9.7
Professions	22.4	26.2	23.2	20.8
White Colar	30.1	25.0	22.8	20.8
Blue Colar	21.6	13.2	13.6	6.7
Total	100.00	100.00	100.00	100.00

SOURCE: INSEE, 1990 population census, survey as of 1/4.

planning considerations. These three conditions are interdependent and for example a location in the east of Paris can be enough for a development that was bourgeois in the beginning to be transmitted less successfully than Maisons-Laffitte or Vésinet.

A Counterexample: The Park of the Château of Raincy

The origins of Raincy, a bourgeois city lost in the working and communist neighborhoods of the Seine-St. Denis, are similar to those of Maisons-Laffitte: the park of a château developed by a prudent businessman.

Jacques Bordier, superintendent of finances since 1649, had a château built at Raincy with the most prestigious collaboration at the time, Le Vau for architecture, Le Nôtre for the gardens and Le Brun for the decoration.[13] In the 18th century "the park was completely transformed in accordance with the requirements of a time when nature was being rediscovered. Time has flown since the rigor and order where reason guided the design of Le Nôtre."[14] In 1812, Napoleon became owner of Raincy. "The park was then recorded as covering 193 hectares including 74 of mature standing timber, 37 of cut wood, 2 of arable land, 1 of kitchen garden and 79 of meadows; all of it enclosed by walls."[15] Then

Table 7. Distribution of residences (houses and apartment buildings) according to the date of their construction

	Type of housing	before 1915	1915 to 1948	1949 to 1967	1968 to 1974	1975 to 1981	after 1982	Total
Metropoliti an Paris	one family housing	12.7	26.1	20.7	12.9	12.1	15.5	100.00
	multi family	23.3	14.9	25.0	19.0	11.0	6.8	100.00
Le Raincy	one family	36.3	35.9	11.6	6.5	5.2	4.5	100.00
	multi family	22.4	23.9	18.2	9.3	15.1	11.0	100.00
Maisons-Laffite	one family	26.1	35.3	20.0	5.6	5.4	7.6	100.00
	multifam ily	12.5	11.6	44.4	15.7	10.8	5.1	100.00
Le Vésinet	one family	35.0	36.1	17.5	5.7	3.8	3.9	100.00
	multi family	13.1	15.7	44.1	10.5	10.4	6.2	100.00

SOURCE: INSEE, 1990 population census.

Raincy, having become the personal property of Louis-Philippe, was put under sequestration and was confiscated after the events of 1848. In 1854, a civil company was formed, under the management of a businessman, Delion, to buy the lots offered by what was then the Administration des Domaines, which was founded in 1855. But very quickly, contrary to what occurred at Vésinet and especially at Maisons-Laffitte, the institutional structure disappeared. Indeed, as of "September 16, 1859, the sales being completed, the Land Company was dissolved and the 700 purchasers had to organize themselves. It was un-thinkable to ask the town of Livry to take charge of the services necessary to the colony, which affirmed its existence as its own community."[16] So the inhabitants of the park asked that it be converted into a township. This was done, by an imperial decree on May 20, 1869; Vésinet had to wait until 1875 to stand on its own. Raincy remains a bourgeois town today with, in 1990, 13.2% workers as against 21.6% for the whole of metropolitan Paris. But because it is located to the east, in the heart of a département where the population is much more modest than in the Hauts-de-Seine or Yvelines, it seems that the collective patrimony made up by the development of the park of the château of Raincy, now destroyed, has trouble maintaining itself as a place as chic as Vésinet or Maisons-Laffitte. Of course, one can still see the sinuous design of the alleys of the old landscaped garden. The beauty of

Table 8. Average Number of Rooms per Dwelling

	before 1915	1915 to 1948	1949 to 1967	1968 to 1974	1975 to 1981	after 1982	Total
Matropolita nParis	2,74	2,81	3,26	3,25	3,34.	3,61	3,11
Raincy	3,92	3,40	3,45	3,90	3,37	3,44	3,59
Maisons-Laffitte	3,92	3,54	3,50	3,30	3,06	3,68	3,52
Vésinet	5,01	4,19	1 3,82	3,64	3,58	3.93	4.16

SOURCE: INSEE, 1990 population census.

the view—still so clear, since it is on a hill whose slope is, in places, rather steep—is diminished only by the great heterogeneity of the properties. Large bourgeois houses[17] sit side by side with very modest working class houses without any particular space being properly reserved for the one or the other.

A STATISTICAL APPROACH TO LOCAL SPECIFICITIES

Maisons-Laffitte and Vésinet kept, because of their origins, a population whose social level is higher than that of the whole of greater Paris.[18] The difference is less clear in favor of Raincy, even if it is still perceptible. Business executives go from 12% for the whole area to 14% in Raincy, 24% in Maisons-Laffitte and 26% in Vésinet. Conversely, the working class represents 6% of the working population of this township, 13% of those in Maisons-Laffitte and Raincy against 22% for the whole of the area (Table 6, below). These figures would be even more marked if one established them only for the small islands of these communities, corresponding to the developments studied. One could then eliminate the center from Vésinet, certainly included within the perimeter of the original exercise in town planning, but whose role always was to provide a shopping center for the city with a dense section of apartment buildings. The difference would be even more clear at Maisons-Laffitte if we could retain only the 40% of the town's population that lives within the Park itself.

The results of the census concerning the levels of diplomas are similar. Thus in 1990, 10% of the population aged 15 and over, in the whole of the metropolis, had a higher diploma than the level of "baccalaureate + 2." This rate was 12% for Raincy, 17% for Maisons-Laffitte and 24% for Vésinet. In parallel, breaking down the census by quarters gives an unemployment rate of 5.5% for Vésinet and Maisons-Laffitte, and 6% for Raincy, against 9% for the whole of the agglomeration. Thus all these indicators of social level converge. But the population of Raincy seems less favored, with everything turning out as though bourgeois enclaves in a proletarian environment were condemned to an evolution that brings them closer to the urban fabric within which they are inserted.

Graph 3. Statistical weight of company executives and workers

The distribution by ages shows a greater weight of the highest age brackets in the townships considered. 23% of the people are over 60 years in Vésinet, 21% in Maisons-Laffitte, 21% in Raincy, but only 16% in the whole of the agglomeration. Conversely young adults, and thus at the same time the 0 - 14 year-old young people, are proportionally fewer: 48% of people aged 20 to 49 years for the whole of the agglomeration, 41% for Vésinet, 44% for Maisons-Laffitte, 45% for Raincy. The more comfortable the population is, the older it is.

The real estate park shows remarkable characteristics. In the agglomeration, 39 % of the houses were built before 1949. But this proportion goes to 72% in Raincy, 61% in Maisons-Laffitte and 69% in Vésinet. However, in the outer regions where the majority of the towns only recently experienced a massive urbanization, the construction dates are much more recent. In fact, our three towns formed part of the former Seine-et-Oise. With regard to residence in apartment buildings, Raincy does not differ clearly from the whole of the agglomeration. On the other hand, Vésinet's and Maisons-Laffitte's urbanization in collective form is more recent: 76% of the residences are later than 1948, against 62% for the agglomeration (Table 7, p. 239). The essential difference is between 1949 and 1967, i.e. during a time when the weakness of town planning regulations and the pressure of an acute housing crisis led to a relative boom in construction.

The occupancy status and the size of the residences tend in the same direction: the habitat in the towns under consideration is specific, and would be still more so if one took into account only the perimeter of the developments of the 19th century. 40% own their homes in the whole of the agglomeration of Paris, but this rate varies between 55% and

58% in the townships studied. The size of the residences is exceptional: 5 rooms or more for 15% of the cases in the agglomeration, but 24% in Raincy, 23% in Maisons-Laffitte and 38% in Vésinet, which appears to be particularly favored there as well. The average number of rooms per dwelling reflects the strong presence of great residences: it goes from 3.11 for the agglomeration to 4.16 for Vésinet (Table 8, p. 241). The logic that might demonstrate that, in the agglomeration, the oldest residences are also the smallest and most decayed, is reversed here. In the agglomeration, the residences built before 1915 count on average 2.74 rooms, those of Vésinet ofer 5. the other hand the averages are 3.6 and 3.9 rooms for the residences later than 1982. Whatever the period considered, the advantage always remains with Vésinet, Maisons-Laffitte and even Raincy, but this advantage is reduced: it is in the extraordinary old housing developments that one must seek the source of the originality of these towns.

FOR EXCEPTIONAL DEVELOPMENTS—EXCEPTIONAL MANAGEMENT

At Maisons-Laffitte, the boundaries of the development of the old park of the château, designed by François Mansart in the 17th century, are announced at the entrance (which is flanked with its original pavillons) by a large sign saying "Maisons-Laffitte Park - Private Property." The characteristics of the roadway system are imposing from the start, with its broad tree-lined avenues such as Avenue Albine (named for the banker Jacques Laffitte's daughter). The urban matrix bears the imprint of the history of the park. François Mansart, who built the château de Maisons for René de Longueil (superintendent of finances), designed the park along two large axes and a half-star from which branch out the alleys intended to facilitate hunting. Then Marshal Lannes, having bought the château and its park in 1804, traced a great circular and radiating composition of pathways organized on the theme of the cross of the Legion of Honor. Their names add to the Napoleonic symbolism: the avenues of Austerlitz, Wagram, Moscow, Marengo, and of Sainte-Hélène converge toward Place Napoléon.

Lastly, Jacques Laffitte bought up the whole of the domain and parceled out the park by defining the areas for construction. This resulted in an urban setting that leaves considerable room for trees. There are no paved sidewalks except the ways along the avenues. The Park seems to overtake the construction; the houses are hardly visible and disappear behind the branches of trees that are hundreds of years old. Few cars circulate although the secluded avenues are open to public, the municipality, in the form of a grant, contributing to their maintenance. But, according to a real estate agent whose offices are close to the principal entry, "the Park is a closed space, it is not a through route, only the inhabitants drive there because one cannot go anywhere other than in the Park." Indeed, it is bordered by the Seine on the north and the east, and by the forest of St. Germain-en-Laye in the west. Only the south of the Park opens on the old village of Maisons-Laffitte whose narrow streets contrast with its spacious green avenues.

In 1994 the economic consortium "Galop" had decided to close the hippodromes of Maisons-Laffitte and Chantilly because of their financial deficits. A campaign of petitions which collected 16,000 signatures, and a complex financial arrangement, allowed the town of Maisons-Laffitte to buy its hippodrome and to sign an agreement on June 1, 1995 with France Galop, the company chaired by Jean-Luc Lagardère who expressed his intention to start horse racing again in France. At Maisons-Laffitte, there were formerly 10,000 spectators for the grand prix ; today there are only 2,000 at the maximum. However, the horse is still omnipresent. In the misty alleys, early in the morning, some 800 racehorses and their stable-lads elegantly tread the carpet of fallen leaves. In addition, since 1990, a decree grants "horses priority over cars", as many signs indicate.

In the autumn, as on this day of November 1993 when the dead leaves fallen to the ground and not yet swept up form a colorful and luminous whole with those remaining on the trees, or in winter, when the snow combines lawns, trees and houses in a blue monochrome, the pedestrian forgets that he is sauntering in a town of 8,000 inhabitants,[19] which represents about the population of Mende, prefecture of Lozère. Noise is long since proscribed since, according to a decree of 1864, one cannot "sound a hunting horn, trumpet, or instrument of comparable nature inside the village of Maisons and the colony." Today a sign indicates that "by a local by-law of March 18, 1933 the playing of ball and football are prohibited." Jean Cocteau, who was born there on July 5, 1889, left a description of this "kind of trainers' park sown with villas, gardens, avenues of limes, lawns, flowerbeds, fountains and plazas. The racehorse and the bicycle reigned there as Master. We played tennis at one another's homes, in a bourgeois world that the Dreyfus affair divided [...]. This all made a clean ground for childhood, flattering the illusion that one lived in a unique place in the world."[20]

But for such a landscape to survive, of course, has required all the vigilance the property owners could bring to bear. 2,800 owners, including 700 from private houses and 2,100 from the apartments, they are still gathered within the Association of Maisons-Laffitte Park, founded in 1869. This association has the status of a public administrative establishment and it is under the supervision of the prefect of Yvelines.[21] Every owner is obliged to be a member, including the legal entities and thus the sports organization "Encouragement" and the Steeplechase Society.[22] The tax collector is the accountant of the Association and so it is he who collects each owner's contribution, a contribution which is added to the town housing tax and represents approximately 1,500 francs on average per year per dwelling (apartment or house). The Park is maintained by about fifteen workmen employed by the Association. The mayor consults the association before making his decision regarding building permits within the park. "However," specifies the Secretary-General of the Association, "We are very attentive to contruction permits. We even have four guards who are former gendarrmes and who are not only charged with keeping an eye on traffic and parking but also construction and work being carried out. There is a risk of becoming like Neuilly, by becoming overcrowded." The schedule of conditions provides two forms of protection: the prohibition of industrial and commercial activities and a prohibition on construction in the wooded reserves, which are the property of the Association. In the Sixties, many apartment buildings were built. "At the beginning of 1963, 10 buildings were under construction and 23 in the planning phase. Their construction tore down hundred year old plantings and ruined the equilibrium of the whole district. They went up without general planning, for small profits, and ignored the building codes."[23] There was widespread dissatisfaction and that was the year that the owners gathered together by creating the Association for Safeguarding and Enhancing Maisons-Laffitte Park. Indeed, in 1963 the mayor was also President of the Council of the Park, the executive body of the Association, and this official plurality of functions gave him a greater margin of freedom to deliver the building permits."[24]

According to an inhabitant, the Association for Safeguarding is also one of the means of being elected to the Association. The Association of Safeguarding has the reputation of being very strict in protecting the historical unity and the natural setting of the Park. "They are truly watchdogs," according to this inhabitant. "There are people among them who are fanatically opposed to any change." This inhabitant of the Park, who has been reproached for not replastering the front of his house, is pleased in addition that apartment houses were built in the Fifties and Sixties because they created a better "sociological balance," since these apartments are more accessible financially. "And then it also brought us sewers, whereas before we had only cesspools, and public lighting, while formerly, the Park was sinister in the evenings, in almost complete darkness."

These apartment buildings have another advantage: they allow older inhabitants to find housing in the same location, in an apartment, when it is time to leave a villa that has become too large. In addition "the old people here," according to the assistant mayor of Maisons-Laffitte, "are in a highly medicalized universe. There are a hundred doctors, hospitals and private clinics; Maisons-Laffitte is one of the most medicalized cities in France."

The real estate agent estimates that "overall, living in the Park is a 'plus,' but there remain nevertheless the problem of distance, insulation and the difficulties inherent in maintaining large yards. The absence of tradesmen here explains why there are properties in the city which sell at the same prices as in the Park."

Because of the emblem of the horse, because of the closed nature of the community, Maisons-Laffitte has a strong identity, a quasi-provincial identity. The same agent says, "We sell 50% of our residences—and 75% of our houses—to people who already live in Maisons-Laffitte. Maisons-Laffitte functions like a provincial town; many old families have been there for a long time. Besides, it is Maisons-Laffitte which attracts, not only the Park; it is a matter of location."

Regulations have been very useful in preserving the park of Maisons-Laffitte. The urban development plans have filled the gaps in the list of restrictions. Today the residency plan (POS) helps. "If there were no POS," remarks Mr. Langlumé, Assistant Mayor, "there would be no more stables but only residences built by the promoters." In addition, many of the avenues are registered with the Inventory of Historic Buildings. That is the case of Avenues Albine and Eglé. The others are classified as sites, and since 1989, all the reserves, the green no-construction zones which are the property of the Association, as well.

At Vésinet, the housing development and the municipality are one. To satisfy the company, Pallu, and the owners, the development was made into a township in 1875. Previously, Vésinet "managed itself, according to its own laws and by means of its own delegates, without the governing townships having to intervene at all, most of the time: therefore when we ask them to fulfill their role, for example with regard to street lights or the police force, they do it with the greatest ill-will possible. However, the inhabitants of Vésinet are taxpayers in the townships on which they depend, although the corresponding charges are ensured by the company. Vésigondins will quickly have enough of this groundless administrative and financial subjection, whereas the neighboring townships will do anything to preserve the gold mine."[25] The new township only comprised the grounds which belonged to Pallu, and Alphonse Pallu was its first Mayor. "Thus, in less than twenty years, [he] carried out his dream: to make a model resdential city from the woods and to become its leader." So that the POS of Vésinet still today owes a great deal to the regulations and restrictive conditions of 1858. Vésinet has remained residential and inhabited by the bourgeoisie. The township still presents a rare landscape in certain places with its lakes, and its brooks bordered with walking paths named for foreign cities with which Vésinet is paired, such as Oakwood Walk in homage to the American city. Not to spoil the tree-lined landscape, many pavements are not paved, in order to blend better with the terrain.

The "English embankments" are rather expensive in terms of upkeep. All the area known as "natural no-construction zones," which includes these "lanes", lakes, rivers and lawns, constitutes a classified site so that "any important modification in the handling of earth-moving, plantings or paths traversing it will be presented first to the ministerial authorization" as stipulated in the Regulation of the POS.

The idea of landscaping, so dear to the Count de Choulot, still presides today in the minds of the responsible municipal parties. They have secured the assistance of a town-planner, Gerard Bauer, whose thoughts on the infrastructure of this residential community are based on "an urban project. In other words, I start with what I want to achieve, then I make the rules." Usually, he says, it is done the other way around. "But it is possible at Vésinet, because for its inhabitants generally Vésinet takes precedence over their individual interests. So some people can accept bending the rules of individual property rights in order to safeguard the ensemble." Giving priority, in certain cases, to landscaping over the rules of town planning means that on behalf of the landscape there can be inequalities in the way identical lots are treated, for example different population density limitations.[27] But these attacks on individual property rights are conceivable at Vésinet for the inhabitants know well that their individual patrimony draws its value only from physical, urban and social qualities that are completely exceptional from the rest of the township.

In addition, since 1965, the city as a whole is registered with the national Inventory of Sites. Exceptions to the usual rules are numerous there. Thus, according to Mr. Lallemand, Assistant Mayor for town planning, "even before the decentralization law of 1982, it was the mayor of Vésinet who delivered the building permits." Everything at Vésinet is special, even the railroad. Its station seems to have grown up naturally between the trees. "The transformation in 1972 of the venerable railroad into the regional subway could have led to a catastrophic "modernization" of the station and its driveways. But the inhabitants, who wished to preserve the pleasant everyday feeling of going directly from the train into the park, required that the impact of access roads and the parking area remain minimal."[21]

As at Maisons-Laffitte, the inhabitants created a Safeguard Association at the beginning of the Sixties in response to what they regarded as a significant densification of Vésinet due to the construction of small apartment buildings. However, there are so few shared residences that the POS had to be amended at the beginning of 1994 because of the consequences "which the city of Vésinet must draw from the fact that 'the provisions of the law of July 13, 1991 went into effect on January 1, 1994,' still called the LOV, the Law of Guidelines for the City, which defines quotas of multiple family residences. The township had a deficit of 735 apartments compared to its quota. "Indeed, if we count, according to statistics of the 1990 census, 6,137 principal residences subject to the tax on homes, 20% of those should be multiple family residences, that is to say 1,227— whereas today there are only 492 of them." Amending the POS was justified by the fact that in Vésinet, to prevent the streets and other avenues from being clogged with cars, it provided 1.2 parking spots per apartment not exceeding one principal room, and 2.2 above that size. However, the

Name (Name of the Villa) Circles and Clubs	Other Addresses	" Profession"	Spouse
Gerard Adam of Villiers (Macui) MBC	Av Foch, Paris 116	writer (author of spy novels SAS)	Christine Loncle
Count Romée de Regnauld de Bellescize (Laurediane)	. pl St-Sulpice Paris 6 . castle of Saint-Léger, Coast-d'Or	Councillor of State Master of Requests to the Council of State	Countess Diane of Bonneval
Fernand Bricout (Skiouros)	Av du Colonel Bonnet Paris 016	Professor at faculty of medicine	Cécilia Médina
Michel Canque (La Restanque)	* Av Thermal, Chamalières, Puy-of-dome * Holley by the Sea GULF Breeze, Florida, USA	Medical doctor	Monique Marcilhacy
François Dalle (Les Quatre Oliviers)	Av Frederic Le Play Paris 7	CEO (of Philips and BNP), Chairman of Oréal, vice-president of Nestlé	Geneviève Clément
Alain-Pierre Duvaux (La Pierrire) ACF-CI-P	Blvd d'Argenson, Neuilly	CEO	Josiane Berliet
Albert Frère (La Bastide de l'Ay) CDC-P	. domain of La Peupleraie Gerpinnes, Belgium .Av Foch Paris 8		Christine Hennuy
Didier Hallenstein (La Grivolière)	rue du Paris, Boulogne-Billancourt		Sophie Bricout daughter of Fernard Bricout (see above)
Georges Hervet (La Beriaude) CI-DV-GM-P	* Blvd Maurice BarrèsNeuilly * Menetou Salon, Cher	Bank Hervet	S.A.S. Princess Marie d'Arenberg (owner of Château Manetou)
Conte Antoine (L'Olivade) RC	* Av Henri Martin Paris 116 * Le Pré Naudin Saint-Viatre, Loir-et-Cher	[large family of many significant alliances]	Nicole Vitry
Mrs. Solange Miot (La Tramontane) P-St- C	Blvd Maillot, Neuilly	Born Soange Hervet, daughter of Jacques Miot, father of Georges (see above)	Widow of Jacques Miot banker, chairman of Francefi
Mrs. Michel Motte (La Bergerie)	Pl. du Palais-Bourbon Paris 7	born Claire Droulers, of a family	widow of Michel Motte, one of multiple descendants of the line of Motte
Mrs. Prevesianos (La Bergerie)	Pl du Palais Bourbon Paris 7		daughter of Mrs. Michel Motte (see above)
Gérard Rebut (Aulx sauvages)	Av George Mandel Paris 116		Brigitte Deleplanque

employ a couple who live on-site. If the association offers some other common services, like
SOURCES : *Bottin Mondain* and Who's Who.

fee-based. The Hervets' nine year old son, for example, has to pay 6,000 francs to play tennis during vacations at the Parks—which his mother "does not find overly expensive." It is clear, however, that the peace and quiet, the services and security have their price.

On the French National Geographic Institute's map at 1/25 000 one can see, a few kilometers from the center of St. Tropez, between the Cap Saint-Pierre and the pointe de l'Ay, a cluster of sinuous roads which serve scattered buildings and zigzag around the sign symbolizing the castle. One easily deduces the presence of a development within the Parks. The Michelin map, less detailed, has one invaluable additional, dissuasive indication for explorers: the main road of this network, the only one shown on this map, is drawn in red, closed to traffic. On the spot, it turns out that indeed a barrier prevents entry to cars that do not belong in the development. A small building permanently houses a security guard who can grant guests or deliverymen authorization to enter in the parks of St. Tropez.

Pedestrians, curiously, are accepted, and have been since the original schedule of conditions established in 1956. However, a sign informs the stroller that he is allowed in only thanks to the benevolence of the property owners. "The Parks consists of absolutely private properties," one reads. Their residents welcome you and offer for your walking pleasure these charming avenues which pass through the most beautiful sites of the headland. They expect, in return, that you respect the peace and the conduct appropriate to this place." Pedestrians are invited to stay on the avenues, not to pick flowers, and not to picnic. The director of the Parks, the person in charge of maintenance and security, considers that this is a pure gesture of goodwill, since the municipality contributes neither to the maintenance of the roadway system nor to that of the water supply, which are the responsibility of the owners. They simply find it "more elegant to open up than to barricade oneself." The same applies to the maintenance of the path along the littoral, partially paved in cement, in the difficult passages, with here and there some steps which help in crossing where the rocks are too steep. This path, which is in any case required, theoretically, all along the sea coast, makes it possible to take the measure of the privilege represented by the fact of having such vast residences, overhanging the Mediterranean, complemented by large parks open to the marine horizons. However, the owners give one to believe that the truly privileged people are the walkers whom they thus authorize to skirt their lawns and to catch a glimpse of their swimming pools. Signs laid out along the path recall indeed that to walk in such a place must be properly appreciated. "We have arranged a pedestrian walkway all along the shore—we wish you to enjoy it pleasantly," is courteously written in the preamble. Then come the recommendations, basically identical to those that appear at the main entry. And with great precision: "Our guards are authorized to write up police reports on any infractions." An ambiguous sentence follows: "Thank you for respecting these provisions in order to help us to maintain this privilege in the Parks." Upon reflection, this can only mean the privilege of the happy walkers who are admitted to skirt the edges of paradise, the territory of the gods.

Surrounding the Château Borelli, the Parks, whose original name was "Parc of the Cap Saint-Pierre," occupies 120 hectares. Those villas that occupy the highest positions, among them that of Mr. and Mrs. Hervet, dominate the gulf of St. Tropez; or they open directly on the shore, which is rocky at this place. The whole property belonged to Jean Bréaud, with his ties to real estate and the financial world, who then proceeded to subdivide his lands at the end of the Fifties. The château, at the highest point of the headlands, was transformed into five apartments, of which some were sold for 18 million francs. More than 150 villas are interspersed, behind the greenery of their estates, along winding and sloping alleys. They are not very visible from the small roads and the presence of foot traffic, according to Mrs. Hervet, does not disturb the owners, sheltered behind vegetation that is abundant and all the more effective since the buildings are generally placed far from the roadways. Cypresses, pines, lime trees, eucalyptus and mimosas form a verdant shell that ensures calm and discretion. So much so that t gardens are not fenced in and the Parks themselves are largely open to the surrounding countryside. But the luxuriant vegetation effectively conceals this preserved space, protected from the devastations of tourism, and gives walkers the impression of being in a public park. Even in the summer, while visitors are crowding on the boardwalks or the beach of St Tropez, there are only few pedestrians in this haven of peace. Essentially, according to Mrs. Hervet, they are people from the surrounding area and ornithologists, the Parks being a bird sanctuary. But a limited number of visitors come especially, off-season, to benefit from the tranquility and the luxuriance of the vegetation. Perhaps the barrier and the guard at the entrance have a dissuasive effect, social timidity preventing people from coming to read the sign that specifies clearly that entry is free for pedestrians. The customs officers' path has more traffic in the summer.

The houses, of which some are vast (for "second homes"), having ten rooms or more, are in very good condition even though most of them are used only one or two months a year. It is true that the list of restrictions requires excellent maintenance of the villas. One would never imagine that Mrs. Hervet, born Princess Marie d'Arenberg, had known places in the family's châteaux, where the maintenance of the gardens and the condition of the woodwork occasionally left something to be desired.

These villas, recently built since the subdivision dates only from the Fifties, are mostly done in the Provençal style and have nothing to do with the whimsical buildings and rococo of the beginning of the century as one sees at Biarritz or Deauville. The Hervet family's villa, rough-cast pink, was designed in 1977 by one of the architects in the style fashionable on the Riviera, Herrerra. It is one single story but on several levels, because of the declivity of the ground. Located at the summit of the headlands, it enjoys a remarkable view of the sea that one can fully appreciate from the salon, "open on all sides." A room for eating and a salon for the children supplement the reception rooms. With six rooms and four bathrooms, one can host family and friends within an enchanting setting, supplemented by a swimming pool, an element from which almost all the villas benefit. Within such a framework, with the service of a couple of guards and a cook brought down from Paris, one might suppose that the conditions have been met so that it may be possible to have a pleasant stay, in spite of the summer mob which invades the area.

The happy owners of these places appreciate above all the calm and seclusion, as the Director of the Parks or the guards gave one to understand. Silence as to the identity of the personalities living in these places is resolutely impenetrable, just as is everything that relates to their nationalities, social and professional details. Fortunately *Bottin Mondain* and its new complement, the *Petit Mondain,* which classifies the people who appear on the society list according to address, by department, are useful, even if they remain insufficient. Fourteen owners were thus identified—that is a little less than 10 % of the total.

All these owners have a residence in Paris or Neuilly, with two exceptions, one in favor of Boulogne-Billancourt, a township that is heavily bourgeois, the other in favor of Chamalières (but in this case there is also an address in Florida...). In Paris the addresses are located in the best districts. Avenue Foch, which is one of the most expensive addresses in the capital, and the VIIth arrondissment are well represented. Postal Code 116 indicates the northern part of the 16th district, smarter than the south, indicated by code 016. Many of these happy property owners are thus neighbors in the city as they are when on vacation. The more so as some belong to the same clubs, two being with the Interallié and four with the Polo.

San Tropez pedestrians supplemented this incomplete information, revealing the presence of Bernard Arnault, President of Groupe LVMH, describing the fabulous residence of a Saudi businessman (invisible from the service road), and insisting on the presence of helicopter pads in certain yards—quite a useful means of transportation at the height of the season.

The Owners' Association, which manages the parks of St. Tropez with the same statutes as at Maisons-Laffitte, does not exert any control over the sales and the purchases of villas. One of them was offered for sale in *Propriétés de France*[33] in these terms: "Parks of Saint-Tropez. Charm, serenity, quietude, southern exposure and sea view. Splendid grounds and small existing house with swimming pool in a private yard, well maintained and with a fine reputation. Building permit granted for 380 square meters." The price level, in practice, is sufficient to ensure a rigorous selection, certain houses having been negotiated at the end of the Eighties at the height of the real estate market for 40 to 50 million. The market has returned to more reasonable levels, but one cannot find a house at the Parks for less than 10 million. The privacy of the place and the constraints of the schedule of conditions contribute to the selection of potential buyers, but the pressure on the area is such, the demand is so strong, that not all the purchasers readily yield to the stipulated constraints and it happens that the Association of the owners must take legal action to enforce the schedule of conditions with newcomers who are insufficiently concerned with preserving the exceptional ssetting.

CONCLUSION: COLLECTIVE FORMS OF MANAGEMENT

The social power is thus also a power over space. This specific form of the power results in the capacity to control the residential environment, as much from the point of view of its social composition as of that of buildings and landscapes. In the 19th century, the Second Empire was a period of intense urbanization. Be it in the Paris area or the vacation resorts, seaside retreats or thermal spas, high society did a lot of building. For residence or for leisure, new procedures appeared which tended to ensure a tight control of the urban processes. Things were done as if it were a question of leaving nothing to chance. Two principal concerns, closely linked, are at the bottom of this urbanistic prudence: on the one hand, the social need to ensure oneself of being among one's own kind, within the borders of a space which one chooses, manages and sets up, and on the other hand the taste for a backdrop to life which is the worthy frame for exceptional existences. To build a social environment and an urban envinment out of the ordinary, those proponents of economic liberalism and individual initiative call in collective forms like the private housing development and the schedule of conditions.

Maisons-Laffitte and Vésinet present this characteristic a priori. Astonishing comfortable social classes, fairly collectively they are committed to the defense of a patrimony that seems indissolubly individual, family and collective. This paradox is comprehensible only if one takes into account the fact that the security of these patrimonies, the practical values as well as the exchange values, are what they are only due to their reciprocal reinforcement. The counter-example of Raincy demonstrates that. The environment counts for a lot in the value of good real estate. Its most precious value lies in its symbolic value. But if the sociological environment begins to be degraded, this value symbolic is threatened. Social activity intended to ensure the best conditions for transmission is then important. One finds at the level of the social group the same fears, in any case the same concerns as at level of the family structure: how to ensure, under the best conditions, the perenniality of the power, of which an exceptional habitat is one of the main factors since it expresses symbolically.

The representation of the common will associates regional planning and high-ranking civil servants, urban planning and the 20th century, whereas those which accumulate all kinds of capital have always known how to control, discreetly but effectively, certain aspects of the urban development to their own benefit. It is true, however, that if it is left to the effects of market forces, this control can escape even from those who have the best assets. Also, as we will see in certain vacation resorts, when family and economic interests are both at stake, the grand bourgeoisie does not hesitate to break the rules of the market in its own favor. Then one sees developing in some spaces a completely remarkable urban protectionism, creating conditions for safeguarding the acquired advantages and secure incomes.

Notes

1. See Susanna MAGRI and Christian TOPALOV, "De la cité-jardin à la Ville rationalisée. Un tournant du projet réformateur, 1905-1925. Étude Comparative: France, Grande-Bretagne, Italie, États-Unis," Revue FranHaise de sociologie 28 (3) 1987, p. 417-451.

2. See Michel PINÇON and Monique PINÇON-CHARLOT, "Propriété individuelle et gestion collective : les lotissements chic," Les Annales de la recherche urbaine, No. 65, December 1994, p. 35-46.

3. George POISSON, De Maisons-sur-Seine à Maisons-Laffitte, Association de sauvegarde et de mise en valeur de Maisons-Laffitte, 1973, p. 67. This work was republished in December 1993 by the same association with the assistance of the authorized trade-union Association of Maisons-Laffitte.

4. Op. cit., p. 69.

5. George POISSON, La Curieuse Histoire du Vésinet, Ville du Vésinet, 1986, p. 62. One may also consult Le Vésinet, modèle d'urbanisme paysager, 1858-1930, "Cahiers de l'inventaire", No. 17 (national Printing works); Imprimerie nationale); Sophie CUEILLE, "Une colonie dans une forêt: le lotissement du Vésinet (1858-1930)", Villes en parallèle, no 14, June 1989, p. 71-75; Jacques CATINAT, Grandes Heures de Chatou et la naissance du Vésinet, Chatou, Éditions SOSP, 1985 (première édition en 1972).

6. La Curieuse Histoire du Vésinet, op. cit., p. 71.

7. Ibid, p. 77.

8. Robert JOHY and Élisabeth CAMPAGNAC, Racines historiques du lotissement, Paris, Secrétariat d'État à la Culture, Copedith, 1976.

9. Eric MENSJON-RIGAU, "La persistance du modèle du château dans les modes de vie et les valeurs aristocratiques, ou les limites de la fusion des élites dans l'univers de la communication au colloque Noblesses et villes, 1780-1950, Tours, Éditions de la Maison des sciences de la ville, 1995

10. Norbert Elias had already noted that "the court gentlemen had created with their 'hotels' a rather specific type of city residence. They were indeed city houses, but it is felt that they derive from the former gentry. The

farmyard still exists, but it has become a simple access road for carriages, a "representative" space. One still finds the stables, the outbuildings, the servants's quarters, but they form a unit with the central building. The garden replaces the surrounding countryside. The country reminiscences of the "hotel" are symptomatic. It is certain that the court gentlemen are townsmen, the town life marked them to a certain extent. But their bonds with the city are considerably less solid than those of the bourgeoisie carrying on a professional activity. The majority are owners of one or several country residences. It is from those that they draw their name in general, a good part of their incomes; it is to those that they sometimes retire. The company they keep is always the same, een if the place of residence changes." *(La Société de cour, op. cit., p. 21.)*

11. George POISSON, "Neuilly-sur-Seine, histoire ", dans : Évocation *du vieux Paris. La banlieue nord-ouest*, Paris, Minuit, 1960, p. 433.

12. On Chatou, one may consult, under the direction of Domenique HERVIER, texts by Laurent ROBERT, photographs by Jean-Bernard VIALLES, *Croissy-sur-Seine, villégiatures en bordure de Seine*, Paris, Association pour le développement de l'inventaire général, 1993.

13. Jean ASTRUC, *Le Raincy, "Forêt j'étais, ville je suis"*, a work published with the assistance of the city of Raincy at the time of its centenary (1869-1969).

14. *Ibid*, p. 57.

15. *Ibid*, p. 103.

16. *Ibid*, p. 134.

17. In 1992 there were 500 taxpayers liable for the wealth tax (ISF) between Raincy and the communities bordering it, Villemonble, Gagny and Montfermeil. Thus in 1983 Raincy counted as many great fortunes as Morbihan and fewer than Savoy. See Jack DION and Pierre IVORRA, *Sur la piste des grandes fortunes*, Paris, Messidor-Éditions sociales, 1985.

18. In the tables from INSEE providing the results of the 1990 census, the area of Paris was indicated as the "urban unity of Paris". We preserved the term " agglomeration ", the name "urban unity" being used to cover the rare cases of isolated cities at the same time as that from the true agglomerations.

19. According to the 1990 census, there were exactly 8,059 inhabitants in the Park, that is to say 36.3 % of the population of Maisons-Laffitte (22,171 inhabitants).

20. Jean COCTEAU, *La Difficulté d'être*, Paris, 1948, quoted by George POISSON, *De Maisons-sur-Seine...*, op. cit., p. 91.

21. This type of association, governed by the law of June 21, 1865, is not common in the urban environment for their first objective seems to be rural and relates mainly to agricultural irrigation work. The association of Maisons-Laffitte Park (ASP) "is by far the largest and brings together the greatest number of landowners," according to the Association's brochure. The jurisprudence confirmed its character as a public establishment and "the strict application to these associations of the rules on public accountability, the general interest inherent to the activities of the association, the right of expropriation, the character of the administrators and agents of the association as public civil servants, the competence of the administrative courts." (*Le Secrétaire de mairie, vol. 1, p. 110*).

22. The Maisons-Laffitte race track and certain driving tracks are part of the Park. These two owners alone represent more than a quarter of the votes. "But during elections," says the Secretary-General of FASP, "according to the statutes no owner can exercise more than 5% of the votes."

23. George POISSON, *De Maisons-sur-Seine... op. cit., p. 119.*

24. Since then, this office plurality was made impossible.

25. *George POISSON, La Curieuse Histoire du Vésinet, op. cit., p. 107. 26. Ibid, p. 122.*

27. The POS report specifies that "the concept of COS (Coefficient d'Occupation de Sols) fixed *a priori* will no longer be implemented in UB areas. The rules give precedence to the concept of volume, which on the

architectural level is more logical. " (p. 32).

28. Gerard BAUER, Gildas BANDAGE, Jean-Michel Roux, *Banlieues de charme ou l'art des quartiers-jardins*, Paris, Pandora Éditions, 1980. A chapter is devoted to Vésinet: "A residential Bois de Boulogne: Vésinet."

29. For example *Julie Lescaut,* produced by Élisabeth Rappeneau, *L'Inspecteur Moulin,* produced for TFI, *Délit mineur, by* Francis Girod.

30. In his comparison of social structures and tax bases, Edmond Preteceille shows that Vésinet and Maisons-Laffitte are not exactly the same type of township. Vésinet is "a posh suburban community," where "only industrialists, large business owners and professions prosper" whereas Maisons-Laffitte is "a community of high status salaried workers" where "the higher executives do very well." Probably the Park, if considered separately, would be in line with Vésinet. In any event, the two townships have the same type of tax structure, characterized by "a very high tax base on developed land and housing, which is logical: the most bourgeois townships are the townships where real estate and land have the most value." On the other hand, the professional tax is very weak there, which corresponds well at their eminently residential character. Edmond PRETECEILLE, *Mutations urbaines et politiques locales*, Paris, Centre de sociologie urbaine, 1993, p. 40 and 138-139.

31. George Hervet, a banker, directed the establishment founded by his ancestor at Bourges, in 1830, an establishment which had prospered magnificently before being nationalized in 1982.

32. The Owners' Association was constituted, in accordance with the schedule of conditions, under the terms of the law of June 21, 1865—the same one that was used for the creation of the Association of Maisons-Laffitte.

33. *Propriétés de France, No. 27*, March-April 1994. This publication, published by *Le Figaro*, offers in a first left, Articles on the market top-of-the-range real estate of an area, on decoration or on a specific house, chosen for the quality of its architecture and its fitting. The second party, longest, is made up of real ads whose descriptions are always detailed and are based on photographs in blow ups which puts in scene residences of dream and castles of fairy tales.

34. The meanings of the abbreviations used in the table: ACF = Automobile Club of France; CDC = Club of the Hundred; Ci = Circle of the Interallied Union; FD = Circle of Deauville; GM = Golf of Morfontaine; MBC = Maxim's Business Club; P = Polo Club of Paris; RC = Racing Club of France; StC = Saint-Cloud Country Club.

CHAPTER VII

Contested Spaces, Defended Spaces

The case of the chic developments of the Parisian suburbs has demonstrated that urban quality is not self-sustaining. To ensure successful continuation, it appears to be necessary for the owners to combine their efforts as much as possible to control the processes of urban development which are always likely to lead to a certain "degradation." From the very beginning of the century, voices were heard among the grand families living in private mansions along the Champs-Élysées denouncing what was already perceived as the beginning of a decline.[1] In the 1880's, the members of the Circle of Deauville had echoed similar fears, not hesitating to speak about "the degeneration of the clientele of our beach."[2]

With the origin of a beautiful neighborhood or a prestigious vacation resort, the presence of high society families, the peace generated by the profusion of space and greenery, the elegance of the architecture, the perfection of a social life sanctioned by one's peers which both aristocrats and grand bourgeois know how to arrange—all explain the prestige of these exceptional places. But a disastrous destiny seems to be linked to fashionable locales, as if their rare qualities contained within themselves the process of their deterioration. For great addresses attract and inflame the covetousness of those who have sufficient economic resources without necessarily having mastered the codes of conduct and the manners of the old bourgeoisie who made these spaces. Today, *nouveaux riches* businessmen and movie stars are perceived as worms in the fruit: a fatal danger to the permanence of quality. Business and the luxury trades, by invading buildings formerly reserved for housing, are emptying the districts of the mid-west of Paris of their traditional social life and are threatening the identifying landmarks of the great families. At Deauville and other resorts, the diversification of the public raises similar concerns.

To stop that ineluctable urban law that says that grandeur always leads to decline, the owners or future owners organize themselves. Faced with town planning that is anarchistic—because it is left to the laws of the market—associations and defense committees for the beautiful districts try to preserve the privilege of their own milieu and the respect for the architectural order through rather specific actions and interventions.

AN OLD TRADITION: THE DEFENSE OF THE BEAUTIFUL DISTRICTS

As of the end of the 19th century, after the Haussmann traumatization, the great families mobilized themselves through learned associations and societies. It was a question of making it so that no one could destroy anything anymore. In some *arrondissements*, the combat goes beyond defending the old stones. That is how it was in the VIIIth *arrondissement* where the Historical and Archaeological Society, founded in 1899, gathered property owners and tenants. They were, of course, concerned about preserving the architectural and urban beauty of their *arrondissement*, and also the well-being and the homogeneity of the neighborhood of the great families. It is true that these wealthy families of the Right Bank were pushed westward by the influence that the banks and insurance companies relentlessly extended on the grand boulevards and all throughout the IXth *arrondissement*. Also, on the other bank, the noble inhabitants of the St. Germain suburb yielded ground before the pressure of the ministries and the embassies. Their departure could mean a good bargain for the families. However, some of them, in particular those whose incomes were essentially land-based, sold their assets to disadvantage after the demise of tenant farming in 1946. Pressed to cash in part of their patrimony, they were forced to sell it off.

Faced with this pressure from the tertiary sector, numerous great families created associations to defend their *arrondissement* or their district. The case of the Rue du Cirque is an example. This narrow and quiet street—for it is used only by the residents—parallel with the Avenue Matignon and the Avenue de Marigny, joins Avenue Gabriel with the Rue de Faubourg-St. Honoré. A commercial gallery was opened between 16 Matignon and 9 and 11 on the Rue du Cirque. Two steps from the Élysée, this street, that has always been very "nicely" inhabited, is still unusually residential in a VIIIth *arrondissement* where a great number of residences have been transformed into offices. The eight apartments of 9 and 11 rue du Cirque were gutted, representing a total floor space of 1700 square meters, that is to say an average of 212 square meters . . .

The stake was not architectural. According to the plan, the late 19th century façades were preserved and, even better, one of the buildings on the rue du Cirque, built in the Thirties, had its façade rebuilt in the same style as the other buildings in order to accentuate the cohesion of the unit. However, fears were all the more acute since the deal, in the beginning, included a salesroom with a bonded warehouse linked to it, which implied heavy traffic—trucks—to which the inhabitants of the street were hardly accustomed. The problem rested equally in the harmful effects which this commercial gallery was likely to cause, not least the possible presence in the street of the population that frequented the Champs-Élysées, which hitherto did not come there. Of course, given the proximity of Avenue Matignon, it was art galleries that were likely to occupy this new commercial infrastructure—and so they did. But, as one of the skeptical owners said, "we know what happened to Les Halles." Such a prospect worried the residents. "From the point of view of our enjoyment of life and our isolation, it is very detrimental because idlers and customers are going to come," stressed this same interlocutor.

The emotion was strong and the association very quickly counted 90 members, 98% of the families of the street being thus represented. The Countess of Brantes, mother-in-law of Valéry Giscard d'Estaing, was among them and undoubtedly she took part in the work of proselytizing, which consisted of delivering an information letter to each residence and then making contact with the families. Their social homogeneity was not unrelated to the mobilization of the inhabitants. This activity strengthened the bonds between neighbors. A conviviality developed and from time to time dinners still bring together "the militants."

Initially, the insurance company AXA, promoter of the transaction, refused to negotiate. The Association of the Rue du Cirque then worked in close collaboration with S. O.S. Paris, created in 1972 by Marthe de Rohan-Chabot. At the time it was a question of trying to prevent the realization of plans, dear to George Pompidou, aiming to allow better traffic flow in the capital.

In 1992, S.O.S. Paris had approximately 800 members. Although its battle does not relate only to the beautiful districts, the Association includes members belonging to the best society. In 1992, its President, Philippe Denis, was a former chairman of several financial subsidiaries of Crédit Commercial de France. He comes from a provincial bourgeois family and he is member of several clubs, such as the Automobile Club of France and the Polo Club of Paris. In his own words, S.O.S. Paris "includes high society and the small fry." Henri Fabre-Luce, nephew of Mme. de Brantes, was at one time the lawyer of this association. Listed among the members are the Clermonts-Tonnerres, Baron Guy de Rothschild, Anne de Lacretelle, the Marquis de Breteuil, the princess de Faucigny-Lucinge. As for less well-known names, the grand bourgeoisie is no less present with, for example, Jacques Cheuvreux, former stockbroker, today Chairman of a stock exchange. In addition, while there are members of S.O.S. Paris living throughout all the districts, they are proportionally more numerous in the beautiful districts: 15% are located in the 7th district, 14% in the 16th. S.O.S. Paris plans to extend its activity throughout the capital, sometimes by supporting district associations, as was the case with that of Rue du Cirque.

The two associations worked together to bring about the intervention of "very powerful political support" in order to destroy or at least to amend the plans for a commercial gallery by AXA insurance company. A first building permit was refused in May 1991. In May 1992, a new plan was accepted. But the new license no longer contains the three-level parking lot under the building as was originally foreseen. Then the associations and the lawyer from AXA made some deals leading to the suppression of two major elements in the plan, the salesroom and the bonded warehouse, which were hitherto to bring significant traffic of 12-ton trucks to an exceptionally quiet street. The gallery will be realized, but with serious amendments to the preliminary design which should limit the harmful effects.

Thus, the most privileged families are not safe from urban " accidents" of this type. Families and business compete for the appropriation of the cherished spaces. But defense associations like those of Rue du Cirque and S.O.S. Paris are only makeshift, and they get involved when urban space is already threatened. In other situations the families of high society intend to control the combined processes of construction and to manage space within the framework of town planning such as that which was carried out under the Second Empire.

ARISTOCRACY AND THE BOURGEOISIE AT THE SEASIDE: THE URBAN DYNAMICS OF DEAUVILLE

There are vacation resorts where the high society families are gathered in collective ensembles that recreate in a certain way the large city ghettos of Gotha. They are the vacation resorts that the high society has always kept for themselves. As it was at the dawning of the beautiful Parisian districts, they built "spas," thermal, seaside and for winter sports. For their leisure, as for their stays in the countryside, the mountains or by the sea, the great families generally prefer to develop virgin land for themselves rather than to reconquer a habitat that is already in use. The small fishing port where one buys an old house without being sure of the neighborhood, that is hardly the approach taken by those of the most comfortable categories which, in these situations again, prefer to decide on their environment and to build in their own image the shell that will house their leisures. Deauville is an example of this sort of town planning carried out by certain individuals for the benefit of high society families.

From Marshes to a Wonderful Resort Address

Deauville was a new city, before the term was invented. It came out of the marshes at the edge of sea through the will of some wealthy businessmen during the Second Empire, with the deliberate plan of offering a setting worthy of high society which was just taking up the idea of the benefits of sea bathing, which it was about to make fashionable. The creation of the city, from 1859 to the First World War, comes shortly after the social success of Dieppe, which was for a time the place of choice for the aristocracy of St. Germain, and that of Trouville, which is separated from Deauville only by the Touques, a modest coastal river. But in both cases the villas and the luxury hotels were grafted onto fishing cities whose popular character prevented fashionable success. Social heterogeneity, which is what lends charm to old Parisian neighborhoods, in the view of many members of the middle classes who enjoy living there, offers few attractions for high society, at least when it is a question of offering the optimal conditions for a prolonged stay.

Astute businessmen, anxious to have a vacation resort at the seashore for themselves and conscious of the profit which could accrue from the new fashion, took their chances on the marshes which, south of the Touques, separated from the edge of sea the small rural village of Deauville, perched on a hill. The town council, quite a modest assembly at that time, agreed on August 31, 1859 to yield to Messrs. Donon and Olliffe these worthless marshes, property of the township, which served as poor pastures.

Donon, a banker, founder of the Caisse d'escompte, directed many companies including the Public Works and Construction Company. Doctor Olliffe was born in England in 1808 and had studied medicine in Paris where he practiced as an expert attached to the British embassy. "He liked the fashionable life and its leaders and, in reciprocity, society, imprinted with a certain Anglomania, accepted him." All the more easily, undoubtedly, since he had acquired a considerable fortune through marriage. The two initiators of the transaction received the support of the Duke of Morny, half-brother of Napoleon III, who played a leading role in the fashionable life of the Second Empire. He contributed in a decisive way to launching Deauville by giving it the seal of approval of someone significant in the regime. In a work on the luxury hotel trade, the authors write that "this policy of creating and/or developing tourism that took place in the years 1850-1860 is particularly interesting to study from the point of view of town planning and the social and economic stakes. As Marie-Hélène Contal stresses, "For Napoleon III, the establishment of thermal and seaside resorts was a support by example, a putting into practice of the imperial plans for economic and urban expansion."[4]

The trio agreed to make Breney the chief architect of the new Corporation of Buildings of Deauville.[5] In 1861, he would become the new mayor of the township, all the power being thus gathered in the hands of an interdependent group. As a disciple of Haussmann, Breney designed broad avenues intersecting each other at right angles, and vast plazas. The first villa was built in 1861. It was the Duke of Morny's, baptized *Sergewna*, in honor of the Duke's second son, the suffix being a homage to the Russian origins of the Duchess.

The grand families fill the space. They buy lots and have villas built in imaginative architectural styles—from Norman to Moorish, with every imaginative fancy of the wealthy owners; architectural inventions, baroque and neo-classical, abound.[6] Business flourishes. "After subdivision and partial development, sales start in 1861 and the prices rise quickly. Since 1863 certain plots, bought at 33 centimes the square meter, are resold on the basis of 8 to 10 francs."[7] However, the parcels are vast, reaching or exceeding 10,000 square meters. On the Duke of Morny's, in 1912, the Royale will be built, a deluxe hotel with over 300 rooms. Of course we should add to the price of the land the cost of constructing imposing villas equipped with all the comforts of the era.

The public in question consists of wealthy families who are making an investment at the same time as fulfilling the desire to have a home at the seashore. In addition, bankers and businessmen buy land much larger than that required for building a family villa, and sometimes in noncontiguous lots: as astute managers of considerable fortunes, they combine a pleasant backdrop for life during the summer holidays with the probable benefit of profitable land and property transactions, while retaining the right of overseeing how Deauville is populated. By controlling the market, the first occupants can manage the arrival of new owners in a way that borders on co-optation. There is no better means of ensuring "the quality" of one's future neighbors. Similar features are found in "English aristocracy's participation in the creation of resort towns," whether spas or seaside resorts.[8]

As in the new cities and new villages being built these two last decades in Île-de-France and on the periphery of the great metropolises, it is not only a real estate product that is offered, but a whole lifestyle. At Deauville, a habitat and an environment are offered which favor the blossoming of the aristocratic and grand-bourgeois way of life. For that it is necessary to ensure fast and pleasant connections with Paris. This was done in 1863 with the inauguration of the railway line and station. The racetrack and the casino open the following year, one year before the houses of worship, St. Augustin church and the

Protestant church. In 1866 the pool is inaugurated.

Deauville was obliged to grant a choice position to the horse. The new hippodrome itself covers 65 of the 357 hectares that make up the city. The Club of Deauville is created in 1873 with the purpose, according to its current general secretary, Count Guy de Jouvencel, of accommodating the owners of racing stables and offering them the conveniences and pleasures of club life like that which they prize in the Parisian clubs. The Club of Deauville still occupies the building that was built for it, facing the sea, its salons advancing in a half-rotunda toward the shore. It remains one of the rare witnesses of this pioneering time, and symbolizes today the originality of Deauville, a seaside resort which rose out of nothing through the will of a few businessmen and wealthy families. It is the story of town planning at work, constructing the entire infrastructure, including the houses of worship and this club headquarters. "To my knowledge, this is the only building that was originally built for the use of a club and whose destiny has not changed in 120 years of existence," stresses the Count de Jouvencel. A new city, Deauville simultaneously produced all the buildings and the equipment essential to its objective of being a fashionable seaside resort.

In 1870 a plan gives the list of the owners of the villas on the Terrace of Deauville, today Boulevard Eugene Cornuché, founder of the current casino and the large hotels of the resort. At the water's edge were Mr. Tenré, a Paris banker, the Marquis de Salamanca, Baron Poisson, Mr. Boitelle, prefect of the police force, the Count de Gontaut-Biron, etc.[9] The villas of the three promoters of Deauville were contiguous and, what is more, the first to be built. Today only some engravings of them remain.

In addition to the Royal Hotel which replaced the duke of Morny's villa, four-story buildings came to replace Olliffe's and Donon's, as was the case all along the edge of the sea.

This edge of the sea is surprisingly far from the first buildings. Actually, the villas were indeed built at the limit of the beach. But twice, in 1872 and in 1876, violent storms tossed up masses of pebbles and silt, moving back the high tide mark by three hundred meters. That did not prevent the resort from being the success that we know. Alluvium, these sandy and not very attractive expanses which henceforth separated the villas from the sea, posed some infrastructure problems indeed, but they did not block the development of the city initiated by Donon and Olliffe. It is very much the case that families staying at Deauville are looking for something other than swimming in the ocean, even if that remains one motivation for their visit. The deluxe hotels, the casino, the hippodromes, and golf were and still are principles by which the everyday life at Deauville is organized for those who are there on holiday, so much so that it is not rare, even today, for someone to comment in a joking tone about Deauvie t "the ocean is there, too."

The villas, the deluxe hotels, the casino, the luxury shops, are all forms of the social crystallized in urban objects. They represent a level and a way of life. They are an objectified form of social reality. Social agents, and in fact those who frequent these places, are also a product of society. They are the social being, incorporated in their mentalities, practices, tastes, and also the bodily postures and the multiple ways of being which unceasingly reveal one's position in society. Urban life can then be analyzed as being the result of the permanent interaction between these two forms of social life.

However, at Deauville, until the Sixties, the wealthy families of the aristocracy and the bourgeoisie lived in harmony with a framework of seaside life not only built for them, but even on the initiative of some of their members. This rare circumstance is always seen best with the passing of time, whereas the urban development introduced some hiatuses between the city and people. Deauville was like Cannes and Biarritz, a holiday resort. The Royale was a vacation hotel where families arrived around July 14 and left again shortly after the Grand Prix of Deauville, traditionally run the last Sunday of August. Today people stay a much shorter time: Deauville has become a town for weekenders, as all our interviews confirmed.[10]

But above all the style has changed. The grand-bourgeois way of life was so much in place that it was unthinkable, at the Club of Deauville, to dine without a tuxedo. Including for the members, in a dining room which was reserved for them alone and which was thus most private public place where the assurance of being among one's own kind was most complete. After dinner, the club members used to go visiting at the casino. That establishment, says Mr. de Jouvencel, "was very happy to accommodate members of the Club of Deauville, who would go there to meet friends rather than to play, to have a glass at the bar, to take a small turn before going to bed. It was very elegant and very convivial."

The Club, which always gathered the elite of the elite in the velvety intimacy of salons which have hardly changed since the 19th century, was certainly the social jewel of the city, but did not stand out there. The deep social homogeneity between the revelers was paralleled by a great permeability between the local establishments. "To such an extent," remembers the Count de Jouvencel, "that, when I was young member of this club, the maître d'hôtel who served as cashier in the restaurant accepted completely that one would take a casino chip out of his pocket to pay his bill. It was used as currency in the Club."

The ties were even closer with the horse world, the Club having even been in charge, until 1920, of managing the races which took place at the race track of Deauville. The majority of the Club members were stables owners or great fans of racing. Still today, the Club has a reserved stand at the hippodrome of Deauville, the way the Jockey Club members enjoy their own stand at Longchamp and at Chantilly.

Baron Guy de Rothschild, a member of the Club of Deauville, is an owner-breeder of horses at a stud farm in Meautry, 3 kilometers from the city. His name is all the more strongly associated with the resort since the Rothschilds have been going there for several generations. "My father," says Guy de Rothschild, "also spent the season at Deauville. He inherited his father's passion for horses. He raised them since his youth."[11]

Besides, it was during the gala reception of the Races, a prestigious evening which is held each year in the sumptuous Ambassadors' Salon of the casino, that Guy de Rothschild met his future wife, Marie-Hélène de Zuylen de Nyevelt de Haar. During this traditional evening in the social life of Deauville, owners, trainers, stockbreeders and jockeys are honored. Their efforts devoted to "the improvement of the equine race" are rewarded by the solemn distribution of various prizes.

The horse world is one component of the ordinary universe of the highest social milieux. One also used to find, during the best period at Deauville, pigeon shooting, very much practiced at the Club, and polo, which was and remains one of the centers of attraction at the peak season at the end of August. The Yacht Club had its Club House built not on the port but on the beach, opposite the casino, which was not always practical for the yachtsman whose boat was moored far away but which offered an ideal site for the judges of regattas. Golf has been available since the end of the last century. Deauville thus had the whole outdoors infrastructure that good society could wish to find at a vacation resort.

This correspondence with the expectations of a privileged public owes much to the personality of those who conceived and built the resort. They were from the same world and what they did suited them as much as those whom they sought to attract and satisfy. The boardwalk, one of the famous features of the city, is a very significant element of this accommodation of the setting to those who are called to live in it. This long pavement of wood, an exotic wood able to withstand bad weather and moisture without suffering from it, several hundreds of meters long, allows promenading, and one can only think of the elegant people who would formerly go to the woods (of Boulogne) or strolling on the Champs-Élysées. The boardwalk thus has the virtue of allowing one to walk along the edge of the sea without fear of twisting an ankle or worrying about the disgraceful contortions associated with losing one's balance. "Until the Sixties," remembers M. de Jouvencel, "we would go by foot to the board walk, the men in white trousers, a blazer and Panama. They had a glass at the Bar du Soleil, at the edge of the boardwalk. It was completely different from today."

Mr. de Mazerand, descendant of the one of the first families to have a villa built at the seaside, always liked to visit the casino. But it is far from matching what it was in its heyday—from the point of view of the stakes played, first of all. "Mr. André Citroën played at astronomical levels, 1 million gold francs!" Even after the Second World War, a certain moneyed aristocracy "could play 2 million at a clip—which represented at the time the value of a villa on the sea." But one needs to know how to maintain one's rank, and money is nothing without the elegance that enables you to express the idea that your position also involves personal qualities. "A woman would arrive for the season with thirty long gowns, one for each evening." Certain families pushed the envelope of hospitality and courtesy to the point of hiring rooms in the deluxe hotels for their guests. The gaming rooms of the casino were also places of high elegance, of jewels and haute couture dresses. There, one could come across the great names of industry, of entertainment, even crowned heads. Deauville was the summer prolongation of the beautiful Parisian districts and sheltered in other forms the same universe of luxury and power.

The Newcomers

Rumor has it that today Deauville "is like Sentier." This generic term is a reference to a population of Jewish families, originating in northern Africa where they already benefited from a rather easy social position, improved further by investments in the clothing industry of the Parisian district of le Sentier. Coming from members of "good society," such an assertion is meant to deplore the replacement of an old bourgeois or wealthy aristocratic population by more recently enriched families, without the manners and the network of relationships that go with social excellence. In other words, they are nouveaux riches. The talk here is no different from that which one hears in the beautiful Parisian districts, where they complain constantly about the presence of neighbors deemed not to belong to the best society.

Whatever the statistical reality of the presence of these new arrivals at Deauville, it is certain that they are made responsible for the fact that Deauville "isn't what it used to be." The bases on which such judgements rest are confused. To show one's wealth, to make a display of it, would be regarded as vulgar, unseemly. It is true that, for example, the proliferation of flashy cars, in glowing colors and with powerful sounding engines, 4 X 4 vehicles with superabundant chrome or small scarlet Japanese racing cars, if not Ferraris, taking great pleasure in making several turns around la Place Morny, the heart of town at Deauville, has all the signs of a deliberate show of material success. The old bourgeois and members of the Club claim to be horrified by this exhibitionism of wealth. But, simultaneously, the same people deeply regret the abandonment of long gowns and tuxedos in the evening at the casino. There is an art and a style to showing off: it should be done with class; it is necessary especially that the assertion of rank be for internal use rather than externally directed: elegance of behavior, courtesy in manners (the practice of hand-kissing), are more a way of being identid with a group than of proclaiming to others that one is not part of their group—which the nouveaux riches, tempted to mark the relatively new and modest distances which separate them from the common run, are always driven to do.

One of the reasons for this quasi-obligatory reference to "le Sentier" resides in the great relative homogeneity of this milieu, at the heart of which the rate of mutual acquaintance is very high. Consequently, the families walk together on the boardwalk, and the young people form bands of friends who occupy the terraces of the cafés and the sidewalks of la Place Morny. The group comes out to be seen—all reasons that make up, in public opinion, the principal cause of what has changed. Of course, the grand bourgeoisie and the nobility were not always entirely discrete. Great parties at the casino, receptions at such and such villa, retinues setting out for a stroll, meetings on the boardwalk and groups in animated discussions were not lacking. What poses a problem is that the new group seems to be competing for space. This conflict is all the more exacerbated in that it underscores what the great families have always exerted themselves to deny or at least euphemize: the modesty and discretion which the wealthy usually affect are indeed scarcely compatible with the magnificence of sumptuous villas, which hide wealth with, in truth, only relative discretion. The exterior lets one guess or imagine that the contents are out of the ordinary. One might then wonder whether the irritation, the nuisance felt by the old families of Deauville in the presence of these new categories, might not be in response to certaunconscious discomfort when faced with the reminder of that which they themselves may have produced with their power and their wealth.

The development of Deauville recalls that of the beautiful districts of Paris: after carrying out real estate transactions of great magnitude, under the direct or indirect control of the best society which built private mansions and investment property, the explosion of the real estate market leads to a great sociological diversification of the inhabitants, solvency being the only criterion of selection. Competition to occupy space becomes very strong then, based only on the fact that beautiful districts and beautiful addresses constitute a mark of quality for those who live there, a kind of geographic designer's label to some extent, the address playing the part of the brand name, the logo affixed by the great dressmaker. To have a pied-à-terre at Deauville can be as much a part of a strategy for seeking legitimacy of social success as a residence in a beautiful Parisian district or at Neuilly. That proves, in itself, that one has the means for it. But also that these means were used with discernment in chong that which could have the most symbolic value—in other words, with an effective knowledge of this symbolic first step toward acceding to social legitimacy—which leads to cohabitation in public places, the casino, the restaurants, the deluxe hotels, on the boardwalks or in the condominiums. For there are criteria for acceptance only for Club membership. All the other places abide by commercial logic: be they seaside cabins and the multicolored parasols which are the photographers' delight, or the tables at Ciro's and Chez Miocque, the fashionable restaurants, whether it is suites at the Normandy and the Royale or access to the tables in the gaming rooms and at the slot machines.

But for this evolution to be possible, the circumstances must lend themselves to it. Improving the conditions of foreign travel supported the adoption of new vacation habits among the wealthy families. Trips abroad multiplied, just as inside their own territory: long stays in the family villa have become a rarity. Deauville, which has become so near to Paris, saw its vocation changing: it became a weekend town. So much so that one may refer to the 21st district of Paris.[12]

Today, even in season, i.e. in August, the city tends to empty out on Sunday evening and fill up again the following Friday. This rhythmic change is accompanied by a democratization of the brief stays by the sea which relate to sometimes not very wealthy people, come to walk on the boardwalk and visit the slot machine room at the casino.

However, the merit of reminiscences of past splendors should be weighed carefully. At all times and in extremely varied places it seems that those who benefit from the highest positions and the most favorable living conditions always express their concern, even their recriminations, against what they regard as a threat of degradation. We have already noted that à propos of the Champs-Élysées: from the very beginning of the century, voices were heard among the great families in the private mansions, denouncing what was already perceived as a decline of the avenue.[13] At the same time, in Deauville, the management committee of the Club echoed similar fears. Thus one may read in the report of their June 8, 1886 session that "in the current state, the races constitute in fact the only true attraction [of Deauville]. Also, from season to season, one can note the degeneration of the customers on our beach. A too-divided public, coming these days almost exclusively from the world of racing, has replaced by number, but not by quality, the elegant society of the first years. There is danger for the future of Deauville. We should have no care more pressing than curing this by all the means at our disposal. In this spirit, we could do nothing better than to give a ball whose success would be certain and which would give a real satisfaction to the elements that we wish to keep around us." On these considerations, the committee took up the suggestion of holding a ball. The social élites always feel pursued by pretenders and are threatened by that. They need to preserve their own environment where they can be themselves—primarily because social homogeneity is one of the conditions of the happy fulfillment of the provisions of their habitude. This remark is valid for every social groups. But the privileged classes, because they have the means that enable them to choose their residential environment, are most attentive to securing control of their living environment. And they readily express fears and objections on this subject.

The danger would appear to be consummated in Deauville today. Mr. de Mazerand considers it regrettable that with opening of the slot machine room, the casino has lost its soul. "Now everyone comes in. While there was a time when, in August, there would be some 200 people waiting near the entrance to the casino admiring, like a true spectacle, the arrival of the men in tuxedos and women in evening gowns, going into the gaming room. There was something dreamlike, magical, about it."

One finds at Deauville the same arguments as those used by the great families of the 8th district of Paris to denounce the transformation of the Champs-Élysées. Thus, a certain carelessness in the behaviors and the attitudes is shocking. "Last year, while coming to Club from my home," says one of its members, still outraged, "I saw, in front of the very door of the Club, some Asians who had opened the two doors of their car and installed a napkin on the sidewalk. It was very smart and very elegant! They sat on the ground around the napkin, there was pie, in a word they were snacking on the sidewalk! In front of the door of the Club, in broad daylight! I had never seen that before! Such things one sees these days in Deauville!" One also sees there families sleeping in cars, taking a nap while letting their feet stick out of the doors. The perception of social hierarchies is thus conveyed explicitly by the maintenance of the body, the style of dress and the way of doing things. And the astonishment, even reprobation, against those whose postures are considered slack, relate to the nouveaux riches as well as to modest people.

Certain places crystallize these problems of cohabitation among social agents equipped with extremely different habitudes. Thus, on the Champs-Elysées, there are fast food establishments, McDonald's and others, where these "fauna" gather (as the privileged inhabitants of the 8th district say) whose presence is taken poorly. These establishments have made only a timid showing at Deauville and the large chains have not yet been established. But a few years ago, the casino opened a slot machine room which plays the same part as the fast-foods of the Champs-Élysées in the representations and the deploration of what is going wrong. This room is denounced as having the effect of attracting a population which formerly did not have a place in the resort, and even less at the casino. In the mind of a number of our interlocutors, it has become one of the factors of what they feel to be the decline of Deauville.

The slot machines concentrate people's concerns. But there are other objects of recrimination, like the pricing policies of the deluxe hotels which, faced with the difficulty of attaining a sufficient occupancy rate, offer special rates which make it possible to spend a week in one of these luxurious establishments for sums quite a bit lower than the official tariffs.[14] The Olympic swimming pool, created on the effluvia of the sea, opposite the Royale and the Club, and the marinas of Port Deauville are considered to spoil the perspectives and views, and thereby contribute to devaluing the site.

It is quite clear for the observer that a rift has formed between the décor of villas and deluxe hotels, designed in the last century for the aristocracy and the bourgeoisie, and a population more mixed than it used to be, among whom those elements the furthest away from traditional high society express a radical discordance with an environment for which they are not made, or rather which was not made for them. A case in point would be in the corridors of the deluxe hotels. Groups of young people in jeans may be chatting, with a volubility that comes across as aggressive within a setting so obviously designed for muted conversations, and patrons go by dressed as average tourists, tennis shoes on their feet and open short-sleeved shirts worn over shorts. In the large gaming room of the casino, the majesty of the place contrasts with the apparent ease of many of the players, in shirt sleeves, no tie, the women sometimes in trousers, and jeans not being rare under the gilt chandeliers, close to the rotunda whicouses the bar, in front of the frescos decorating the walls, in the deep armchairs of the corner-salons. The sharpest contrast is when this segment of the public is seen opposite the croupiers in impeccable tuxedos, with always dignified behavior and with precise and elegant gestures. Already in the Fifties, according to a former small banker of the Royale, when staff members went to the casino, they were recognized because "we, at least, did not commit breaches of comportment." If tennis shoes and beach behavior are prohibited, including for access to the slot machines whose room is clearly separated from that of the gaming tables (roulette, black jack, chemin de fer, baccarat), the style of dress and the postures have more to do with relaxation than with elegance. So much so that, on behalf of those who belong in another social universe, and who have been around a bit, the lamentation is systematic. As one aristocratic woman stresses, in the restaurant casino which slightly overhangs the gaming room, "it is not enough to have money, one still needs to be well-bred." From the table where she dines with her husband, she expresses all her contempt for the negligent comportment and how she misses the *toilettes* of the olden days that contributed most of the charm of the evenings in this place. No doubt that which might be felt as a contempt of class expresses above all an upbringing based on self-control, an assertion of culture and codes against the slack behavior that others assert in the name of "naturalness."

But it is precisely the beauty of the décor, its widely recognized quality, which attracts also these newcomers, nouveaux riches readily stigmatized by those whose lifestyle they disturb. Like the others, they are not insensitive to small flower gardens, the cheerfulness of brightly colored but harmonious parasols, the morning trot of horses going

192

out for training. "It's like a dream," they tell us. The majesty of the casino, magnified by an excess of electricity, attracts crowds of these new people, frequently amateurs of the slot machines or the gaming tables. That is part of the celebration, of this "fabulous and festive environment" where they like to find each other, weekend after weekend. The proximity of Paris and the pomp which remain despite the changes in the public allows the resort to continue its pronounced success, even if some people have already deserted it.

The city evolves only slowly, its transformations may be delayed compared to those of society overall, and it can thus establish separations between urban forms and the social realities which shape them and generate them. Thus the mediations are too complex and the forces too strong for the harmonies that sometimes manage to be established between the urban environment and the social agents to endure. At Deauville that is expressed by these gaps between the décor of the fashionable life of former times, which endures, and the social agents, i.e. also the bodies modeled by society, whose training does not allow them to slide softly into this shell produced for others.

Managing the cohabitation

Families of the nobility and the old bourgeoisie, entrenched long since at Deauville, newly rich Parisian families and those more or less modest people who go to Deauville for one weekend at the seashore, employees of the Group Lucien Barrière,[15] the municipality—headed since 1962 by Michel d'Ornano, then, since 1977, by his wife Anne d'Ornano: all have to manage this social heterogeneity. Dubious and delicate work, as a seaside resort, Deauville is subject to trends, to the vicissitudes of changing epochs. It is easier to change one's vacation resort than one's residence—except for the great families who preserve part of their memory sheltered there from the spray and winds in the large houses of the last century. But as their positions crumble, their hegemony in this city built out of the marshes is no longer absolute and they have to be creative.

The procedures by which the social juxtapositions are managed vary according to the location, the circumstances and the stakes. The customers of the deluxe hotels have changed. In the halls of these establishments, various types of customers rub elbows—even if all, by definition, have comfortable incomes. They are also mixed up on the various floors and, although the rooms are sufficiently soundproof so that your neighbor can turn his television all the way up without annoying you, sometimes the environment of the corridors leaves something to be desired when, for example, children are allowed to transform them into playgrounds. Never mind that the attitude of some of their parents can seem exaggeratedly relaxed. Therefore a kind of internal area has been cordoned off in these establishments. Such a floor would be classified as *élite*, for society, and one would avoid placing there families whose way of life was too relaxed. On the other hand, the followers of traditional elegance, of hand-kissing and strictly raised children would enjoy assured calm surroundings and neighbors in harmony with that which creates distinction. Such a plan only extends to the hotel itself that which has already been the rule for a long time at top restaurants—the maîtres d'hôtel take care to place each customer at a table by taking account of his personality and those of his neighbors. In addition, not all the tables are equally pleasant and strategic in terms of the view they offer of other patrons and the outside. There, too, it is a question of treating each one with diplomacy according to his position, known or, more difficult, evaluated and estimated based on his appearance and manners.

The casino, which is accessible to a broader audience than the deluxe hotels, offers even more occasions for confrontations between different ways of life. Since July 1988, the slot machines have attracted new customers. But, for legal reasons related to security issues, the casinos can have only one public entry—so that the players, whether they are going to confront the "one-armed bandits," to sit by the gaming tables, or to take part in a society dinner, all pass through the same hall and climb the same staircase. Confusion could be at its peak at certain moments during the arrival of the guests for the gala reception for the Races. But in these circumstances there is all the same a great correspondence between one's social position and that which one must occupy in the space of the casino. The social distance is considerable, explicit, the risk of error is nil. Each one knows, or thinks he knows, his place. In extreme cases such stark asymmetry of the relations leaves no choice but condescension accepted or avoided. In other circumstances, these places become emblematic of the social inequalities and can be the theatre of a verbal confrontation, as on Thursday, August 26, 1993 at the time of a demonstration against the threat of dismissal organized by the association of French trade unions, the CGT. The demonstrators blocking the entrance of the establishment brandished signs with slogans su as: "The bourgeoisie slaps its cash on the tables in the casinos where insolent luxury is on display."

The casino offers sometimes quasi-surrealist social proximity. Consider the afternoon of August 28, 1993, when Guy de Rothschild was signing and selling his latest book.[16] Installed in a strategic spot on the landing at the top of the casino staircase, the author spent the afternoon behind his table waiting for readers-customers-admirers. The situation had something incongruous about it. Admittedly, the author appeared relaxed and he pleasantly answered the questions of a journalist from the local daily newspaper, while showing the greatest kindness towards the readers to whom he was dedicating his work. But during this time, the slot machine players were going by in numbers, throwing a distracted glance at this character, anxious, as they were, to go to try their luck. And the whole afternoon, as usual, one heard the metallic clinking sound of the coins released by the machines, the noise having only a rather remote relationship with the real profits of the whole of the players. The author had undoubted not planned on this juxtaposition, but there was something extraordinarily strange in this unexpected meeting between one of greatest fortunes of France and the aural illusioof abundance generated by this tintinnabulation of currency. The distinguished euphemisms of inherited and controlled wealth were answered thus by the somewhat desperate search for immediate profit, in a kind of grasping shortcut that exhibited all that the old bourgeoisie dreads about proximity with the nouveau riche: the impudence and the cynicism of recently accumulated money which is not afraid of being seen and noticed. A member of the Automobile Club of France and the Club of Deauville, Baron Guy de Rothschild is certainly not newly rich and his Jewish origins, which he displays, affirming strongly his solidarity with his community, do not prevent him from forming part of "the best society."[17] It is quite true that religious affiliations are of little weight compared to the mark of excellence which the age of one's fortune provides, and the family from which it comes. Cleavages and antagonisms are established socially: the grand bourgeoisie founds its unity on its position in social space, not on a religion. It is as newcomers, as pretenders who find themselves, in the recent years and at Deauville, mainly of Jewish origin, that the new habitués of the resort disturb those who are already in place. As for the more modest tourists, Sunday picnickers, the carelessness of their dress and their behaviors, at least as the members of the Club of Deauville see it, cause an immediate and wholehearted reprobation.

One understands better how it happens that certain institutions that seem a little out of date are still quite alive. The Club of Deauville thus offers a harbor of good taste and distinction. Open only in August, i.e. during the local tourist season, it has 282 members, only men in the image of certain Parisian circles and clubs. It is true that about half of them (133) live in Paris, but only in the beautiful districts, i.e. in 16th, 8th, 7th and 17th districts, by descending order of the number of members concerned. There are about sixty addresses in the provinces and forty foreign, but only three at Deauville: it is understandable that the Club is open only in August.

The weight of the nobility is important in this institution. The Presidents have always held a title and, in 1993, the Duke de Noailles occupied the position, the Vice President being the Duke d'Audiffret-Pasquier. Among the 282 members, 82 had a family name that appeared noble, of which 56 were enhanced with a title. This is, however, far from the percentage of the nobility at the Jockey Club, and the Club of Deauville has a goal to recruit more widely. It is true that it is the only one in the place and that the good society has no other choice. The Club constitutes a kind of abridged list of high Parisian society. One finds personalities from the political world (Édouard Balladur, who has a villa in the center of the resort), leaders from the luxury trades (Claude Guerlain, Kilian Hennessy and Henry Racamier, former chairman of the House of Vuitton), industrialists and businessmen (Jean-Luc Lagardère, Jean-Louis Hachette and Guy de Rothschild) as well as many foreign personalities who make it possible to give an international character to the social capital managed in this type of institution.

The family of d'Ornano has been present there for three generations. Michel d'Ornano, although not belonging to an old Deauville family, offered the advantage, for managing the municipal affairs, of bearing a great name of the imperial nobility. His wife, Anne de Contades, comes from a family of older nobility. One and the other contributed by their elegant presence to furthering the work of the families of the nobility and the grand bourgeoisie. It is possible that their son will take the succession: he has just entered the Club of Deauville where his father and his grandfather had been members. It is thus a family in conformity with the ideal of the great families interested in the future of Deauville who control the municipal power.

Induction into Club of Deauville is the rule. A Club is not an association to which one may make a membership payment in order to have access. So that, the criterion of fortune being secondary, the newly wealthy families are isolated, in fact, sometimes to the benefit of families with lower incomes, whose degree of nobility or bourgeoisie compensate for relative misfortunes in business.

Also, according to the Count de Jouvencel, the Club of Deauville is one of the rare havens of peace for the families having a certain position to maintain. "To be here," he says, "in one of these salons to which the patina of time gives a slightly quaint character and which are a specialty of Clubs, that is peace, one is at home, one is among one's own kind, one does not suffer. I can tell you that the majority of the members who come here park their car in the courtyard for their whole stay and each one goes by foot from the Club to the racecourse; it is very pleasant." To be at home means "to be among people of good company. With people who will hold their fork like you and me, who know how to behave at the table." No doubt the respect for table manners has such an importance because of the place which lunches and dinners occupy in the social existence of these groups where the management of the network of relations is a priority task. Like all the big Clubs, that of Deauville offers restaurant services to its members who have the freedom to invite there, under their responsibility, anyone they please. Another reserved space, that of the private stands at the hippodrome, where the respect for standards of conduct are imposed: " No member can enter these stands," Mr. de Jouvencel takes care to specify, "if he does not have a tie." No doubt this attention to the small things which make all the difference is at the heart of what appears to be a constant in high society: deploring the degradation of manners and the changing customer base in certain places with a chic reputation. It was seen that the committee of the Club of Deauville has been concerned about who was visiting the resort, since 1886.

The shared enjoyment of an activity where passion mixes in can suspend social distances, at least temporarily, during the time of the activity itself. Deauville Yacht Club was such a chic place; it is still one of the Clubs mentioned by *Bottin Mondain*. It was founded in 1928, rather tardily compared with the date the resort was founded. The industrialist Louis Bréguet was one of its most active organizers. Today the composition of the club has diversified. One still finds great fortunes there, but also engineers, managers, even representatives of more modest professions, including a master carpenter. In 1992, out of 246 members, only 5 bear a name of noble appearance, which is out of proportion with that of the Club of Deauville. Sailing, like hunting in other parts, transcends the class differences. If, at the Club, the social excellence of the members is acknowledged and even emphasized as that which makes the institution special, the President of the Yacht Club shows himself very anxious to let it be known that what attracts its members is a taste for the sea and for boats. The club gave up its buildings at the edge of beach, near the Royale, far too distant from the docks and the boats for true lovers of the sea. Besides, the boats are the only second hom of some of the members, who thus live, when they are at Deauville, in the comfort (relative) of the sailboats.

Thus, on the ground of a common passion, socially distant agents can meet. The races and the horse are another example. The horse world, on the side of the owners, remains obviously related to high society. The races of Deauville were founded in 1864 by the Duke of Morny, in the very early days of the resort. There are in fact two hippodromes, that of la Touques, of which 65 of the 72 hectares are located on the township of Deauville, occupying 21% of its surface. In order to complete the other racecourse located in the township of Clairefontaine, Deauville had to buy 25 hectares. They are places where the seaside life and the fashionable life are organized, as well as at the casino or on the golf courses. Grands prix, polo championship, sales of yearlings, young thoroughbreds one-year-old to a year- and-a-half, all these events attract a large public and concentrate the good society.

Thus on this August 29, 1993, the day of the Grand Prix of Deauville, which is the peak of the season, the firm Lancel (luxury luggage) had tents installed and an open air buffet beside the stands. Guests in cocktail dresses and wide brimmed hats, light suits and panamas, arrive by foot from a not very distant parking lot where they left their vehicles. From time to time, a helicopter deposits some individuals. Under the amused or admiring glance of many idlers who arrived two hours in advance of the first race in order to benefit from the free spectacle of this fashionable assembly, the guests move with confidence toward the buffet, and nibble while chatting and drinking the champagne which is liberally offered to them. All that, to the tune of an orchestra, which envelops them in the music of a café-concert, and within sight of the entire public delighted by this scene. "This makes eight years that we are coming here," says a very modest couple. "We arrange to come the last weekend of August for the Lancel prize. Our aim is not the races, it is to see the outfits." The wife of a small Breton farmer says she loves "the procession of these ladies, the grand toilettes, the hats. For me, it is the pleasure of a spectacle. Deauville, it is famous in any case. But yesterday evening, it was 1400 francs entry fee [refering to the gala reception of the Races]. We were not at the party, that is not for us."

Simple white wooden barriers, about a meter high, delimit the sacred space where the common folk cannot enter. But the happy elect, far from being sheltered from view, appear on the contrary to be on display, offering the rare spectacle of a society gathering and a luncheon, sheltered under tents but quite as exposed to onlookers as the arrival buffet had been. It all seems as though one were there to be seen. People let themselves be photographed and filmed by the press, but also by the hangers-on who benefit from the occasion to fix some images which appear exotic to them. The contrast shown between the two publics does not seem to pose a problem. The well-cut 3-piece suits are met with short-sleeved checked shirts, the thick, tired silhouettes with svelte and slender figures carefully emphasized by tailored clothes: the world of prêt-à-porter is contrasted to that of made-to-measure. But it all happens in a relaxed environment, as if the fact of finding themselves together, albeit on two sides of the barrr, expresses a complicity stronger than the social divisions, around the festive and shared taste for this so specific atmosphere of the racecourses where, in spite of this social demarcation of space, each one having its own stands, its own places, a kind of community is expressed, temporary but real—an atmosphere which is also found at the rendezvous of the hunts, at the automobile Grand Prix of Monaco. In situations where competition, in a kind of symbolic representation of society and its conflicts, erases the differences that will reappear at once when the winner is designated—a kind of social mass where the dominant and the dominated celebrate one moment together, the social organization which produced them and gives them life. The social layers that owe their position to their academic capital are absent from these situations. Thus, at the heart of one of the smartest beach resorts, there is room for these moments and these spaces where contradictions are denied, or rather, social antagonisms are sublimated.

Fashionable ceremonies, the care taken with the floral decoration of the streets, the meticulous maintenance of the beach and the multicolored parasols, the luxurious meals at the casino, everything is done at Deauville to maintain an atmosphere, an environment worthy of the prestigious past of the resort. The city keeps a specific cachet, with the flowerbeds, the trotting of the horses early in the morning on the paving stones as they leave for training on the beach, the electric excess of the lights of the casino. But these efforts to ensure continuity are limited by their own logic: the prestige with which the families of high society endow the places that they choose ruins their urban value in the long term. Social success is soon followed by a more ordinary success. High society and the crowd are hardly compatible. Deauville, like the grand boulevards in earlier times, or the Champs-Élysées today, has been submerged by a more varied population, which no longer belongs exclusively to the higher real of siety. There is no value judgment inherent in this established fact. It is enough to note that in this domain, power over space is limited by the laws of the market: the extreme enhancement of the value of certain spaces carries within itself the germs of their evolution and their social change.

PAID HOLIDAYS AND SOCIAL SECURITY

There are other vacation resorts which owe their evolution to the Welfare State and its social policies. Paid holidays, whose influence is felt only in a marginal way at Deauville, and social security have deeply affected the aspect of other beach resorts and thermal spas by allowing visits by social categories which, until these social attainments, could not afford it. Exceptional places, the spaces arranged by and for the grand bourgeoisie are thus submitted to the covetousness of the pretendants, of the new rich, but also at that of the less moneyed social categories.

Arcachon: the Seashore and the City of Winter

Not such a long time ago, the resort of Arcachon planted its villas, Neogothic and Rococo, Basque and Moorish, along the edge of sea. In this diversity specific to seaside towns and the spa towns of the Second Empire, the grand bourgeois of Bordeaux had its residences. Victim of its own celebrity and popular acclaim, its villas have been disappearing from the shoreline, replaced by buildings without charm, with a view on the bay, vacant for months at a time. There remain some witnesses of the resort's glorious past, such as the villa Saint-Yves of the de Broglie family. Or the imposing villa where Christel Baseden spends the summer, a few steps from the property occupied by her grandparents. " Look," she says, "at my grand-parents' villa. They fought for generations to keep it, but in our generation we know that it will be over. In ten years it will certainly be a new building. There are five children. Let us say that three of them wish to keep it. They must first compensate the others. It is an amazing budget. And then there is the work that needs to be done. Then there is always a promoter who arrives at the right moment with a beautiful offer and people jump. Everyone rails about it, we always criticized those who let themselves be tempted, but we will do the same thing, we will not be able to do any differently." Undoubtedly, it would have required that the mode of management of the urban problems be more collective, as it is at Maisons-Laffitte or at Vésinet.

The destiny of the City of Winter, on the heights of Arcachon, stresses *a contrario* the importance of collectivizing the measures of defense of patrimony, although in a way different from what occurs in the smart developments of the Parisian suburbs. Indeed, the collective defense of the urban patrimony was organized, in the City of Winter, only after the departure of the grand bourgeois families, and the rescue of the villas was accompanied by a renewal of the population. An average bourgeoisie, which has comfortable incomes but which does not belong at the highest layers of society, thus replaced the old wealthy families which were involved in the origins of the district. The City of Winter is an example of the transfer of patrimony from the grand bourgeoisie to the comfortable middle class, and of the access these classes gain to the "spacial" capital of the grand bourgeoisie.

On the heights of Arcachon, because of the vivifying quality of its air the City of Winter was intended to shelter patients suffering from lung diseases during the bad season. However, in order to preserve the fragile bronchi from the winter rigors of the ocean, the Pereire brothers established a sinuous layout and used the dunes to shelter the wealthy patients and their families, all convinced of the fortifying virtues of the broad oceanic air. In the same architectural imagination as that of the beachside villas, this very original real estate unit, whose unity lies paradoxically in the surprising diversity of the forms and the decorative elements, a charm supported by the magnificence of the gardens and their luxuriant vegetation.

Ownership of a villa in the dunes, sheltered from the winds at large but deprived of ocean views, often went hand-in-hand with ownership of another residence, preferred in the summer, at the edge of the bay. Little by little, the importance accorded to the benefits of the salubrious air and at the same time mistrust of the sea breezes decreased, and the villas of the interior were forsaken in favor of those residences at the edge of the water. So that, toward the Fifties, the City of Winter was in a state of neglect, many villas having been abandoned. It would not have taken much for this exceptional architectural ensemble, a fine representation of the resort architecture of the last century, to disappear in favor of small buildings of vacation flats. Tradesmen, liberal professions, teachers sometimes, bought the old houses whose condition was often not very engaging. The president of the association for new owners belongs to the average segments which did not inherit a villa, but who seek, through a restoraon effort, to be able to live in houses with a prestigious past. The dilapidation of the villas was partly due to the fact that they were built very quickly, according to techniques of quasi-prefabrication. On the lands acquired and parceled out by Émile Pereire, he, as an astute businessman, accelerated construction. "They used the technique of prefabrication (the word was not invented yet). The former furnishing company, the Compagnie du Midi, was contracted to manufacture elements which were transported by rail to Arcachon."[18] Carefully hidden by decorative abundance and the variety of styles, the rudimentary character of the main construction did not turn away the new occupants who made the City of Winter their principal home, all working at Arcachon or in the surrounding area.

But this sociological reassignment of the villas has not come about without difficulty, especially when it was a question of preserving the integrity of the whole site. The fight over the Villa Teresa is revelatory of conflicting interests. This villa, one of most majestic in the place, on high ground in the middle of a vast park, was put up for sale a few years ago. It was acquired by a promoter whose intentions were to tear it down to vacate the ground and to build 24 apartments whose profitability was assured. But the new inhabitants of the City of Winter mobilized themselves; they created a preservation association and, with the support of ecological associations, they succeeded in having the villa classified, in *extremis*, in March 1980, in the Supplementary Inventory List of Historic Buildings. The Villa Teresa, thus saved, was transformed into a hotel while preserving its appearance and thus its charm. Even better, its new owners gave it back its former majesty by restoring the ornamental panels of ceramic tile which had decorated the entry and which had been plundered, as well as the monumental banisters of the main staircase whose wood had been used for heating by shivering squatters. Then the City of Winter was registered among the picturesque sites of the Gironde, under title of the law of 1930. "There are 285 villas in the City of Winter," says the owner of the Villa Teresa. It is like at Vésinet, except that here it is the dunes that were subdivided and developed. We are in contact with the city of Vésinet, which forwarded to us its new POS." But while the will to protect exceptional urban sites may be shared, it remains true that this urban resort patrimony was given up by the grand bourgeoisie to the benefit of another social group.

Biarritz in search of its identity

Biarritz, victim of its own success, has undergone considerable transformations. This spa resort is today in search of its identity. The current mayor, Didier Borotra, appears to have defeated the outgoing mayor thanks to a program that was the principal factor in rehabilitating the resort's image by emphasizing the symbols that recall its prestigious past. Thus the casino, built in 1929 by the architect Alfred Lamblé, was restored "with strict respect for the Art Déco architecture of 1928, but modernizing all the functions: a theatre, meeting rooms, a gaming room. The casino," continues Michel Veunac, Assistant-Mayor responsible for public relations, "is more or less the symbol of the philosophy which guides the current municipality in a spirit of urban development articulating both modernity and tradition."

For some, the identity of Biarritz was built during the Belle Époque and between the wars. For others, it is Eugénie de Montijo, then the imperial couple who, as Morny created Deauville, launched the resort. For the former group, the role of the imperial couple at Biarritz is more myth than identifying landmark and legitimate symbol. The latter group considers it regrettable that the tourist folders are too discrete on the Napoleonic origins of Biarritz and agitate, as does the Biarritz delegation "Friends of Napoleon III" (which has a hundred members in the city) for the resort to dedicate at least an avenue to the Emperor. There is a parish Ste. Eugénie, inaugurated in 1856 and one Avenue de l'Impératrice, but nothing is devoted to the memory of her famous husband. However, even if it were only due to the size of the local delegation of the Friends of Napoleon III, the memory of the Emperor is long-lived in the resort. More than at Arcachon or Deauville where, to our knowledge, there does not exist a similar delegation. It is true that the role of Napoleon III was only indirect there.

In fact, in Biarritz, nobody is unaware that the splendid Hôtel du Palais was built at the beginning of the century on the site of the Villa Eugénie, which Napoleon III had had built in ten months in 1854 on a very nicely located site overlooking the ocean—which makes it possible today for the dining room at the international deluxe hotel to offer an exceptional panorama between the sky and the sea, between rocks and seafoam.

It is in this establishment of great reputation, bought up in 1956 by the municipality and whose director is himself a member of the Friends of Napoleon III, that this association holds its meetings, using the conference and banquet halls. The Napoleonic memory is revived each year by the presentation of the Napoleon III Prize, which is decreed in cooperation with the town of Biarritz. It is given in the salons of the Hotel du Palais under the Presidency of S. A. Prince Murat and Didier Borotra, mayor of the city. Each year, the Friends of Napoleon III take part in three masses celebrated in the imperial vault, bequeathed to the municipality, at the time of the anniversaries of the death of the Emperor, the Empress and the imperial prince.

It is likewise within the sumptuous setting of the Hotel du Palais that the Imperial Ball is given, which magazines like L'Éventail and Point de vue readily review. In 1990, it was chaired by the countess of Barcelona, mother of the King of Spain, Juan Carlos. "Biarritz has been international since Napoleon III, who was particularly open from this point of view, his wife being Spanish," points out Mr. Bognar, President of the local delegation of the Friends of Napoleon III. The Spanish presence is still attested by that of Marquis Pedro de Carvajal, which is reproduced in one of the photographs published by *Point de vue.* "The guests in period costume," notes *L'Éventail,* "revived for one evening the pomp and elegance of Biarritz under Napoleon III."[19] This VIIth Imperial Ball was not given solely in the honor of remembering the Emperor and his family but, like many events of this type, it also had a charitable purpose since it was arranged to benefit the work of an organization dedicated to alleviating difficult childhoods.

According to Jean-Claude Lachnitt, Secretary-General of the Napoleon Foundation, "the life of the imperial couple was not so fashionable and protocol-driven at Biarritz. The Empress preferred that Court etiquette be reduced to a minimum." However, all of international Gotha was attracted by the new resort. "Stunned Biarrots would see arriving successively Queen Isabelle of Spain, the King of Wurtemberg, Léopold II of Belgium, the sovereigns of Portugal, Prince Jerome Bonaparte, Prince Albrecht of Bavaria, Count Walewski, the princes de Metternich, the writers Prosper Mérimée and Octave Layer, not to mention the illustrious Bismarck, the Iron Chancellor who enjoyed an idyll with the charming princess Orloff."[20] Clearly, the success of Biarritz owes much to the attachment that the imperial couple felt for it.

This quarrel around what identity to give to the resort is tightly linked to its chances for a future. The emblematic search for a past laden with prestige, recalling the hours of a resort's glory where the great ones of this world stayed, is a way of signifying the exceptional quality of a place where the pressure of tourists, having become massive, risks ruining its attraction for the first social categories which had made one of it their preferred places.

Deauville, Arcachon, Biarritz: these three examples show how much the beach resort infrastructure of the French coasts was tied to the economic development of the Second Empire. Coinciding with the appearance of the fashion for sea bathing and with the implementation of the rail network, solid bases were thus launched for a tourist pattern to become entrenched along the littoral. A development which, through the hesitations and the inflections of history, has not been contradicted up until our times. To these seaside examples we should add, for the sake of completeness, those of the thermal resorts and the mountain resorts. The Second Empire shaped many tourist dimensions of the national territory.

Thermal resorts: Enghien-les-Bains and Vichy

If the introduction of paid holidays had their share in the development of Deauville, Arcachon and Biarritz, by allowing in those categories which hitherto hardly had the possibility of visiting the edge of sea. Social Security changed the traffic pattern at the towns around mineral springs. It was thus at Vichy and, to a lesser degree, at Enghien-les-Bains, whose role as a thermal spa never reached the same renown as that of the first city.

At the beginning of the 19th century, Enghien became a mineral water spa town in fashion with the Parisians to whom it was so close. Located to the north of Gennevilliers and Épinay-on-Seine, it is today enclosed in working class and industrial suburbs and constitutes, like Raincy, a bourgeois enclave amid lower class territories. That was not the case at the beginning of its success, when the small hamlet, then isolated, was invaded in summer by the well-to-do families which came to seek a little cool air on the edges of her lake, at their homes that were not yet called secondary. The thermal resort of Paris was created in 1821, on the initiative of Mr. Peligot, administrator of the Saint-Louis Hospital. The center, inaugurated in 1846, allowed those wishing to try the waters, and other visitors, to flow into this new vacation resort. Enghien obtained the status of a township in its own right a little later, in 1850. It was necessary to wait another half-century for the founding of the racecourse, in 1879. first casino functioned from 1901 on, and the current establishment, at the edge of the lake, goes back to 1934. The resort seems to have started slowly and to have reached its cruising speed only gradually. It is true that it was not the object of concerted town planning like Deauville, or like Maisons-Laffitte or Vésinet. The apogee of the resort was perhaps reached toward 1936. That year, 15 families listed in *Bottin Mondain* give Enghien-les-Bains, Seine-et-Oise, as their place of residence, which is a lot since one counts 22 mentions for Maisons-Laffitte and 37 for Vésinet, but far fewer and often none at all for many other townships.

Still today, Enghien remains a chic place, with its casino and its theatre, and its deluxe hotel—which is part of the same Lucien Barrière chain as the establishments of Deauville. From 1968 on, similar in that respect to other bourgeois towns in the Parisian suburbs, like Maisons-Laffitte, Vésinet or Neuilly, Enghien see its population decreasing. It went from 12,000 inhabitants in 1968 to 9,735 in 1982—which is all the more remarkable since the closest cities, Deuil-la-Bars in particular, saw a sustained high growth rate. It is true that, "for households of modest or average incomes, it has always been difficult to find housing at Enghien."[21] However, if the town still has the attributes of a fashionable vacation resort today, with its deluxe hotel on a lake that covers 44 hectares, its casino and its race track, it has the also appearance of an average city with its multiple functions. Its marked residential function is coupled today with a commercial function whose influence goes beyond the strict township limits. The medical function remains, with the thermal spa, which accommodated 4,000 who visited for the cure in 199. The exploitation of sulphurous water is, furthermore, the legal condition for maintaining the operation of the springs, and thus forms the basis of the Groupe Barrière's interest in hydrotherapy. But this medical function was democratized when Social Security took over responsibility for the cures. In the same way, because of the immediate environment and because the township is within some none too attractive suburbs, e recreational traffic has become more socially diversified.

In spite of specific qualities linked to its urban environment, the development of Enghien is similar to that of other towns with mineral springs, and singularly to that of Vichy. According to Doctor Pilloy, who practiced as a doctor in this city, the resort has returned to its original status, losing that that had been grafted on, that of vacation resort. The large deluxe hotels, including the one that had sheltered the Vichy government, were closed, sold and transformed into apartments. For this doctor, [France's] de-colonization was not insignificant in this decline. "The customers completely changed with the disappearance of the colonies. For the colonials came in numbers to Vichy to take care of their livers inflated by drinking parties [...]. Vichy lives today only thanks to the people under the care of Social Security. And such customers don't spend much." At Vichy, as at Biarritz, there are symbolic fights that aim to confirm such and such image of the resort. The association of the Friends of Napoleon III is also very active, although it has fewer members.

Having made his retirement at Anglet, close to Biarritz, Doctor Pilloy is experiencing a similar development, that of the relative democratization of spa resorts, paralleling that of the thermal resorts. His new residence is an apartment set up in a vast villa that used to belong to a wealthy South American family, the Santos-Suarez. The Santos-Suarez, who used to give parties attended by King Farouk in their residence, were ruined at the casino, points out Mrs. Pilloy. The park was parceled out, and as at Deauville, Arcachon, Vichy and Enghien, densification was accompanied by profound changes in the population, whether permanent residents or families on holiday.

It seems that the strong element of these evolutions resides in the upheaval of the field of hydrotherapy, consecutive with its accessibility to the modest social categories taken under the wing of the Social Security system, and irresistible tourist pressure related to the generalization of paid holidays. If it is true that these vacation, rest, or leisure destinations created by high society really constitute a patrimony in a collective form, the social assets of modest workers, and even of the middle class, are leading to a transfer of the spacial privileges of the grand bourgeoisie.

But the latter are not without resources: thalassotherapy arrived at the appointed hour. Thalassotherapy is less widespread—the people who seek treatment in this sector are four times fewer than those for hydrotherapy (approximately 150,000, for more than 600,000, figures respectively from 1992 and 1988). It is covered less by Social Security and so its public is less democratized. Thus paid vacations and Social Security are fundamental to the development of preferred places. One finds in chic spaces a kind of urban curse which causes fashionable places, the places of wealth and the stylish life, to become the object of competitions, fights to take them over.

In addition to the general processes of democratization of ocean front and thermal spa resorts, made more accessible by the social services, explicit claims on the more enviable spaces have been, here and there, threatened as the *de facto* monopoly of the upper classes is called into question. Thus, in the Fifties, a youth movement made its slogan "the Riviera within everyone's reach," a watchword that had concrete consequences.

In 1952, the CLAJ (Youth Clubs of Leisures and Activity), a movement born in the heart of the Youth Hostels, inspired by progressive and at one time Christian motivation, became purchasers of an abandoned old white villa, between Nice and Monaco, at Cape-d'Ail, at the edge of the Mediterranean, one of the most sought-after locations of the Côte d'Azur. This villa is one of the 1956 residences, from St. Tropez to Menton, which enjoy the privilege of having its feet in the water.[21] The villa acquired by the CLAJ is of course surrounded by residences, one more luxurious than the next. Appropriately baptized "Le Grand Large " [literally, "The Big and Spacious", but rhyming with "Grand Lodge"] is open to the sea on all sides. Using white marble abundantly, it shelters a great foreign fortune and offers in its two-hectare garden a swimming pool whose overflow spills in a cascade to the sea. The remote owner of the villa of the CLAJ, Mrs. Théodora de Janotta, lived in Brazil and could not have cared much about the personality of those who bought this ivy-covered house. Thus came the peaceful invasion of young working class men and women who undertook the reconditioning of the place. "On all sides the 'Sunday millionaires' emerge, as Enrico Macias would call them a few years later [...] . On the walls, sandpaper and palette knifes scrape the skirting of plaster pink and all the scales of the past, the snobbish and nostalgic past of the Riviera of the Russian princes, the English lords, wealthy from war and commercial traffic, the old Bugattis and the rococo casinos."[25] The young people doing this work are often local. They think they, too, have a right to this "corner of paradise" at the seaside. After the renovations they will enjoy "the supreme pleasure of being able to slip, into this shell of luxurious residence, their own popular and merry fulfillment." The pleasure of the forbidden, of reaching the inaccessible—but which does not come about without raising the indignant protests of certain neighbors, disturbed still today by precisely that proximity which they had intended to flee by establishing these preferential places. Young people of the CLAJ seem to have been sensitive to the differences in attitudes between the grand bourgeoisie and those who were perhaps newly rich. "The famous neighbors remain discrete. Winston Churchill, Boussac, we will never see them! Sacha Guitry, the great lord, refused to sign petitions against the Villa Thalassa, an International Youth Hostel. The others, runts of fortune, skinflints of fame, agitated in every direction, with the mayor-promoter and the real estate agent taking the lead. The intermediate classes are always keenest to defend their piece of property."[26] The transaction would be re-published in 1956. This time the CLAJ acquired "a splendid villa belonging to the marchioness of Boisgelin! The Villa Sperling is located in the high class district of Cimiez, which is next to the heights of the Regina Palace [in Nice]."[27]

However, it is rather in the form of what was called "the social work châteaux" that the process would be extended.[28] Part of the patrimony of the wealthy families would be sold this way to municipalities, factory councils and other mutual benefit associations which made them into vacation houses, or convalescent homes. It is not insignificant that these very markedly social activities were established in places that were not intended for that purpose. The choice of these buildings could not have been based solely on considerations of functionality, which may be questionable, even if available space is a consideration. There are also symbolic effects in such choices of location.

One finds thus, in another form, the difficulties inherent in maintaining the real patrimonies of the wealthy families in their entirety. Be it the family's château, or the villa at the sea, various pressures make the transmission of these goods questionable. As far as vacation resorts, the question arises of whether new areas have been opened up by these families. A district on the heights of Marbella, a certain Swiss resort, a certain village in Sardinia, seem today to play an important part in the siting of these vacation resorts. In addition, Biarritz and Monte Carlo still have beautiful remnants.

Beyond these vicissitudes related to the auxiliary homes and family homes, it is the permanence of a great part of the patrimony which is concerned, all the more important since it is priceless—that which holds the family memory, constitutes the foundations of its symbolic capital and thus supports all the other forms of capital.

These difficulties also affect vacation spots that the upper classes have always preserved. These "holiday" patrimonies can represent a significant part of the patrimony of use, whose incomes can be appreciated materially, in the use of an asset of great value, but also by the symbolic, even emotional, return that they can provide. For, as with the château, family residences at the sea shore are the cases in which the magical memories of childhood are piously preserved—but also those of the family/society life of long stays at the beach. Symbolic profit is added to the emotional profits of having a residence in an exceptional setting and which benefit in addition from a social environment without par. Here as well there is a designer label effect and, as in the beautiful Parisian districts and the developments of the residential suburbs west of Paris, the value of the vacation residence depends on the social quality of well-selected neighbors. To maintain such locations at the level of urban perfection represents a social effort which would be useless to attempt single-handedly, and which, even taken in charge collectively, is not always crowned with success.

Notes

1. See *Quartiers bourgeois, quartiers d'affaires, op. cit.*, p. 101-107.

2. See Michel PINÇON and Monique PINÇON-CHARLOT, L'aristocratie et la bourgeoisie au bord de la mer: la dynamique urbaine de Deauville *"Gene//ses,"* 16, June 1994, p. 69-93.

3. Roger DELIENCOURT and Jean CHENNEBENOIST, *Deauville, son histoire*, s. n., Imprimerie Marie, Honfleur, T. 1: *Des origines à 1914*, 1977, p. 107 (T. 2: *De 1914 à 1977*, 1982). Roger Deliencourt, a doctor, was assistant mayor of Deauville since 1947. Thus he was assistant to mayors Robert Fossorier and Michel d'Ornano. Jean Chennebenoist, instructor at the city's academy, also had responsibilities as an advisor in the municipality directed by Michel d'Ornano in 1971. These works of local history provide a multitude of precise and extremely useful information.

4. François ASCHER, Jean-Louis COHEN and Jean-Claude HAUVUY, *Luxe, habitat, confort: les références hôtelières*, Paris, Institut français d'urbanisme, université de Paris VIII, 1987. Marie-Helene CONTAL, 1854-1936, *Création d'une ville thermale*, Paris, Institut français d'architecture, CEP, éditions du Moniteur, 1982.

5. This corporation is in the hands of a small number of owners. "The 1859 purchasers," writes É. Acacie, "the Duke of Morny and the architect Breney, form the core. We are left to think that Deauville was for its promoteurs and for the principal shareholders of the copmpanies a speculative deal." Élisabeth ACACIE, "La naissance d'une station balnéaire sous le Second Empire", *Villes, histoire et culture*, URA CNRS 1010, No. 1, December 1994.

6. "This exoticism announces the contemporary seaside Utopia. By convening the Arab, Asian and Scandinavian styles, Persian palaces and Swiss chalets, in a place where they do not belong, the voluntary anachronisms of this heterogeneous architecture standing beyond the boardwalk or on the dunes set the development apart from the rest of the world." Jean-Didier URBAIN, *Sur la plage. Moeurs et coutumes balnéaires*, Paris, Payot, 1904, p. 280. For the history of English and French seaside resorts, see Alain CORBIN, *Le Territoire du vide. L'Occident et le désir du rivage*, 1750-1840, Paris, Flammarion, coll. "Champs," 1990.

7. Gabriel DÉSERT, *La Vie quotidienne sur les plages normandes du Second Empire aux Années folles*, Paris, Hachette, 1983, p. 24.

8. David CANNADINE, "L'aristocratie et les villes dans l'Angleterre du XIX-me siècle : les stations balnéaires," *Urbi*, 1, 1979, p. 33-46.

9. Among the other proprietors: Messieurs Hauttement, Delahante, Dalloz, Bourgoin, Jouhet, the Duke of Sesto (who had married the Duchess of Morny, her husband being deceased in 1865), Prince Demidoff, the Count de Kersaint, M. de La Lombardière. This plan was kindly furnished to us by M. Agnes, archivist of Deauville, who also helped us to understand the broad outline of the history of the city. We hereby thank him kindly.

10. In addition to reading works on Deauville, this study is based on ethnographic observations carried out during a prolonged stay during the summer of 1993. About fifteen interviews were conducted with families that have homes at Deauville, with people in the hotel industry, members of the Club of Deauville, and the city archivist.

CHAPTER VIII

The Duty to Pass It On

Keeping the patrimony within the family over the generations does not happen automatically. It is an occupation unto itself, with specific symbolic and economic strategies geared to maintaining and retransmitting that which was received, and to transmitting that which one has acquired oneself. According to D. Kessler and A. Masson, inter-generational altruism is rare, legacies of precaution being more frequent than legacies of transmission. What is inherited has more to do with the cautious savings of the legatees than with an accumulation intended to be bequeathed. But there is "a limited hard core of transmitters" whose base is restricted to the most well-to-do households.[1]

The transmission of assets is not only transmission of a patrimony but also transmission of a social relationship. "What establishes the institution of the heritage is the transmission of a relationship; *it is a relationship of transmitting a relationship,*"[2] that means that the heir must be suited to inheriting, that the heir must even be suitable to be inherited by his heritage.

Transmitting major assets is a collective process, an ensemble of negotiations between the generations, the parents and the children. It is one of the reasons why the *nouveaux riches* are under suspicion from the old families, because they have not yet shown their capacity to pass on this relationship. "Wealth is intrinsically honorable and confers honor upon its owner. As a further refinement, from that point forward there would be more honor in having wealth that was passed on by ancestors or other predecessors than in acquiring it through one's own efforts."[3]

The transmission of patrimonies will be taken here as a social relationship and a collective process within the family group. The preceding chapters have concentrated on the fact that, in the great families, the individual is not considered on his own account, but according to his place and his role in the family structure. He is only one element of a whole which transcends him.[4] What matters is the family's perenniality, even if, over the course of generations, it may produce some heirs who are poorly prepared or inept at assuming their responsibility. Prudence is necessary when considering the counter-examples that come to mind, so great is the system's capacity for recovery.

We know the famous case of Wittgenstein who, having given up his considerable heritage, made his sisters and his brother the beneficiaries, thus ensuring collective continuity although the individual line was broken. But even if the economic dimension of the transmission is renounced, it seems as though the moral and cultural aspects cannot be rejected. The paternal plan, also built on the basis of a rupture, in a certain way was assumed by a son who seems to have internalized its essence. It is not so easy to refuse to be the child of one's parents, and the will to break away does not always guarantee a consequent criticism of what is transmitted.[5]

GIFTS, COUNTER-GIFTS, AND CONTRACTS BETWEEN THE GENERATIONS

In the majority of the French families, one hardly broaches the subject of heritage. The silence can be explained, in the most modest surroundings, by the fact that there is little or nothing to pass along. In the intermediate groups, the average sectors of the cities, there seems to be a very great denial of the transmission of the goods to be inherited. "The absence of conversation about heritage," affirms Anne Gotman, "results first of all from the fact that the prospect of inheriting is strictly associated with the very event of death [. . .]. Death, covetousness and submissiveness—such are the principal reasons for the silence that the family imposes on the heirs—an absolute discretion not only verbal, but also of thought. This is a rule that is adhered to unanimously as to the prospect of heritage: that must not happen, no one expects an inheritance. Better, one does not expect anything. Inheritances appear to be not so much forbidden as as a unthinkable."[6] One may also see an analogy between heritage and the symbolic exchange carried out in the form of the gift and the counter-gift along the lines suggested by Marcel Mauss. [7] Respect and filial love, which are morally owed to the parents, constitute the essential return gift for a transmission that can be received without guilt after the death of beloved people. The parents' posthumous gift cannot be received with serenity without the anticipated counter-gift of filial devotion, and thus without keeping silent about the inevitable prospect of death and inheritance. The relationship is magical: death and transmission take place automatically, but one avoids discussing this topic. That is one of the properties of the economy of symbolic exchanges: "It is *the taboo of clarification* (price is an example of this, par excellence). To say what is what, to state the truth of the exchange or, as they say, 'the truth of prices' (when a gift is made, we remove the label . . .), would be to destroy the exchange. One notes, in passing, that the conduct that follows the paradigm of the exchanging of gifts poses a very difficult problem for sociology which, by definition, is explicit: it is obliged to spell out that which happens naturally and which must remain tacit, unspoken, as though under penalty of being destroyed as such."[8] Heritage is an exchange which thus generally goes unspoken.

Links in the Lineage

It is different with wealthy heirs. Respect for one's ancestors, the duty to transmit in one's turn, the fact of living themselves as a link in a lineage, of feeling oneself to be only the usufructuary of goods which, fundamentally, do not belong to you, of which you are only the agent—all that is not lived spontaneously, as though it were obvious, but must be learned. So much so that Jean d'Ormesson, in his foreword to the autobiography of Victoire de Montesquiou, affirms that "it is a terrible handicap to be born with so much past."[9] Because this past, one must take it on, be worthy of it. Thierry de Valréal is unable to take away from the family, by sale, the paintings and the château that he inherited. "When I look at all these things, I do not think one minute about the money, I do not put values on all these objects." Patrice Fustier and his wife Helene de Nervaux-Loys are joint owners of the domain of Courson in Île-de-France. Like many lords of the manor or owners of historic buildings, property that has been in the family for several generations, they feel "responsible for an escrow account in Courson, which is entrusted to us but which is not really ours. Our park is the product of six generations of amateurs in the art of gardening."

Marquis François des Monstiers thinks that he became aware of being a link in a lineage by the age of seven or eight years. "Because they told me, about the house, 'You know, it is not yours, it will only be lent to you. And you must leave it on behind you.' We are never owners," he concludes today at the age of eighty two years, "we are only tenants. But we are responsible for these goods, for the time that God lends us life. It is a very heavy moral burden which I felt even before being proprietor of this house, for it is a concept that was inculcated into me as a very young person." M. des Monstiers talks about a Renaissance château the way the aristocrats of the Jockey Club, of which he is a member, talk about a house. "In families like ours," he explains, "one never speaks of a château but of a house, because, actually, it is the family aspect which takes precedence. Thus in 1928 my parents celebrated the seven-hundredth anniversary of our house, since our family's acquisition of this property goes back to about 1228. It has remained in our family, from male to male, until today." The house is the objectification, the materialization of the lineage, the favorite place for the accumulation of the family capital, a specific form of social capital.[10] This recording of the lineage, crystallized in the house, is also in a symbolic way a certain mastery of the past and future—which very few social groups can think of.

The farming community is one of the rare milieux that shares this privilege with the aristocracy and the great old bourgeoisie. The monograph of a family of peasants in the Pyrenees, the Mélougas, put together by Frederic Le Play at Cauterets in August 1856, shows that due to a major effort to socialize and inculcate the children, from the earliest years, the house of the Mélouga family and its agricultural properties retained their integral form from generation to generation. For, according to Le Play, "it is always transmitted to eldest of the children (boy or girl)". The house thus remains associated with the Mélouga family, in a strong intermingling between economic capital (dependent on the assets) and the symbolic capital, accumulated around the surname, since even when the eldest is a girl, her fiancée, to marry her, must agree to bear her name. The other children may remain unmarried at house and contribute to the domestic and agricultural work, or leave with the help of a dowry.

In a somewhat similar scenario, as Le Play says, few legal means are implemented to thus preserve the patrimony in its entirety within a family. That is only possible because "each member of a community, appreciating early on the advantages which go with the conservation of a patrimonial asset, subordinates all his behavior to this feeling and inclines himself with respect to intentions of the father of the family."[11] The Mélouga family was an example of the family-stock whose extension seemed to Le Play the most effective means to fight against the rise of individualism and the growing social disorganization. The objective of this monograph was to show Napoleon III the mistakes of the Civil Code of 1804, related to the obligation to divide the family property evenly among children. On this point, Le Play must have benefited from the agreement of the aristocratic families—and in any case would benefit from it today, so sharp is their resentment with regard to this aspect of the code.

Pierre Bourdieu's works on "celibacy and the condition of peasants" in Béarn shows that, still in the middle of the 20th century, many aspects of the system of transmission in favor of the eldest are maintained. "The compensation granted to the juniors is only a concession forced by the requirement of equity. The successional custom resolutely favors safeguarding the patrimony, bestowed upon the elder, without sacrificing, as in former times in England, the rights of the juniors."[12] "At the same time lineage and patrimony," adds P. Bourdieu, "the house, 'the maysou', remains, while the generations which personify it pass through."[13] In the same way, Élisabeth Claverie and Pierre Malmaison's works on Gévaudan,[14] or the observations which we could make in French Basque Country, would tend to prove the significance of this system of transmission, which is preferred in the south and especially the south-west of France, where the eldest one (or whoever is designated as such, in the case of Gévaudan) must at the same time manage the house and the activities which are linked to it, on the material level, and defend the honor of the family and the house, this time on the symbolic plane.

The ability to conceptualize the future over the long term appears to depend on the possibility of referring to a past, as rich and extensive as possible. The grand bourgeois or aristocratic residence is, from this point of view, a true sanctuary of the family past: memories not publicized but preciously preserved; old books, collections, furniture, jewels, family portraits, works of art, curios, everything makes sense because everything has a history. "When the metaphorical relationship of the home and the domain to the family which lives there, used to live there and will live there is the tightest, when one can speak equally of a great family or a great house, a term begins to indicate simultaneously the material residence and the permanent presence of which it is the site and the symbol," writes Marc Augé.[15] The ambiguity of the term "house," which can indicate a construction or those who live within it, the building or the family, was noted by Emile Benveniste, who notes the generalized tendency in the Indo-European world "to identify the social grouping with its material habitat," and thus the contaminations which he observes between the two roots, however distinct, dem- (family) and *dem(¶) (to build).[16] But this history, this recording of the family memory in a place, it must be continued—that is one of the meanings of "noblesse oblige." And this duty to continue what the ancestors bequeathed is of an economic nature—these are goods with high monetary value—but also of a symbolic and emotional nature.

Clarifying the Stakes

If the concepts of gift and counter-gift can help us understand the game and the stakes between the generations in the majority of the social groups, it is different in the upper classes where the inescapable transmission is neither denied nor euphemized. Admittedly, there is indeed a social act that is connected to the gift, in the sense that what is transmitted appears to be given without anything in return, and as being dissociable from the person of the giver. Usual expressions like "the family possessions" or "my aunt's vase"[17] testify to that.

As regards heritage, the gift/counter-gift is established in a strong interpersonal relation, as F. Bloch and M. Buisson write: "If the donee feels he is seen as the subject in this 'something from oneself' which is passed in the gift, then he will receive it as an invitation to give something in turn. If the donee feels, on the contrary, that the gift is not really intended for him, that he is not really recognized by the giver as a person having his own subjectivity, then he will avoid, will refuse the relationship of which he feels captive: which, within the family framework, is not always simple!"18 All the upbringing, in the great families, explicitly prepares one for this passage of the relay. There is a lot to pass along, economically and symbolically; clarification is impossible to circumvent. It is important that the gift be well received and that it can generate the counter-gift, i.e. the perpetuation of the name, the permanence of the line. Because of this, the nature of the relationship between the generations is contractual rather than taking the tone of a gift/counter-gift. The latter type of relationship is magical because it is denied, but it can not the meet complex requirements of these transmissions which are exceptional in both volume and their composition. Bank services for the management of fortunes also strengthen the level of clarification of the transmissions between generations. "We know," writes Bank Paribas in an advertising text published in *Le Courrier du Jockey Club*, "that we have not been unworthy of our mission when we hear a son who is pleased with his father's financial management . . . which, in fact, was a little bit that of our bank."

In the television documentary devoted to the Rochefoucauld family,19 the Duchess of Liancourt discusses the educational methods which she applies to prepare her son, François-Xavier, to inherit the title and the castle of the dukes de La Rochefoucauld: "We try to raise him in a simple way. There are two facets to his education. There is first of all, the everyday life with the valuable example of his parents, but there is one more, for he will need to learn that he forms part of a family that is a thousand years old. This is why we chose for his godfather Jean-Domenique de La Rochefoucauld, the family historian. We very much count on him to teach him what his family has been and for him to ensure continuity." When there is lot to inherit, formalized injunctions and moralizing speeches are very much present. Between the generations, in the dominant milieux, the structure of the exchange is not repressed—it is made explicit at the individual level and at the collective level. The inculcation of moral and cultural effects is not incompatible with the fact that one sees the following calculation made: "Someone gives you something, you must accept it but you will have to return it, you are only a usufructuary." It is possible to display openly the reality of the relationship, to clarify who are the current holders and who are the successors to the heritage, and even the consequences of the death of one's parents, because it is never a question of receiving only a legacy. At the same it is time a charge, a duty, that of ensuring the passage of the relay at its turn and of making sure that the line will survive in the apparent immortality of the material and symbolic patrimony. The group of peers, nobility or grand bourgeoisie takes care that their heirs fulfill their mission well and do not stray. The prodigal son constitutes a symmetrical figure to, and is as much detested as, that of the newly rich.

According to Article 578 of the Civil Code, "usufruct is the right to enjoy the things owned by another, like the owner himself, but with the charge of preserving its substance." And the owner, in fact, is the family throughout its duration, the lineage in its transcendent reality.

The Living and the Dead

For there to be transmission and reception of the heritage under good conditions, belief in the lineage is essential, and even a certain idealization, even "a sacralization" of the family which must be seen as a source of enchantment. "Why," asks Christiane de Nicolay-Mazery in the introduction of her book, *La Vie de château,* "did I want to take you along with me through the French countryside for a year? Not to show you historical residences, but to have you share the intimacy of houses that I loved, of family houses, preserved from generation to generation, where each one has left his imprint. Houses which warm the heart, sweet to those who are born into life, and a solace to those preparing to leave it."[20] Death is part of life, but to engrave one's own disappearance in the logic of the lineage allows one to assume it with more serenity. "As a very young person, thanks to the photographs which I discovered in family files, I internalized the fact that the succession of the generations is an irreversible process," confides Christiane de Nicolay-Mazery. "I would look at such and such aunt or uncle at five years, then at the day of their marriage and finally on their death beds. A few moments later I would find a grandmother or a great-grandmother fixed thus by the photographer at the various ages of life. So in this way I internalized the ineluctability of the cycles of life, and their apparent resemblance." Familiarity with the preceding generations varies according to social milieux. It is possible that the memory is proportional to the size of the patrimony. In a condensed and thus simplified form, one may suggest that misery makes one live in the present, and opulence, in eternity. Which is not the least of its charms.

The richest families organize during their lifetime at least part of their succession. According to Anne Laferrère and Luc Arrondel, according to a study carried out starting from a sample of the statements of succession of 1987, "within the 1% richest, close to one out of three successions are distributed unequally. Wealthy people thus seem to partly organize their "succession" while they are alive and, more often than other households, fix the shares intended for each heir (apart from what is reserved to them by the law)."[21]

215

The transmission of material goods between the generations within the family must allow each one to take the torch as in a relay race, each runner being permanently confronted with the double nature, economic and symbolic, of the inherited goods. Quasi-techniques of education prepare everyone for the inescapable turnover. The *livres de raison*, books in which the successive heads of household record events, reflections and counsel for the use of future generations, constitute true handbooks for the perfect heir. Thomas Mann has the Buddenbrooks' play an important role in the formation of his heroine. "She turned grey at the importance with which they discussed the most modest events here, the history of the family . . . Her head in her hands, leaning on her elbows, she read with increasing devotion, proud and serious. All her past, however restricted, proceeded there complete. Her birth, her childhood diseases, her first class, entry into Miss Weichbrodt's boarding school, her first communion . . . Everything was recorded by the consul, in his small cursive tradesman's hand, thoroughly, with an almost religious respect for the events in themselves: didn't the least of them result from the will of a God who had marvelously directed the destinies of the family? . . . What would the future bring, for her name, this name which she had received from her grandmother Antoinette? All that would be read by the future members of the family with the same piety that she experienced in following the events of the past."[22]

Even the category of ancestor must be formed, it does not come about by itself: the entire business of mourning must be carried out under optimal conditions in order for the dead to become ancestors, as Mark Augé so rightly says.

"When the dead person has become an ancestor, the heritage can again become patrimony, transmitted and to be transmitted; the identity can anchor itself simultaneously in the evidence of the antecedents and the descendants, the past reconstituted and the future previewed—in the image of other people, in either case."[23] The place given to death in the great old families contributes to making the dead into ancestors. Death is not completely the same, subjectively, i.e. socially, when it comes to taking one's place in the succession of the generations. You know that memory of your lifetime will be celebrated in many ways, through the portraits in the gallery of family paintings, through the trumpets of the hunt that will be dedicated to you and which, sounded at the end of a day of hunting will, for a moment, have you live again in the thought of informed huntsmen and traverse a corner of the forest again where you accumulated so many memories.[24] The transmission of the patrimony is indissociable from the construction of the lineage and family memory. Without patrimony to be transmitted, there is little living memory. "The memory of the poor," wrote Albert Camus, "is already less nourished than that of the wealthy; it has fewer landmarks in space since they seldom leave the place where they live, fewer landmarks in time as well, over a gray and uniform life. Of course, there is the memory of the heart, which one may say is all the more sure, but the heart itself wears with sorrow and work, it forgets more quickly under the weight of tiredness. Wasted time is found only in the rich person. For the poor, time marks only the vague traces of the path to death. And then, to bear up well, one does not need to remember too much."[25]

These bonds between the living and the dead are woven from the earliest childhood. Here is how Christiane de Nicolay-Mazery describes her childhood in the family castle in Sarthe: "Through the portraits, personal objects and furniture: so many of my ancestors had sat down in this armchair, they had lived in this room, walked in this alley . . . I felt the presence of a whole world which seemed to me very much alive. There were also many letters written by my ancestors who were thus at the same time dead and alive. In the attics where I liked to go, all the generations mixed, I did not distinguish between the old and the new. And yet I knew neither my great-grandparents nor my grandparents, but they *were there*. I read in the library the letters which my grandmother wrote to her husband and those of my great-grandmother expressing her concerns for the marriage of so and so." For Christiane de Nicolay-Mazery her ancestors were active, and she was active with respect to them: "I wanted to know who they were. I sought out the resemblances, the signs of temperament, of character, the sense of responsibility, certain types of humor which I found in the living ones." In the underground passage which leads from the château to the village church is the family vault "where were my grandparents and my parents' future place was. There were already "holes" for us." Death is well assimilated when it is made present by the ancestors who mix so thoroughly into the everyday life of a small girl. Death is dealt with collectively by the family but also by the servants and the villagers. Christiane de Nicolay-Mazery's father died in 1991. For his burial the church offered the memory of the great-grandparents immortalized in the designs of the stained glasses. "Six men who worked on the property carried the coffin. The village was quiet, all the shops closed, a little as if the father of the village were being buried."

From the moment of birth, more or less fixed customs and rituals regulate the recording of the baby in the lineage. "The christening robe is our family's," says Christiane de Nicolay-Mazery. "My children were baptized in the christening robe of my father and his brothers, which had served my paternal grandmother as well. Above the dress I added a small white coat which had been worn by my father-in-law. The wedding veil is also a family veil, as well as the jewel that holds the veil. Formerly it was also used above the confinement bed. One put it on for visits. The funeral drapery is also a family heirloom, a large blue velvet cloth embroidered in silver thread, which one places over the coffin. We re-upholster the baby cradle from generation to generation. My children's was a white wrought iron swinging bassinet with white organdy. It was my father-in-law's cradle—we used it for my three children. I kept it and it will be used again." Admittedly, as with some other practices, this transmission, more charged with symbolic meaning than material value, is found in other social milieux. Cradles, for example, often pass from generation to generation. But it is rare that this registering of the essential moments of family life—birth, marriage and death—are handled so systematically and forcefully with objects from the past, the family symbols from old times, thus recording the individual existence in the passage of time. Accumulated with all the rest, this fetishism contributes to the cult of the family.

It seems as though, in these rituals, this worship of memory and the omnipresence of the past, everything works together to give the dead, as soon as possible, the status of ancestors, and to the living, that of perpetuators of the lineage—undoubtedly because if, as Marc Augé writes, "the dead are a burden, but ancestors are reassuring."[26] But also because this transfiguration, privilege of the great families that have the essential resources for this very particular worship of the dead, is one of the founding elements of the symbolic capital which is specific to them.

The ancestors of the des Monstiers family rest in the vault of the château of Fraisse, but they are also painted or photographed throughout, in the salons, the corridors, the gaming rooms and the reception halls. Louis des Monstiers, the current owner's elder grandson, will be called upon to take the succession. For him, the ancestors are very present, so much so that he is always ready to tell some pleasant anecdote about them. He also searches for the resemblances between the living and the dead. The gaze of his ancestors, immortalized on the canvases that decorate the walls of the salons, seems to him to be an injunction not to break a chain started in the 13th century.

An Heir Capable of Inheriting

Louis des Monstiers, 27 years old, is ready. He holds a DESS [graduate degree] in regional planning, which he says should give him a more complete view and enable him to better direct Fraisse. He loves the château, cradle of his family, marvelous frame of his childhood. He is always doing something there, waxing the bindings of the old books, planting two lines of trees to visually isolate the tennis courts, dreaming up restoration projects for "the old castle," the part of the buildings which date from the 15th century. He says he does not really exist as "Louis," but as "a des Monstiers." "We" takes precedence over "I". Tradition is thus one of the pillars of the successful transmissions. Probably in these traditional settings, in any event deeply rooted in a long lineage, that the biographical illusion about which Pierre Bourdieu speaks is the least present[27]. For the weight of the heritage is such that it has the last word on the heir as an individual. The heir is first of all inherited by a heritage that is the fruit of the ancestors' work, which must be passed on in turn. The repetition of the same first names from generation to generation also counters the illusion of individuality. There is a double process in the family, through names, by both the first name and the patronym, which subjugates individuality with, for compensation, a considerable symbolic profit.

For the stronger and more structural the determinants, the more they tend to go unperceived and the more, consequently, they can be lived positively. Quite simply, because then there tends to be harmony between the habitus, the internalized systems of predispositions as a second nature, and conditions of practice.[28] The environment is sufficiently powerful to induce in the actors the attitudes, expectations, needs, and plans that best conform to these conditions. The practice can then be lived, paradoxically, as a mode of realizing one's own vocation, the achievement of oneself, while at the same time it is the product of a habitus perfectly adapted to the conditions which generated it. Louis des Monstiers is dedicated to Fraisse and firmly intends to devote himself to it in the fulfillment of his own identity, that of the lineage from which he comes. To question the awareness of these choices would not call into question this certainty of being where all the family history encourages you to be. The feeling of freedom and plenitude in the conduct of one's existence could not be complete than under these conditions where even the meaning of existence is given to you by your birth. If the members of the great families exert a certain charisma, a certain seduction, which are attested by successful condescension and paterntic relationships, it is also because of the manifest ease of their behavior or, as it is often called in our interviews, because of the feeling of freedom and of serene realization of oneself which accompanies this harmony, this homology between the individual and the world where he acts out his life. [29]

The Weight of Inheritance and Its Symbols

But sometimes the heritage can seem heavy—especially when negligent ancestors have impoverished a patrimonial property without which it seems that the principle of the lineage itself is threatened. Albert de Mun is the great grandson of his homonym who lived from 1841 to 1914. The earlier one was a politician and a catholic leader with national influence. "Admittedly," Albert de Mun states today, "the heritage is all the stronger in that it is a constant reminder of my duties. " It is no less so if the grandson feels a certain amusement at finding himself on the avenue which bears the name of his great-grandfather, and thus his own. The avenue Albert de Mun, in the 16th district, goes along the gardens of Trocadero and his eponym's name was also given to a bus stop, so that this patronym, except in the event of a strike by the RATP, resounds every day in the ears of travelers. But this importance of one's name, which is not completely one's own since it is the symbol of

219

the lineage, is also an existential difficulty, a reminder sometimes too insistent of your status as a link in family continuity. "You have no real importance, except that that you have to transmit. The name is sacred because in fact it does not belong to you, it belongs to the family," continues Albert de Mun. "I will admit to you," he concludes, "that I regret not having changed my first name at work, when I was twenty years old." This denial of individuality is also one of the bases of this courtesy that some will call condescension, so frequent in the old aristocratic or bourgeois families. As much the newly rich is given to think that he owes nothing to anybody and that he is a self-made man, by the force of his character and of his talents, so much the heir to a prestigious line knows that even his name, even his first name, he owes to the ancestors and that he was made by all those who preceded him. The identity and legitimacy, for oneself and for others, then contribute to the success of the transmission.

The nobility, perhaps even more than the old bourgeoisie, uses family first names that the successive generations pass on at the same time as the patrimony. These first names are symbolic goods of the highest importance since they recall the membership in the lineage. Their attribution seems to be the rule at the des Monstiers. Louis carries the first name of his paternal great-grandfather. His father Jean-François holds the first name of the bishop of Bayonne, Jean des Monstiers, who was an ambassador of François 1st, then of Henri II, and who rebuilt Fraisse in the Renaissance style, and of his own father. Thus, for 22 generations, 20 eldest sons were named Francois, either as a single first name, or together with another given name.[30] The eldest daughter of the current Marquis François des Monstiers has the first name of Quitterie in memory of Quitterie de Fraisse who, in the 13th century, married Urban des Monstiers, "and since she was the last of her family, it faded into ours," as they say today at the des Monstiers.

The stained glass window in the family vault is dedicated to him. In the list of ancestors which indicates those who are buried there, it appears on several occasions. One of the statues of the old church is supposed to represent Saint Quitterie. These first names, present again in the painting galleries, are thus mixed into the patrimony and constitute one of its dimensions. For catholic families, they are furthermore a permanent reference to the history of the Church and its saints, thus registering the living ones in another lineage, that of the continuity of the community of believers.

The family name is symbolically represented by the coat of arms which is abundantly reproduced on buildings and documents of all kinds. The blazon of the des Monstiers was originally argent, three fesses gules (i.e. it contained horizontal bands, white and red). Then it was "quartered" (i.e. divided into four parts), the quarter sinister chief (top, right) and the quarter of angle dexter base (bottom, left) being charged with lions passant from the Chastillon family coat of arms, whose last heiress married a des Monstiers. The emblem of this family, which, in direct line, has disappeared today, thus was able to survive.

These coats of arms are found today on the door of the old castle, from where they watched over more than six centuries on the main courtyard. Jean-François of Monstiers carries a signet ring with a motif from these coats of arms. The stained glass dedicated to Saint Quitterie is also decorated with it. The blazon appears at the head of the text given to the visitors to Fraisse on the occasion of the Open Days of Historic Buildings. It decorates the fireplace in the winter dining room, restored by the grandfather of Marquis François of Monstiers in 1905. In other words, this family symbol is omnipresent on all the forms of the patrimony. It is one in the most manifest ways to register its power in space. It is also a means of reminding family members of their membership in a group and the duties that go with it. The armorial bearings are an obligatory accompaniment of the name and, in a symbolic and therefore effective form, they ensure its permanent presence in the most varied places, from the over-mantel oe fireplaces or the flooring of the reception rooms to the plates and tablecloths which may carry the initials and the arms of the family.[31] This "marking" of space and daily objects is not specific to the great families, but it is much less present in the families of the middle and popular classes, which do not have the same symbolic supports to carry it out. The nobility is armed best for that, but the grand bourgeoisie does not scorn to resort to this type of practice, for example with the *ex libris* of bibliophiles.

Inheriting is also Giving

All this social business of constructing the lineage explains why, contrary to what Anne Gotman shows for other, far less wealthy, social groups, heritage in these surroundings does not come across as usurped goods. The entire education explicitly prepares the heir to receive it, and in turn to forward it at the proper time. The meaning of the heritage is not receiving but, paradoxically, giving—for to inherit is not to benefit from the work of the former generations, but to add to it one's own. That, at least, is how they see it, and it is true that the younger generations are spoken to far more about duty than about acquired rights. Which does not forbid the enjoyment of a comfortable fortune, but according to rules and with the responsibility of passing the relay. The exhortations of the Consul Buddenbrook to his daughter, tempted by a matrimonial alliance contrary to the interests of the family, are edifying in this respect: "We were not born, my dear daughter," he writes, "to carry out what our short sight regards as our small personal happiness, for we are not individuals free, independent, endowed with a personal existence; we are, so to speak, the rings of a chain and, as such, we cannot be imagined without the series of those who preceded us and cleared the way for us while following themselves a tested and worthy tradition, with rigor and without diverting their gaze from the goal. Your way, it seems to me, opens in front of you for the past many weeks, clear and strictly traced, and you would not be my daughter, neither the grand-daughter of your grandfather who rests with God, nor a true member of our family, if you alone seriously thought of following, in revolt and inconstancy, your personal and irregular paths."[32]

The family plays a predominant part in the training necessary to successfully pass the baton. But in the academic sphere, certain establishments also continue the work undertaken within the framework of the family. School is not a universe foreign to the family domain as may be the case for the children of the popular social sectors. On the contrary, the families are very much present and active in the institution, as we saw for the École des Roches. The parents are often alumni. From the secondary level onward, young schoolmates show a true *esprit de corps*. They build in this separate space, in the same way their parents did, a social space of relationships, a form of durable social capital which, starting from this very select school setting, redoubles that of the former generation and prepares them to succeed it. So the heritage of excellence is also passed along collectively. These exceptional schools are primarily special places for recording the privileges of lineages. At the École des Roches, the heirs learn individually and collectively to work their way into the succession of the generations.

This idea of continuity enduring beyond the generations is fundamental. Heritage does not have "a macabre value," as Anne Gotman described it for other social groups, because in the milieux that have been wealthy for several generations it is, on the contrary, the symbol of life triumphing over death. But recent developments of society, beginning with the agricultural crisis and the development of financial capital, are likely to upset the successful transmissions.

WHEN SECURITIES BAIL OUT REAL ESTATE PROPERTY . . .

The château du Fraisse is at the center of an agricultural territory of 750 hectares with farms, agriculture, cattle breeding and more recently, sheep. "My parents, like many of the people of the time," explains the Marquis François of Monstiers at the age of 82, "lived on incomes from certain capital investments which were essentially land and agricultural.

I do not think that my parents had a stock portfolio. No! There was the property of Fraisse, a forest in Charente which belonged to my father, and my mother's dowry of Parisian apartments."

However, alliances with the business bourgeoisie are numerous in this family of the old nobility. René des Monstiers, the maternal grandfather of Marquis François des Monstiers, 33 married Suzanne Firino, whose family was then called Firino Martell, "when my cousins had the Cognac house," under the terms of a decree going back to 1921 authorizing the amendment of the patronymic name. Their younger daughter, Andrée des Monstiers, married Maurice de Wendel. "But there was no share of Martell nor of Wendel share in my parents' patrimony," specifies M. des Monstiers. "Initially, because my grandmother had been evicted from the Martell House, as was commonly done at the time, and instead of associating her with the house they compensated her, I do not know exactly how. And then, it was not because my aunt Andrée had married Maurice de Wendel that my parents became participators in the Wendel business. No, my father's fortune was land and real estate, he had no interest in finance. Besides, it was not at all within my parents' land-based and rural mindset. It should be remembered that there had been financial crashes, the Suez story . . .

Some people lost their fortune. I believe that for my grandparents' generation the only sure securities were earth and stone. Those were, in any case, the foundations of our fortune. Or even, more precisely, stone consolidated the earth. The Parisian apartments were rather secure investments with fairly regular returns—which was not the case later on, because the laws have rendered this type of investment much less attractive."

Other alliances of same type were still contracted thereafter: Marquis François des Monstiers married Jacqueline Darblay, whose parents, in the paper industry, were friends of the family. "My parents had many Parisian relations, owing to the fact that they lived part of the year in Paris, in one of their apartments on the rue du Colonel-Combes [. . .]. I met my wife at a luncheon at Darblay where I was invited as a friend of Stanislas Darblay. My future parents-in-law had a property near Paris, at Saint-Germain-les-Corbeil, where I used to play tennis on Sundays. That is how I met my wife."[34] She had in her dowry some Darblay shares and some real estate in Paris, in particular some apartments in a town house in the VIIIth arrondissement which she inherited upon her parents' death and where several of the seven children of M. des Monstiers and Jacqueline Darblay live still today.

When François des Monstiers took up managing the domain of Fraisse, it was profitable and the income that the family received covered the maintenance of the château. This flourishing situation, during which it was possible to have a lot of repair work done, lasted until about the beginning of the Seventies. Then agricultural incomes fell and today the farm is largely overdrawn, so that Marquis François des Monstiers must bail it out every year. The 750 hectares thus cost more than they pay. But it is quite out of the question to sell, at least for the moment, for that would be to cut off a hallowed part of the patrimony, that upon which the family identity and perenniality are grounded. Mr. des Monstiers certainly blames European politics but also the land taxes, which go up to 200,000 francs, and the social fees which, levied in proportion to the area under cultivation, reach the same amount.[35] It goes without saying, that to be able to face such expenditure Marquis François des Monstiers must still have considerable capital. "Fortunately, I succeeded in putting together a portfolio by selling the apartments which came from my mother. I invested in quoted stocks and this portfolio gives me a certain flexibility. The land costs me a fortune!" Lastly—but M. des Monstiers did not say it—it is perhaps not a so bad a situation after all. Who can predict an always-radiant future if the investments are held only in financial instruments?

The Château must be Self-Financed

A château like Fraisse is a money pit. The lords of the manor like to stress that life in a castle is not always rosy. First, there is the relativity of comfort. In winter you have to retire to the heated rooms. There are still many such at Fraisse, but others remain frozen for six months, not to mention the corridors and the staircases. The château's water comes from a spring. But in the event of strong rains, which was the case in April 1994, the water becomes turbid, still drinkable, however, contrary to appearances.

The solidarity tax on wealth and death duties (always considered to be too high) and the reduced incomes no longer allow the same level of maintenance and certain aspects are completely forsaken. That is what happened to the kitchen garden: there is no longer enough staff to take care of it and, after being reduced in size with the passing of years, it is now only a nostalgic memory in Louis des Monstiers's mind's eye, as he tries step by step to get things back on an even keel and, by judicious plantings, to make the grounds surrounding the château attractive again.

In the castle itself, the trophy room reminds us that they used to go out to hunt at Fraisse. It is out of the question today and the stables are abandoned. The grandfather's kennels are nothing but a memory. There would be much work to do, here and there, in particular at the old château, that of the 15th century, which is threatened with ruin. Admittedly, it is out of the water: the roof is in good condition, having been rebuilt not too long ago. But the main beams that supported the floors of the first stage have subsided. The interior of the building is in ruin. However, one of the sons of Marquis François des Monstiers, Stanislas, would like to restore this old house and make it his own. But the expenses would be considerable.

Each generation made its contribution to the common work, restoring here, adding on there. Marquis François des Monstiers's grandfather refurnished the dining room and the winter salon, installing woodwork and redoing the fireplaces: a date painted on one of them, 1905, preserves the memory of this act. Sybil des Monstiers, Louis' mother, remade a room by changing all the fabrics hung on the walls, the armchairs and the canopy bed. The new fabric is identical to the original, having been created from the same design by a specialist. These very well appointed rooms are the pride of the house and one visits them during Open Days. In the same way the guestrooms were restored, with modernized bathrooms, thus expressing a sense and a taste for hospitality.

But all that is expensive and is undertaken only drop by drop, compared to the needs. Therefore the des Monstiers, and those on whom rests the duty today to maintain and transmit, Jean-François and his son Louis, reflect upon ways to make the castle self-sufficient from the financial point of view, i.e. to make it so that it produces sufficient income to provide for its own maintenance and restoration needs. Opening up to the general public is considered in this sense. It is a subject readily taken up with the guests passing through; their opinions are solicited. On the Open Days of Historic Buildings, on which occasion the château has been receiving visitors for approximately ten years, there were 200, then 300, and this year, on Sunday afternoon alone, 500 visitors jostling under the frescoed ceilings. These are, for the most part, country people who, once a year, can entertain the idea of life in a castle.

How many would come if the castle were open to public regularly? The area is not very touristic. It could certainly become that, but it hasn't yet. Louis, who has a taste for botany, dreams of a Renaissance garden, in accordance with the intentions of Jean des Monstiers, Bishop of Bayonne (a diplomat under Henri II and a humanist), who built the house.

It is necessary "to make Fraisse work," as those who live in it like to say. To make the château work by opening it to visitors, perhaps by organizing, as they do at Courson, "plant days," by offering its stables and its outer buildings for receptions, weddings and seminars, by renting part of the arable lands to a golf club.[36] But competition is strong; many castles having been opened to the public in recent years. Michel d'Arcangues, by opening the family residence to prestigious hosts for upper crust receptions, "tries to modernize the traditional tool. The challenge for people who acquired patrimonies, great houses, is to try to maintain them in active life and not to make them into symbols of the past or a former glory, completely out-of-date. The house must be transformed into a working tool, a productive tool." Always with the goal of avoiding breaking up the estate, Michel d'Arcangues recalls that "the creation of the golf course also responds to the desire to avoid losing the lands, which the series of successions can end up parceling out until exhaustion. The golf course is, now, indivisible." Still it is necessary that the château, the house, not lose its spirit, and remains the family cradle. Patrice Fustier considers it regrettable that certain lords of the manor consider them, him and his wife, to be "like merguez [sausage] vendors." "You prostitute your house!" they reproach them—because from now on, for the price of a simple entry ticket, anyone at all can open the door and enter into the intimacy, the hallowed family space, even to foundation of the very construction of the house. Faced with the contradiction of this exposure of the family intimacy to public, the owners of châteaux then do not hesitate to enlarge the family to the nation. These historical goods marked by the great moments of the formation of the French nation belong symbolically to everyone; it is thus normal to open them. The satisfaction of the lords of the manor at showing their domain is supported by the feeling they have of fulfilling a kind of civic duty that, beyond the financial incentives, legitimates the move. Pride in taking part in developing a historical heritage that exceeds private interests, and opening it to the public, gives these interests an exceptional symbolic value. By making it possible to preserve the ancestral patrimony and by increasing the number of individuals in a position to perceive,rough its objectified form, the exceptional quality of the family, opening a château to the public can, far from reducing the prestige of a name, consolidate it.[37] The most difficult shortcoming to accommodate it is the lack of family land, a real estate patrimony, château or large residence, which crystallizes the family memory—for a profound anchorage in a territory plays a decisive part this social construct which is the family.

These châteaux classified as historic buildings can also survive the family, either via the State, as was the case of the Château de Champs, at the edge of Paris, which was bequeathed in 1935 by the Cahen family of Antwerp, or by establishments like the Institute of France, or by private societies, hotel chains in particular, such as "Relais and Châteaux" or "Les Hôtels particuliers." The transmission must thus be considered on the scale of the group and not at the level of the individual or the nuclear family. The definition of the relevant limits of the family varies, besides, according to the social milieu.

The Family as a Social Construct

In a patrilineal society, the males transmit the patronymic names. Mr. and Mrs. de Rochetaillée had three daughters, but no son. However, Mr. de Rochetaillée is the only descendant of the name, which is thus threatened with disappearing. "But you can restore the name," he clarifies. Which is very important in such cases, as for the Rochetaillées, where the name of the territory and that of the family are one and the same. In that case, preserving this patronym with double meaning is important for the family identity. It is possible that the husband of the eldest daughter would take over the name, a patronym that can be legally amended, for valid reasons, such as the continuation of a famous name.

Article 61 of the Civil Code specifies indeed that "Any person who can show justification of a legitimate interest can ask to change his name. The request for renaming can be for the purpose of avoiding the extinction of the name carried by a predecessor or collateral of the applicant to the fourth degree. The renaming is authorized by decree." The law underscores the degree to which the family is a socially established and controlled construction. And how much, therefore, no doubt, the republican State endorses the symbolic capital represented by patronyms belonging more or less to history; as if, fundamentally, the great names were also part of the national patrimony.

Adoption, often of a nephew, is another means used to perpetuate a name in the process of extinction. The Marquis de Vibraye, owner of the Château de Cheverny, having no heir, thus adopted his own nephew Roland de Vibraye, the son of his younger brother. But he died accidentally in 1967 at the age of twenty-five. The Marquis de Vibraye then adopted, the following year, the elder son of Roland's sister, his grand-nephew, Charles-Antoine de Sigalas. From now the elder son of Arnaud de Sigalas and Helene de Vibraye is called Charles-Antoine de Vibraye. French law indeed provides for simple adoption, which requires the agreement of the various parties. According to Article 360 of the Civil Code "simple adoption is allowed, whatever the age of the adoptee." However, if the adoptee is over thirteen years, "he must grant the adoption personally." With regard to the name, Article 363 specifies that "simple adoption confers the name of the adopting party to the adoptee by adding it to the name of the latter. The court can, however, at the request of the adopting party, decide that the adoptee will bear only the name of the adopting party." According to Article 364, "the adoptee remains in his family of origin and preserves his rights in it, in particular his hereditary rights." Countess Anne de Bryas, owner of the Château de Mauvières, says she "knows of a young woman, the eldest of three girls, who married and who wanted her first-born, a boy, to bear her maiden name, so that is does not die out. The young woman's father thus legally adopted his grandson, to assure the continuity of the name."

L'Éventail of November 1989, in an Article on the Château de Cheverny, published the family photography of its current inhabitants. According to the caption, it is "the Viscount and the Viscountess Arnaud de Sigalas, surrounded by their five children, *Charles-Antoine de Vibraye*, Amaury, Aliénor, Gabrielle and Alexandre de Sigalas." In other words, the future heir to the domain, who will take over the name, is introduced quite naturally among his siblings with the patronym for which he will be responsible.[38] This practice of simple adoption is sufficiently frequent so that, at the beginning of an interview, one may tell you as if it were self-evident: "My father-in-law was adopted by his great-uncle so that the house would remain in the family with the same name."

Managers of fortunes, in addition, have many concerns with illegitimate children.

More than in other social groups, apparently, there are still marriages contracted in a deliberate way in order to make alliances between patrimonies. Now, divorce is proscribed because it would put into play the solidity of these same patrimonies—so that each one knows of the existence of illegitimate children, born of extra-conjugal loves that the cynically contractual character of certain marriages causes and inclines one to tolerate. These "natural" children are generally well accepted, since under these circumstances things relating to love and those to marriage are clearly distinguished. On condition, however that these children are "well born," i.e. the non-legitimate father, or mother, is from the same social milieu. If he belongs to the family or to the peer group, often the parent will even be selected as godparent. The concept of the family seems to be more concerned with effectiveness in the primary responsibility of transmitting the patrimony and safeguarding the lineage than with fussing over respect for the law of blood and that of moral principles that one may have thought to be more intangible.

In families where the patrimonies and thus the economic and social stakes are considerable, the processes are made clear through speech and injunctions. One achieves a certain cynicism, at least a rather great clarity, as to nature of the relationships, via a rational use of the law, which is put to use much more than in other social milieu. There is a legal culture which forms part of the cultural capital of the group. The frequency of law studies is remarkable. This legal culture makes it possible to use the law to advantage, even in the bosom of the close family, to benefit the perpetuation of the lineage.

GOOD LUCK AND BAD IN TRANSMISSIONS

Structural conditions, independent of individual will, can influence the success or the failure of transmission. Family compositions are one example, some being more favorable than others to the maintenance of lineages and patrimonies. The Château du Fraisse and its arable lands were able to remain in the des Monstiers-Mérinville family for several centuries, as it was possible to make the transmission in a direct line, from male to male.

A well Established Lineage

That was also the case for the Fontmichel family, at Grasse. According to the current head of household, Herve de Fontmichel, a lawyer, former mayor of Grasse and regional adviser, the permanence of the family rests on two pieces of real estate passed down in direct line since 18th Century—places of identity, memory and prestige for the family group. They are the private mansion located in the heart of the old town of Grasse, acquired July 10, 1774, and a property in the Grasse countryside, an old country house bought in 1765—two properties now classified. "These are the two geographical establishments that give this family permanent local legitimacy," concludes Herve de Fontmichel, who sees four reasons for this permanence. The first lies in the considerable means that this family has controlled for a long time. "This family is of acquired nobility. My family is not at all of old feudal nobility, it is a family ennobled through public office. It always had relatively significant means, accompanied by a very high cultural level, with very definite tastes which contribute to this family continuity." The fortune was founded, first, thanks to "work in the legal profession, then by ownership of a fleet of ships at Marseilles. One of my ancestors, who had a genius for international commerce, threw himself into maritime trade with Guyana, Africa and the Far East." Then this fortune was partially invested, in the following generations, in real estate and arable lands, "of which not a few were confiscated during the French revolution; but some remained to us."

The second reason for this successful transmission lies in the fact "that there was only one division, between my grandfather and his sisters. Since 1773, the fortune was of course touched by death duties and some major expenses that obliged my ancestors to sell things from time to time. But from the point of view of succession, one can say that there was only one noteworthy division since the beginning of the reign of Louis XVI!"

Admittedly today, father of four sons, Herve de Fontmichel, himself an only son, faces a patrimonial situation more difficult than his ancestors'. But—and here lies the third reason for his optimism—he hopes that the chain will be able to continue unbroken, alleging that he educated his children as he himself was. The father and the sons accept the idea that they are not, or will not be, really the owners of the family patrimony which is the property of a collective entity, the lineage, each member who makes it up being at its service. "I consider that the properties, the paintings, silverware and jewels which come from my family, do not belong to me," muses Herve de Fontmichel, "but belong to my family. In addition, our children are raised in same viewpoint. I consider the patrimonial goods as things of which I am the agent. I do not have the right to separate anything that I inherited; nothing. That which I inherited is inalienable by principle." Thus the lands of Mandelieu, which gained in value because of the expansion and the real estate pressure on the Riviera, are simply rented out. "I cannot sell them, I can only rent them, so I benefit from the expansion of the Riviera, but only by means of rents."

Lastly, a fourth element that appears to favor transmission, according to Herve de Fontmichel, lies in the classification as historic buildings of the family's two principal properties, the private mansion in Grasse and the domaine of Saint-Vallier a few kilometers from there. The classification has contradictory effects. It adds culturally and thus symbolically to the value of the classified building. But, at the same time, it devalues it monetarily because of the very heavy constraints that then weigh on any maintenance or rebuilding work and on the possible uses of the buildings. "Which is not important," says Herve de Fontmichel, "since, as I see it, I have not to use them so much as to bequeath them to the following generation."

Châteaux that have Disappeared

Among the varying elements that can explain the very different destinies of certain lineages, one might consider the historical risks and the tragic events stemming from social and political upheavals. Wars and revolutions started a number of patrimonies. Everyone remembers the Russian loans. The World Wars sent part of the real estate patrimonies up in smoke; those châteaux that escaped massacre were plundered, and assets, especially foreign, can be devalued or nationalized.

Taking into account the prevailing conditions must moderate common talk about the deterioration of great fortunes by bad heirs, incompetent to handle the responsibilities inherent in the management of a patrimony. The habitus of the heir, even one perfectly modeled as the agent responsible for receiving and transmitting, may be confronted with circumstances so out of step with the conditions under which the arrangements had been made, that the responses could fail in their attempt to overcome the risks of an economic situation for which nobody can claim to be prepared.

These risks may be combined with a propensity to spend money to satisfy an expensive passion, and the conjunction of difficult periods and these predilections for magnificence endanger the transmission of the economic patrimony. Society life and patronage have led to ill-considered expenditures that have won out over a family fortune. Natalie Champin and her brother, Albert de Mun, a journalist who specializes in the field of tourism, still wealthy, consider themselves to have received "only crumbs" from the preceding generations, so considerable was the family patrimony. Natalie Champin, 63 years old, holds the memories of past splendors in the form of painted plates in her dining room, representing family properties which are no longer theirs. The artist, Princess Chachavadze, was a friend of Natalie Champin's parents. She is often recorded in the journal of dinners held by Aude de Mun, born Vauréal, mother of Mrs. Champin and her brother Albert. "It was very sad for me, for I saw many properties leaving my family, on the paternal side as well as on the maternal side." The Château de Sassetot-le-Mauconduit— her paternal grandfather's property, a home enjoyed by Élisabeth of Austria who stayed there on several occasions—opens the series of the plates and of lost residences. Henri de

Mun and his wife, born Perquer, daughter of a ship-owner from Le Havre, owner of many commercial boats and haciendas in Argentina, were the occupants. Other occupants during the last war, American and especially German, left this Seine-Maritime residence and its farms spread over 650 hectares in a quite poor state. According to Natalie Champin, everything "was completely devastated." Upon the death of their father, Natalie Champin and her two brothers, Pierre-Henri (now deceased) and Albert, sought to sell this asset which had become too burdensome to maintain. It took them ten years to find a buyer. "We experienced an immense feeling of sadness because we had seen so many properties leaving that that was always an additional rupture." In fact, this castle of the 18th century, bought by a law firm, was transformed into a hotel and has the honor of being in *the Guide of Routard.* It is described there in these terms: "An elegant pink façade nestled in the greenery of a large English park of 10 hectares; in the hall, a beautiful double staircase. Built in the XVIII century, the castle was used as a residence by the Empress of Austria (Sissi, to close friends). Entirely restored in 1988, it offers spacious rooms that are less spacious, but more comfortable, with fitted carpet, TV and bath. Each room has its own personality, but all are furnished with taste, overlooking the park".[39] One can well imagine that there is a certain discomfort for the former owners thus to see their grandfather's castle lauded by the Parisians for the charms of nature and old stones. Each portion of the patrimony that gets away from the family poses a problem of conscience: shouldn't one have been able to do better, was this abandonment truly inevitable?

The family cradle has disappeared. It was a beautiful death to some extent, since the stones of the Château de Mun, close to Bigorre, were used, according to Albert de Mun, to build the houses of the village. But that is a very old story and the more recent losses have not healed so well. The third plate of the series represents the Château de Lumigny, in the Seine-et-Marne, where the great-grandfather, Albert de Mun, lived—one of the most active and most visible opponents to the law on separation of the Church and the State in 1905. His castle was sold too.

The old hunting rendez-vous in the Sologne, the great property of Fonsbelle which belonged to the maternal grandparents and where Natalie Champin spent the best years of her adolescence, had been bought by the family with the 200,000 gold francs that the investments in "the flagship industries of the Middle East" used to bring in every year. Today it belongs to an aunt, but keeping it within the family appears to be very much in doubt, for the cousins who will inherit it hardly seem to have the means, nor the intention, to handle the expenses inherent in such a property. It is true that the family does not have a fiber of management capacity. "Fonsbelle," remembers Albert de Mun, "went to my mother's sister, since my mother inherited some stock and a factory which manufactured . . . I do not know what!" This indifference to what is "only" the income-producing patrimony is not the general rule. Often the heirs are careful to keep a well-informed watch over their assets and especially over those that bring in a part of their means of existence. The lack of interest in the bursar's office, for these income patrimonies that are not companies inherited from the ancestors who founded them, is one of the surest indicators of the difficulty of transmission. For the assets of pleasure, even of very great value, cannot get by without the assets of revenue, which alone make it possible to enjoy and to maintain them within the patrimony for the benefit of future generations.

The plates also accept as decoration two city buildings, located one on the Avenue Foch and the other on the Champs-Élysées. Nibbled away, apartment after apartment, nothing of it remains, for the family at least. The private house on the Rue de Chanaleilles, in the VIIth arrondissement, two steps down from the Matignon hotel, received in heritage by a great-aunt whose husband was owner of *Journal des Débats*, was sold to the brother-in-law of Onassis, Niarchos, who still holds title to it although he makes only very rare appearances there.

This great-aunt, who was also a Nalèche, was the godmother of Natalie Champin, who was always astonished to see her meticulously collecting antique art objects and furniture that she protected with covers that were as unaesthetic as the camouflaged objects were superb. "Nobody ever saw them," so that upon the death of the collector, the heirs "entered a cave like Ali Baba's. I discovered splendors filling every cupboard," remembers Natalie Champin. "And we gave all her clothing, all her dresses, all her satin shoes to the costume museum. It was extraordinary! For me, making an inventory of this house with my mother was truly enchanting."

The inventory of the family's goods, to be complete, must also mention the mansion on the Avenue George Mandel, which has also been sold. Indeed, Albert de Mun remembers that "the building that cropped up next to ours was built in the place of a house which had belonged to my great-aunt de Nalèche and where my mother played as a child in the large gardens." Lastly, of course, on the Avenue George Mandel remains the building that holds the apartments still in the family's possession, where brother and sister live today. There remains, however, another property in the family's patrimony real estate, brought by Natalie Champin's husband, deceased, who was in the oil industry. It is a great family property located on the edge of Annecy Lake. In spite of difficulties and especially burglaries, Natalie Champin decided to keep this house. All the beautiful objects, the works of art have been appraised, recorded and insured. For the hemorrhage must stop here. Transmission must now begin again and the following generations must receive something to affirm their identity and to preserve the memory of the family history.

It remains to be understood how a catholic family, where the dynastic spirit seems to have been always present, did not succeed better at ensuring the transmission of a real estate patrimony to which all its members were attached. The war obviously played a decisive role in the loss of the Château of Sassetot-le-Mauconduit. Moreover, for two generations, the attitude was more consuming than producing. They lived off their revenues, while at the same time, in the opinion of every manager of fortune, simply managing one's assets without a firm commitment to making them bear fruit by seeking new investments leads to an inexorable erosion of the patrimony. Natalie Champin's paternal grandfather "enjoyed life, went out a lot, dressed well, hunted, and traveled." Albert de Mun thinks that "the fortune was wasted by carelessness. When there was a tax problem, or anything to be paid, they sold something, and they sold at the bottom of the market because they were in a hurry. The value was thus not reflected, reinvested, in spite of having a businessman who handled our affairs; they were not managing the fortune, but reducing it . . . ". The history of fashionable life in Paris bears a trace of the magnificence of this family. Gabriel-Louis Pringué, in his *30 Ans de dîners en ville*, says how highly he valued the evening parties at the Countess Henri de Mun, born Annie Perquer, the paternal grandmother. "She received many artists, literary men;" he writes, "and the conversations at her place were particularly brilliant. I often found Maurice Rostand there, whose burning, animated, descriptive and madly spiritual conversation entertained us. "[40]

The Champin family, in the person of Natalie Champin's sister-in-law, found another source of money worries. "She had a salon where she hosted poets, writers, musicians; it is she who launched Pierre Boulez. But she received them sumptuously. In her house in Haute-Savoie, she had no fewer than seven servants taking care of this house." This generous patronage ended up getting the better of the personal fortune of this friend of the arts.

"My sister and I," remarks Albert de Mun in conclusion, "we grew up in a milieu where money seemed natural and we thought, obviously, that there would be no problem for us in the future. Isolated from reality, separated from people's problems, from social relations, we lived in a cocoon and we were not involved at all in real life."

Other families present analogous cases. The Blin company in Elbeuf declared bankruptcy in 1976. "They did not convert to modern materials and wanted to continue manufacturing exclusively wool. They lived high, and lived well, on the company. After my grandfather's death," recalls Caroline de Ricqlès, "my grandmother still went in for the grand lifestyle: driver, taxis, luxury hotels; she adored life, she was so expensive that at her death she had practically exhausted the remainder of the family fortune. So Mom left us a little money, but not much."

Of all this industrial life there remains at Elbeuf only the college André Maurois installed in "the Castle," Blin Park on the rue de Lorraine, and the industrial buildings converted into public housing projects which carry the name of the company, "Blin et Blin."

On the Ricqlès side there was also a factory at Saint-Ouen, producing the Ricqlès mint, which was sold ten years ago to a German group. But, says Caroline de Ricqlès, "it was no longer the family's factory since the beginning of the Thirties, although it always remained in our name. At that time, indeed, an uncle had put his hand in the till and to make up the deficit, rather than request anything from the banks, the family had not found any better solution than to give up a significant share of the capital to an outside group. So that my father is the last of the Ricqlès to have worked at Ricqlès."

So transmission is not automatic; but it is enough that certain appearances are safeguarded, that the patrimony is not reduced to nothing; particularly in its symbolic and cultural components, so that a re-establishment is possible. Thus, in the case of the two families cited, membership in the grand bourgeoisie is still a reality, even if the size of the patrimony cannot compete with that of the greatest fortunes. The fact of the matter is that membership in the dominant social elites cannot be reduced to the possession of only one type of capital. As the very great recent fortunes do not ensure *ipso facto* membership in the grand bourgeoisie and the Clubs, so the loss of a significant part of the material wealth does not mean inescapable rejection into the hell of the ordinary world.

PASSING ON A TRADE

Sometimes the patrimony contains a form of capital which one could call professional. It relates to the knowledge and skills of the trades and branches of industry. Transmitted partially by academic institutions, it can also be passed on between generations when it depends on the family. This is not a privilege limited to the upper classes. We might cite the foundry trades which, until recently, before the combined effects of de-skilling and the economic crisis, were based on on-the-job training, often ensured by the father or an uncle, and led to the training of craftsmen proud of their expertise.[41]

In the grand bourgeoisie these forms of initiation to the trades are not rare. It is still a point of convergence between the dominant classes and dominated classes, the middle class owing more to the "education" capital.

To be an heir is also built by learning to work in the business world, to master the information of a given professional sector, to manage a certain area. And, in a society where unemployment touches 12% of the working population, it is the privilege of knowing that you have the possibility, if not the duty, of succeeding your father in managing his business or continuing in the branch of industry where he excelled, while profiting from the social capital accumulated by several generations.

Emmanuel Touton has worked for twenty years in his father's wine brokerage office, in the district of Chartrons, in Bordeaux. "It is my father who completely formed me." The broker, in the wine trade, is a pure intermediary between the owner-wine grower and the trader. Owing to the fact that the wine houses are less and less family-run and are more and more often bought up by industrial or financial groups or institutions, the trade of broker has changed a great deal. "There are no more loyal customers," complains Emmanuel Touton. "There is no more contract. Back when I started here, if a broker introduced himself to an owner with whom one was accustomed to working and proposed to give him fifty centimes or a franc more per bottle, the owner called you and asked you what you think. And, finally, for a franc less, he preferred to sell to the broker who was accustomed to following his production. Today all that is gone, there is no loyalty and no law!" The on-the-job training, in the company of elders in whom one can have confidence, taking into account the family ties, helps one learn to face new market situations. Knowing this relatively closed world of Bordeaux vineyards is a decisive element in the successful exercise of the wine trade. Thus, as early as possible, a clever father initiates his sons to the secret and the art of a trade where involvement in a network of relationships is one of the critical elements of success. "Wednesday afternoon, my father would take me along to the office. His great pride, his great dream, was to have his three sons in the office. He wanted us to work with him as soon as possible, he was never concerned with our studies." On this last point, the change is certainly appreciable: until almost the Sixties a diploma was not something that was required at all costs—a good knowledge of the mysteries of the professional milieu was apparently sufficient. But, since then, with the complication of the financial networks and their internationalization, the great families have all taken off in the race for academic excellence.

Emmanuel Touton's elder brother left to work in the United States, also in the wine trade, whereas the other went into public relations. "All my father's hopes then rested on me. I was practically obliged to join his office." And in his turn, Emmanuel Touton nourishes the dream of seeing his own son coming in behind him. The dynastic spirit is very present in the grand bourgeoisie of Bordeaux, tied to wine or to wood. This vitality of the lineages, which goes with the agricultural character of the activities, with their bond with the soil, marks every aspect of life, which here, more than elsewhere, is centered more on the locale and on alliances with local families, and makes a point of pride, almost an ideal, of this transmission "in the old way" of know-how and the secrecies of the trade.

Guy Schÿler, father of two daughters, does not have a male descendant to take the succession of the business which today bears the name Alfred Schÿler Fils & Co. He decided to make an arrangement with the Duclot company, which continues and maintains the name Alfred Schÿler Fils & Co by, among other means, marketing a brand called "Pavé des Chartrons ", which is the official wine of the French Academy, and of the embassies of the United States and Great Britain. Prince Sadruddin Aga Khan and many other personalities are its customers. This name symbolizes the wine trade linked to the district of which Xavier Arnozan Court, formerly called Pavé de Chartrons, forms the heart. Guy Schÿler still lives there. He wrote a comment on the label of his preferred wine, where one may read that "the Pavé de Chartrons has been my residence at Bordeaux and that of my ancestors since 1739. Montaigne, Montesquieu and Mauriac stayed here. It is both my family tradition and the excellence of the grand wines of Bordeaux that inspired me in the choices that went into this bottle. I am certain that the elegance and the discrete breeding of this wine will bring a note of refinement to your daily existence."

Guy Schÿler is also, through his mother Valentine Guestier, the descendant of another dynasty of Bordeaux wine merchants whose company, Barton and Guestier, dates back to 1802. "My two uncles, Daniel and William, died without issue, and the name of Guestier is extinct," Guy Schÿler says with nostalgia. He has dedicated this work to that dynasty: the work is dedicated "to my mother who had so strongly insisted that I take the name of Guestier . . .".[42]

Guy and Nicole Schÿler, his wife and the great-grand-daughter of Sir Richard Wallace—who donated his large collection to the British State, known today as "the Wallace collection," and who was the owner of the château du parc de Bagatelle in the Bois de Boulogne—live in a vast apartment in a private house on Xavier Arnozan Court, where the various Guestier generations left their traces and memories.[43] The walls are covered with paintings, seascapes, landscapes of the 18th century and many portraits of ancestors. Pedestals and commodes hold collections of bronze animal figurines and enameled snuffboxes, and books—lots of them—including a whole series devoted to General de Gaulle, and two volumes on the Second World War dedicated to Nicole Schÿler by Sir Winston Churchill.

Guy Schÿler and Nicole Wallace met at Arcachon, their respective grandparents having neighboring properties there. Through the transmission of a professional patrimony, be it of vineyards or the wine trade, or the pine forest, the area of Bordeaux, through the permanence of its activities, allows the great families to found true dynasties and, in the manner of the great royal families, to designate successive heirs bearing the same first names, by sequence numbers which are in fact of reference marks in the generations. There is thus among the Guestiers Daniel I, II, III, and IV. The area of Bordeaux is one of those that allow great families to assert their solidarity, which goes as far as concerted endogamy.[44]

Transmission and Conversion

The conditions are not always met for the transmission to be carried out under favorable conditions, so that it may continue beyond the generations. The Château d'Arbieu, close to Bazas in the Gironde, is an example that shows that in such a case a conversion is necessary. Engaged by the head of household, it is intended to be taken up and continued by the actions of his heirs.

What is transmitted then is especially a capacity for innovation that makes it possible to face economic and social risks.

At the side of the road, the guard house stands, neo-gothic in style. A gravel driveway wends its way up the hill, passes in front of a pond teeming with life, crosses a hint of a brook, and comes out at the level of the swimming pool overlooked by a tall dovecote, and ends at the main façade of the château, which turns its back toward town and looks out upon an immense lawn where playing balls await the feet of children. Large trees frame it, including cedars, and it seems more freshly mown than an "English green." There are mynah birds, from Asia, even better performers than parrots, and the owner of the place is teaching them the *Marseillaise*.

The Château d'Arbieu is the property of Count and Countess Philippe de Chenerilles. Five guestrooms make it possible to cover the castle's upkeep. The domain is hardly profitable any more and, what with European grants, the lands provide a better return when left fallow. But it is necessary to look to the future and to employment suitable for the five children. Therefore Mr. and Mrs. de Chenerilles conceived a plan to create a campsite on their vast estate, at the other end of the property. A top quality facility, that goes without saying, taking advantage of the four-star classification. Such an installation could offer incomes for two children and turn to profit on what is only idle land today. "It would be a very large camp-ground of approximately 24 hectares, with playing fields. Each place will be 200 square meters, opening on the woods and without any visible neighbors. There are so many campsites on the coast that to make tourists come to Bazas, we need something special. So there will be a putting green, a squash court and an open-air theatre." For the junior son, who has discovered a vocation for the hotel and restaurant trade, Mr. and Mrs. de Chenerilles also plan to establish a restaurant. "I would like to find a situation inside the estate for them," summarizes Mr. de Chenerilles.

Thus an agricultural estate, condemned for insufficient profitability, will finish well all the same by surviving as a tourist site and by providing the heirs a part of their income. A similar process is at work at the Château d'Arcangues, in the Pyrénées-Atlantiques, with the installation of a golf course and the residences linked to it. The agricultural vocation of the fields has been abandoned, and without any heartbreak: the important thing is to pass down the château, the element that, at the heart of the property, ensures the conservation of the family memory. And that also requires, when external revenues are not sufficient, making the estate itself work in new ways, but always with the intention of keeping it within the family patrimony.

FAMILY GOODS AND FINANCIAL GOODS

Thierry de Valréal stressed how different is his relationship to the inherited belongings, marked by the family and his childhood, which he will try to preserve and transmit, and his more relaxed relationship with those things that he acquired himself. When it is a question of securities in the form of stocks or other financial instruments, rather than material goods, there is no such imprint, this presence of those who are gone, and their last wills materialized in things. Consequently, far more individualistic dreams, less indebted to the family, can be carried out. Isabelle de Solane inherited material goods, upon the premature death of her mother who came from a rich family of industrialists, but especially a capital account which enabled her to concretize one of her dreams, to live on and inhabit a barge. "The boat," she acknowledges, was a certain kind of ability to preserve my independence, to be able to live with a small dose of poetry which I needed in my daily life." Isabelle de Solane has four brothers and three sisters, and she belongs to a catholic milieu that strengthens the spirit of family. Purchasing the barge creates a kind of distance, for "it is precarious," she confirms, "it doesn't have a stone foundation, it is not real estate since it is movable, one does not have to appear in front of a notary. And neither does one say to oneself, when buying a barge, 'I will leave that to my children.' It is a precarious boat, it can sink, it can catch fire. Buying a boat is completely irrational, and it is expensive, on the pretext that the moorings areas are great places, very privileged, in Paris, at la Concorde or at Neuilly. But is nothing like an apartment in Paris where all the newspapers, every six months, tell you how much your apartment is worth. With a barge it is much more random."

However, keeping one's distance, especially symbolically, has its limits. Indeed, on the one hand, the barge was always moored in a beautiful district, "for I cannot live anywhere but in a beautiful area, I would not feel at ease." And, in addition, Isabelle de Solane plans to resell her barge and return to live in the family building in the VIIth arrondissement where her father still stays today, with two of her brothers and her three sisters. And this, so that her young son will have a family. "My son," she confides, "is perfectly in agreement with this plan, for he shall have his family, the only one that he knows. Since he is not recognized by his father, it will be an important family presence for him."

The composition of the patrimony has a decisive influence on the way in which its transmission is seen and taken on. When the heritage is composed to some extent of financial securities, the beneficiary can feel much freer to do what he feels is appropriate and sometimes that can be an occasion to mark one's distance from the family standards. Emotional and symbolic logic seem stronger in the case of material goods.

One identifies with a stock portfolio less than with a castle. However, these last decades, the importance of financial, and thus abstract, capital has increased. Some families have seen this passage from industrial capitalism to banking and financial capitalism, like the Wendel family that made its mark in the French iron and steel industry.

Veronique de Montremy is the grand-daughter of Andrée des Monstiers, the wife of Maurice de Wendel. Although an inhabitant of Marceau Avenue in the VIIIth arrondissement, she spent part of her childhood with her maternal grandparents in Lorraine. She thus grew up and was shaped in what she calls "the Lorraine industrial kingdom," of which she would be one of the princesses. It is difficult for her to dissociate the memory of the Château de Brouchetière, at Joeuf, where homes were still numerous in the Sixties, and the luxurious way of life of the mines and the factories that her grandfather took her along to visit and whose noise traveled all the way to the rooms of the castle. "It was an astonishing place! It was the countryside but there were two centimeters of dust on the leaves, you could hear the blast furnaces and see them at the end of the park, the noise of the factories and shuntings of trains. You could hear the mine when they dumped the ore . . . It was not at all like the châteaux where our cousins and our friends went. I remember very well," continues Veronique de Montremy, "the first time that I visited a factory, I was six years old, I found it sublime—with fire, the noise; it was twisted, made into wire, made into sheets. I found that fascinating, and then the castings . . . It gave the impression of being in a separate world."

Everything came together within a framework so charged with symbolic value, for a successful transmission of the patrimonies, the family being associated with the château and with an industrial territory which was animated by thousands of workers. "Then, of course," concludes Veronique de Montremy, "when all that stopped, I realized that we were not at all a royal family, and that was kind of a blow . . . We don't go to Lorraine any more, except for funerals. We have nothing anymore. It's dreadful. This country, of which one imagined oneself to be the very essence—now we are no longer even part of it!" The Wendel family is not impoverished, for all that, and it appears in thirtieth position in the lists published by *L'Expansion* which classify the wealthiest families according to the size of their patrimony. At the beginning of the 19th century the Wendel family became established in financial society. "Since 1830-1840," says Veronique de Montremy, "my great-grandfather François de Wendel died and left two girls and a boy. His wife then created the company, "Sons of François de Wendel." Then, when her Charles son died, in the 1860's, it became the company Grandsons of François de Wendel, a limited partnership which owned industrial and real estate properties of the Lorraine iron and steel industry."

It is true that history did not spare the family. During the Revolution, the forge of Hayange was sold as a national asset after being put under sequestration. As a consequence of the Franco-German war of 1870, the Treaty of Frankfurt in 1871 placed the Wendel factories in German territory. During the Second World War, "Nazi Germany declared all the Wendel factories and mines Germanized under the trade name of Hermann Goering Werke: and at Liberation, they were returned to the family patrimony."[45]

The Grandsons' company took the form of two family holding companies; only descendants of the founders, and their spouses, can be shareholders.

"The holding company Grandsons of François de Wendel has remained, but all the real estate patrimony left with the Société de Wendel. We aren't called the Grandsons any longer, but there are two companies which are controlled by specific rules," the aim being to keep the capital always under the control of the members of the family. The two family holding companies "control 51% of the shares of Marine-Wendel, which holds 45% of the bonds of CGIP [Compagnie générale d'industrie et de participation], whose portfolio includes shares of Cap Gemini, de Carnaud, de Cedest . . . CGIP is worth 4 billion francs on the stock exchange, 1 billion being in the hands of the 350 Wendel shareholders. This sum does not take account of the family patrimony elsewhere." Marine-Wendel is directed by Ernest-Antoine Seillière de Laborde, son of Renée de Wendel and Jean Seillière, and who was the official representative in several ministerial cabinets including those of J. Chaban-Delmas and P. Messmer. In the board of directors report to the general meeting of 1994, Marine-Wendel recalls that it is "heir to an industrial past that goes back to 1704." "No longer having interests in the iron and steel industry, since 1990, where it had previously achieved its growth, Marine-Wendel, on the initiative of its principal shareholders, has chosen new avenues in growth sectors." That is, through the control of CGIP, packaging, international real estate, and advanced technologies (data processing services and medical diagnosis). In other words, a good diversification, accentuated further in 1993 and 1994 with the takeover of Reynolds (pens) and Stallergènes, specialized in the treatment of allergies.

Such variety does not have any objective beyond "balancing [. . .] risks on a broader basis. The de Wendel empire, concludes Rene Sédillot, was struck by the dramas of iron and steel industry. The family takes refuge in anonymity, behind Sacilor, the majority of which goes to the State, then behind the patronyms of the sons-in-law, Celier or Seillière, executives at a portfolio company, and the General Company of Industry and Participation, CGIP. They are fading into initials."

The Wendels' case is not unique; other families have created similar companies. Thus the Biches, whose limited partnership companies is supposed to enable them to preserve control of the family group. After the death of the founder, Baron Bich, his son took the succession and "neither is any turbulence to be expected for the capital of the group" since the family holds "39.3% of the capital (and still more in voting rights), 17.6% being in the hands of physical people and 21.7 % are held indirectly through a limited partnership, MBE (Marcel Bich Enfants) 48 ". By contrast, the Guichard family, which was the originator of the Groupe Casino, had to propose to its shareholders, on October 28, 1994, abandoning the status of limited partnership, which it was since its creation in 1898, for that of a corporation. Antoine Guichard, the founder's grandson, does not have a successor within the family.

Managing the family patrimony through financial capitalism can indeed provide a certain security, but it can pose other problems. The number of people having rights tends to grow, in the Wendels' case. According to Henry Coston, "84 members of the family were present or represented at the general shareholders' meeting [of the company known as the Grandsons of François de Wendel] on June 20, 1939, (they were about thirty more in 1949)."[49] Veronique de Montremy currently estimates there are between 350 and 400 shareholders at the two family holding companies who divide among themselves, according to Gabriel Milési, 25 million in dividends.[50] At that rate, management loses some of its transparency and risks becoming less consensual. But more serious is the loss of identity that comes with this new form of patrimony, disembodied, abstracted, reduced to coupons and dividends. Veronique de Montremy thinks that for all her cousins who will never have known Lorraine and who, because of their family ties with the Wendels, nevertheless can be shareholders in these partnerships, perhaps family cohesion will no longer be easy. "In the ten years ahead, it will be more complicated for we will not be able to maintain the fiction that the shares can only be bought and sold among ourselves. Before the war of 1940, I believe there were only 35 shareholders. They all knew each other. But now, when I go to a meeting of the Grandsons, it is full of cousins between twenty and twenty-five years old whom I do no even know! It has become a purely financial company where everyone is a cousin, sometimes a very distant cousin." For the moment, family cohesiveness is the rule and all the decisions "are made unanimously. Nobody ever votes against. Fundamentally, they are afraid to break family cohesion. In addition, recent measures were taken according to which, even if somebody had more than 40% of the capital, he could not have more than 40% of the votes. Which means that if one opens to the capital people external with the family, they will not be able to go against the majority, which will remain in the hands of the family."

The company's family character is still well marked. On the board of directors of MarineWendel, in addition to the chairman, Ernest-Antoine Seillière, a descendant of the Wendel's on his mother's side and linked by her father to the Demachy Bank which had been founded in 1780 by the Seillière family, but which was taken up at the beginning of the century by the Wendels, one will notice that the President Emeritus is none other than his uncle, Count Pierre Celier, who is also a tax inspector, married to France-Victoire de Wendel and who is thus also the uncle of Veronique de Montremy. The Lorraine iron and steel holding company is represented, at this same council, by Hubert Leclerc de Hauteclocque, son of the Marshal Leclerc, Philippe de Hauteclocque, who had married a Wendel grand-daughter.

"With the Wendels," says Baron Seillière, "there are four of us from the family in the company: Pierre Celier, François de Wendel (grandson), Henri de Mitry and me. We gave ourselves a rule such that, when anyone from the family is candidate, a headhunter studies the file. Recruitment must be completely professional. Only one thing must be taken into account: the development of the group's affairs."[51]

This example shows that the conversion of industrial patrimonies, and matrimonial alliances with the name changes that they entail, erase the tracks. Only by analyzing very carefully the nonevident family ties, one may see more clearly the extent to which the great families of the past are still present in the business, and sometimes to a greater degree. The investigation would have to be pushed still further to realize, for example, that Ernest-Antoine Seillière is the grandson of Maurice de Wendel, and Pierre Celier his son-in-law.

Veronique de Montremy wonders about the transmission of her patrimony, both real estate—apartments in Paris—and furniture, as one has just seen, to her own children. The work of inculcating of moral and cultural values cannot be slackened for she wishes her two daughters to continue the lineage with dignity, but this time with far more abstract benchmarks: "a solid portfolio of shares!" Her daughters will indeed not have known the territorial bases of the de Wendel fortune. A true teacher in itself, the territory contributes to the shaping of the sons of the family who, later, will be suited to assume all the components of the heritage, including financial. Today, notes Veronique de Montremy, "we spend our time choosing stocks, we are not industrialists anymore. We used to be industrialists, including mentally. It was something tangible that was used for something. It was industry—

and now we have passed over into service, in the tertiary sector. We get shares which we re-sell with the idea that it is necessary to be mobile, fluid." The rooting in a soil, the Château de Brouchetière, in the midst of the factories as other homes are in their own milieu, that is finished. Transmission does not happen anymore to fits own accord: the family memory risks becoming fluid like its assets.

Notes

1. D. KESSLER and A. MASSON, "Le patrimoine des Français: faits et controverses," *op. cit.*, p. 160. See also Luc ARRONDEL, "L'approche économique de l'héritage: modèles et tests," *Communications,* "Générations et filiation," 59, 1994.

2. Daniel BERTAUX, *Destins personnels et structure de classe, op. cit.*, p. 75.

3. Thorstein VEBLEN, *Théorie de la classe de loisir,* Paris, Gallimard, coll. "Bibliothèque des sciences humaines," 1970 (1st edition 1899), p. 22.

4. Ernst Kantorowicz analyzes in a historical context the constitution of royalty, of political power, in a king of flesh and blood, which ended with "cries heard at the burial of the kings of France, at the Abbey of Saint-Denis: "The king is dead! Long live the king!"" (p.296), cries which clearly indicate dynastic and legal continuity. Kantorowicz describes "the construction of a philosophy which made transparent a fictitious immortality by the intermediary of a mortal man, its temporary incarnation, while the mortal man became transparent thanks to this new fictitious immortality who, created by man—as is any immortality—was neither that of eternal life in another world, nor that of divinity, but that of a political institution nothing less than terrestrial." (p. 315). To a certain extent, the same applies to aristocratic and bourgeoise lineages. (Ernst KANTOROWICZ, *Les Deux Corps du roi,* Paris, Gallimard, coll. "Bibliothèque des Histoires", 1989.)

5. See Anne GOTMAN's article, "Déshéritage, dilapidation et filiation: Wittgenstein, *Communications,* "Generations and filiation," No. 59, 1994.

6. Anne GOTMAN, *Hériter,* Paris, PUF, 1988, p. 137 and 139. "The employee of today *leaves to* his children more than he passes on, and gives up his goods to them more than he passes them on," writes Anne Gotman and Anne Laferrère in their Article on "L'héritage," in *La Famille, l'état des savoirs,* Paris, La Découverte, coll. " Textes à l'appui," série "Sociologie" 1991, p. 247.

7. Marcel MAUSS, "Essai sur le don," *Sociologie et Anthropologie,* Paris, PUF, 1966.

8. Pierre BOURDIEU, *Raisons pratiques, op. cit.,* p. 181-182.

9. Victoire of MONTESQUIOU, *Je Suis née un dimanche, op. cit., p. 10.*

10. "In the custom of the Ancien Régime," writes N. Elias, "the concept of 'family' applies more or less to the haute bourgeoisie, while the concept of 'house' is reserved for the king and the high aristocracy." (*La Société de cour, op. cit.,* p. 28). The concept of lineage founds the very existence of the noble families. See Guy CHAUSSINAND-NOGARET, *La Noblesse au XVIIIme siècle. De la féodalité aux Lumières,* Paris, Complexe, 1994. "In extreme cases," writes the author, "members of the nobility do not have an individual existence, a

specific 'me', they are only links in the chain that form the race. " (p. 12).

11. Frédéric LE PLAY, Émile CHEYSSON, BAYARD, Fernand BOTEL, *Les Mélouga. Une famille pyrénéenne au xix' siècle*. Postface d'Alain CHENU: "La famille-souche, questions de méthode ", Paris, Nathan, collection "Essais et Recherches," 1994, p. 63.

12. Pierre BOURDIEU, "Célibat et condition paysanne," *Études rurales*, No. 5-6, April-September 1962, p. 58.

13. *Ibid*, p. 37.

14. Élisabeth CLAVERIE and Pierre MALMAISON, *L'Impossible Mariage. Violence et parenté en Gévaudan aux XVII, XVIII et XIXe siècles*, Paris, Hachette, coll. "La Mémoire du temps," 1982.

15. Marc AUGE, *Domaines et châteaux*, Paris, Le Seuil, coll. "La Librairie du XX-me siècle," 1989, p. 172.

16. Emile BENVENISTE, *Le Vocabulaire des institutions indo-européennes*, Paris, Minuit, coll. "Le Sens commun," 2 volumes, 1969, vol. 1, p. 307.

17. See Anne GOTMAN, "Le vase, c'est ma tante," *Nouvelle Revue d'ethnopsychiatrie*, No. 14, 1990, p. 125-150. On Mauss' theory on gifts, see Jean LOJKINE, "Mauss et l'essai sur le don. Portée contemporaine d'une étude anthropologique sur une économie non marchande," *Cahiers internationaux de sociologie, vol. LXXXVI*, 1989.

18. Françoise BLOCH and Monique BUISSON, "La circulation du don entre générations, ou comment reçoit-on?," Communications, No. 59 ("Générations et filiation"), Seuil, 1994.

19. Marianne LAMOUR, *La Famille la Rochefoucauld, une famille millénaire*, Planète, May 1994.

20. Jean-Bernard NAUDIN, Christiane de NICOLAY-MAZERY, *La Vie de château*, Paris, Éditions du Chêne, 1991, p. 3.

21. Luc ARRONDEL and Anne LAFERRÈRE, "Accumulation and transmission des grands fortunes," a presentation submitted at the XIIIth Journées d'économie sociale, Nantes, September 16-17, 1993, p. 10. See, by the same authors, "La transmission des grands fortunes. Profil des riches défunts en France," *Economie et statistique*, No 273, 1994-3, p. 41-52. In this article they also emphasize the inequalities in transmitted patrimony, since the 1% richest deceased transmit 19% of all patrimonies. "The variance is enormous among the extremely wealthy: the bottom of this group leaves 4.8 million francs, and the richest, 434.8 million francs"(p. 43). One may also consult Jerome ACCARDO and Philippe MONTEIL, "Le patrimoine au décès en 1988," *Résultats* (INSEE), No. 390 (the series "Consommation - modes de vie," 71, April 1995).

22. Thomas MANN, *Les Buddenbrook*, Paris, Le Livre de Poche, coll. "Biblio", No. 3192, p. 197.

23. Marc AUGÉ, foreword to Anne GOTMAN's book, *Hériter, op. cit.*, p. vii.

24. Michel PINÇON, Monique PINÇON-CHARLOT, *La Chasse à courre, op. cit.*, p. 59 and 199-202.

25. Albert CAMUS, *Le Premier Homme*, Paris, Gallimard, 1994, p. 79.

26. *Domaines et châteaux, op. cit.*, p. 18.

27. Pierre BOURDIEU, "L'illusion biographique ", *Actes de la recherche en sciences sociales*, No. 62-63, June 1986, p. 69-72.

28. On this topic, see Michel PINÇON, *Besoins et habitus*, Paris, Centre de sociologie urbaine, 1978.

29. See Pierre BOURDIEU, Le mort saisit le vif. Les relations entre l'histoire réifiée et l'histoire incorporée ", *Actes de la recherche en sciences sociales*, No. 32-33, April-June 1980.

30. On the choice of first names in other aristocratic families, see Éric MENSION-RIGAU, *Aristocrates et grands bourgeois, éducation, traditions valeurs*, Paris, Plon, 1994, p. 103-107. On the choice of first names one may read Philippe BESNARD and Cyril BARN, "La fin de la diffusion verticale des goûts? (prénoms de l'élite et du vulgum) ", *L'Année sociologique*, 1993, p. 269-294. See also Michel BOZON, "Histoire et sociologie d'un bien symbolique, le prénom ", *Population, 1*, 1987, p. 83-98. "One can say that there are true inventories of   lineages' first names, relatively discreet," writes Mr. Bozon, "especially in regard to those intended for the eldest. For the first names have at the same time an internal function. Some of them are

reserved to the elder successors, while others designate exclusively the juniors, and an emblematic function, directed toward outsiders, the first name of the elder symbolically redoubling the significance of a patronym."

31. "Everyone is free to adopt the armorial bearings of his choice, subject to the rights of third parties, i.e. on condition of not taking a blazon already in use by a private or legal entities, for the blazon, being "the name, in design and color," enjoys the same protection as the [written] name. The civil courts have jurisdiction in disputes related to the usurpation of armorial bearings. One can protect his blazon by depositing his design with the Office of Artistic Industrial Copyright: the protection and the exclusiveness of the design involve those of the blazon which it embodies." *Quid*, Paris, Laffont, 1994, p. 564. Common practice among the nobility is that, if a castle happens to change owners, the new family preserves there the arms of the family which preceded it. It is thus at Sannat, but also at the Château of Arbieu, at Bazas, in the Gironde, under Mr. and Mrs. Philippe de Chenerilles, where the coat of arms which remains is that of the Saige family, for whom the great-grandfather of Mr. de Chenerilles bought Arbieu. This use is an indicator of the importance of the house, holy sanctuary of the family. The men wear the signet ring, but the women also have their sign of recognition in bracelets. "Usually, people have charms for their children or their ancestors," states Christel Baseden. "Me, I put on all of my Dad's badges from when he was little."

32. Thomas Mann, *Op. cit.*, p. 184-185.

33. "I am des Monstiers on the paternal side and on the maternal side," explains the interested party, "since my maternal grandmother was also a des Monstiers, having married one of her des Monstiers cousins. " His maternal grandparents, owners of the Château de Voisin in the Ile-de-France area, sold it to buy the Château de Sannat 25 kilometers from Fraisse, still in the hands of this branch of the family today. Thus, when he was a child, the Marquis François des Monstiers could go from one château to the other by a road which his father had made through a forest forming part of the domaine to make the comings and goings easier.

34. "The Darblays, members of the *conseil de régence* [of the Banque de France], no longer control the paper mill which bears their name. However, the family counted among the largest fortunes in the country and its history illustrates the vitality of French capitalism of the pre-war period. The ancestor was a postmaster. His two sons joined together in grain trading. One of the two was appointed deputy of Corbeil in 1841. The other, an engineer, devoted his life to the improvement of flour. From the grain mill, he went to a paper mill before becoming a deputy in his turn in 1852 [. . .]. In 1932, the family bought up Grand-Couronne, in the suburbs of Rouen, the new paper mill being founded five years before by the State thanks to funds poured in by Germany as reparation from the war. It was amalgamated a little later with the Papeteries de la Chapelle founded by a Swiss industrialist not far from there. Because it had not developed a resolute investment policy since 1958, the company, whose capital came under the management of Paribas and FIDI (Institute of Istrial Development), deposited its balance-sheet in 1980." Gabriel MILÉSI, *Les Nouvelles 200 familles. Les Dynasties de l'argent, du pouvoir financier et économique*, Paris, Belfond, 1990, p. 18. The *Bottin Mondain* of 1995 indicates two addresses for Stanislas Darblay, avenue Frederic-Le-Play in the VIIth arrondissement, and the château de Saint-Germain-les-Corbeil at Corbeil-Essonne.

35. Thus, the family allocations are calculated on the basis of the cadastral income and not on the wages paid.

36. At the time of the Plant Days at Courson one can see how extensive is the concept of patrimony. It must include, for example, the parks and the gardens, which constitute land but also a cultural and symbolic patrimony. The art of the garden, like any art, is also a space of economic profits and symbolics. See Francoise Dubost, *Vert Patrimoine. La constitution d'un nouveau domaine patrimonial*, Paris, Éditions de la Maison des sciences de l'homme, coll. "Ethnologie de la France," 1994.

37. Furthermore, the concept of patrimony has a collective meaning which has converted some individual and family goods into national and historical goods. Practices as socially significant as the hunt also acquired the

status of national patrimony. In any case, it is the intention of huntsmen to thus preserve hunting, and the democratization of the practice as well as the popular success of LAISSER-courre is part of that trend. See *the Hunt, op. cit.*

38. *Bottin Mondain* adopts a similar presentation besides.

39. Guide du Routard, *Week-Ends autour de Paris,* Paris, Hachette, 1995-1996 edition, p. 99.

40. Gabriel-Louis PRINGUÉ, *30 Ans de dîners en ville,* Paris, Édition Revue Adam, 1948.

41. See Michel PINÇON, *Désarrois ouvriers. Familles de métallurgistes dans les mutations industrielles et sociales,* Paris, L'Harmattan, coll. "Logiques sociales ", 1987, chap. II: " Un beau métier ".

42. Guy Schÿler, *Guestier. Souvenirs familiaux et documents, Bordeaux,* Arts & Arts éditeur, 1993 (prix Georges Goyau de l'Académie française 1994).

43. On the history of this mansion, see Albert RÉCHE, *Dix Siècles de vie quotidienne à Bordeaux,* Paris, Seghers, 1983, p. 221.

44. On the transmission of companies, one may read the series of articles in by *Le Nouvel Économiste* on heirs to industrial empires (Michelin, Lagardère, Aguelli, etc.) No. 1005 of July 13, 1995 to No. 1011 of August 25, 1995.

45. Rene SÊDILLOT, *Les Deux Cents familles, op. cit, p. 49.* See also Jean-Noél JEANNENEY, *François de Wendel en République : l'argent et le pouvoir* (1914-1944), Paris, Le Seuil, 1976, and Rene SÊDILLOT, *La Maison de Wendel,* 1704-1958, Paris, RISS, *1958.*

46. "Fortunes françaises ", une enquête de Pierre BEAUDEUX, *L'Expansion,* no. 340, 23 September 23 to October 6, 1988.

47. Rene SÊDILLOT, *Les Deux Cents familles, op. cit,* p. 59.

48. "Shortly after the death of its founder Marcel Bich, Bic confirms its intention to sell Guy Laroche," *Le Monde,* Thursday June 2, 1994, p. 26.

49. H. COSTON, *Dictionary of the bourgeoises dynasties . . . op, cit.,* p. 585.

50. Gabriel MILÉSI, *Les Nouvelles 200 Familles . . . op. cit., p. 56.*

51. *Ibid,* p. 161.

CONCLUSION

Heirs to prestigious lineages, wealthy aristocrats and the old stock grand bourgeoisie owe more to their heritage than to their personal merit. But a heritage is earned. It is necessary to bear the name that falls to you, and the richer it is in symbolic value, the heavier it is to bear. Admittedly, it is better to have to face this responsibility than to have to prove oneself or, even more, than to have to fight to tear one's way out of misery. But a name is built over the long haul, through several generations. To enter the restricted club of the elite takes that which cannot be acquired—time. Or, at least it presupposes great patience and the ability to accept seeing one's efforts not fully bearing their fruits except for the generations that will follow.

Getting into the coterie takes time. Leaving it does too. The credit that has accumulated around a name is not ruined in the blink of an eye. It should be deserved, this name, but it is in the vital interest of the clan to defend from all challenges the irreplaceable capital which it represents. Therefore, one will do anything to recover the wayward heir, the irresponsible, the delinquent who, by his life on the margins and his mistakes, risks destroying all the forms of capital accumulated by a patronym. The honor of the name is at stake; people will do anything to preserve it. That explains why, ultimately, there are very few failures in the social reproduction of the elite: someone will always find a special place for the one who, in spite of the good cards he held at the start of the game, did not know, or want, to play correctly and who is found to be losing ground. This "adventurer" threatens the unit of the family group and, through the network of which the family is an integral part, the entire social group, due to the extent to which the capital of a reputation, based only on the name, creates a loyalty among all who share that name.

Thus, more than for any other social group, because the stakes are so interdependent in the wealthy circles, it is important to study the social system that the individuals comprise, the brotherhood of the great families. Common sense impels one to represent these families as autonomous units, whereas they are actually part of a whole, that of the dominant positions.

One never feels the strength of the group so strongly as when the group is marginalizing one of its members. Christel Baseden thus found herself banished from the group when, at the age of eighteen, she married a son of the northern bourgeoisie and not, as was expected of her, an heir to the high society of Bordeaux. This society had been counting on the young Christel, as on all wellborn girls. "She had a price" and she was invited everywhere, "extraordinary parties, long dresses, châteaux to knock you off your feet." But, "when I announced my engagement to somebody who was not part of our tribe, that was finished. I did not receive one more invitation. That was a lesson that I will never forget. It was as though the families of Bordeaux had said to themselves: 'We invested in her, in order for her to marry someone from among our people.' It is then that I realized that I meant something to my social group, which I had not understood—and which I discovered at some cost to myself."

But as one will do the utmost to recover the one who is slipping away, when there is a good name to be preserved, so when it is a question of a nouveau riche like Bernard Tapie, or Bernard Jansoulet, called 'the Nabob' and hero of a novel by Alphonse Daudet,[1] the penalty for any deviation from the standards of the group will be the most brutal rejection. In the case of the contemporary businessman as in that of the hero of a 19th century social novel, high society cannot accept in a lasting way those social agents who, while certainly generously provided in economic capital, lack seniority. A quick fortune and high media visibility lead to the sharpest rejection as soon as the first reversal appears. Friendships, political relationships, press contacts are then turned against the one who was going to set the world on fire and had thought that being rich was enough for joining the club of the dominant ones. Then the group reacts as a mobilized class that, in concert and without any need for dialogue, socially destroys the disturbing element that came to interfere with the game.

The existence in the wealthiest families of sizable patrimonies to be managed and transmitted calls for such a high level of formalization, clarification and codification to make this transmission a success that the mobilized group becomes a class. The similarity and the proximity of the ways of life and the ways of presenting themselves are not enough to make mobilize the class, as Pierre Bourdieu stresses. "The people who live in a defined space," he writes, "are closer (by their properties and their dispositions, their tastes) and at the same time more inclined to make themselves close, and are easier to bring together, to mobilize. But that does not mean that they constitute a class in the sense of Marx, i.e. a group mobilized by a view of common objectives and in particular against another class."[2] Nonetheless, that is what appears to happen among the wealthiest families. Fortunes, and good fortune, in lives that are not lacking in those qualities, form the objective basis of a mobilization simultaneously for one's own kind and against the others. What does one think in the best neighborhoods, at institutions like the rallies or the Clubs, at the employers' federations like the CNPF? That one is well off in comparison to a class that speaks of itself and defines itself against, or at least apart from, the others.

Existing only on paper, as theoretical objects, to really exist, the social classes must be built socially, and that is a process both conflictual and historical. It is different for the grand bourgeoisie whose real and not only theoretical existence appears more established. One can even see in the obsession with transmission a demonstration of this will to build continuously the class. Admittedly, that is not seen in this terminology. But there hardly exists another social group sufficiently conscious of itself and its interests to manage its territories, its relationships, and the matrimonial alliances of its children with as much vigilance . . .

This work of building the group could even be a pure product of the grand-bourgeois habitus. In a splendid paradox, that would suggest that, in the same motion which makes them deny, ideologically, the existence of social classes, it builds a real class because the group of peers cannot survive, develop and thrive except by removing intruders, in other words all those who, in the social space, occupy other positions, including if one takes into account the criterion of time.

There was, in Marxism, a social task of building the dominated classes as classes, and in particular an assertion of the originality of the working class, which acquired organizations that proclaimed the existence of the class and made it come true by means of this very proclamation. The practice, thus, fulfilled the theory. We know how that evolved— as Marxist theory waned, it produced a counter-effect, the dominated classes being less than ever today groups apart.

Recourse to the concepts of marginality and exclusion signifies the retreat of the dominated classes' forms of organization—whereas, in parallel, the grand bourgeoisie affirms itself as a class by denying the reality of classes. The triumph of liberal ideology is undoubtedly all the easier since the grand bourgeoisie can be satisfied with the practice: it can function as an organized class acting according to its well understood interests without having to build the theory of its social reality and its practice. The habitus of the members of the dominant fractions of the dominant classes has only to carry out its potentialities to make manifest, in practice, a class which has no need to declare itself as such, and especially need not do so in order really to exist.

THE END!!

Notes

1. Alphonse Daudet, *The Nabob,* Paris, G. Carpenter and Co, 1883.
2. Practical Pierre *BOURDIEEU Reasons, op. cit.,* p. 26.

BIBLIOGRAPHIE

Articles et ouvrages généraux

ACCARDO, Jérôme, and MONTEIL, Philippe, "Le Patrimoine au décès en 1988", *INSEE Résultats,* no 390 (série Consommation -modes de vie, no 71, April 1995).

AGUILAR, Yves "La Chartreuse de Mirande. Le monument historique, produit d'un classement de classe", *Actes de la recherche en sciences sociales,* no 42, avril 1982.

ARRONDEL, Luc, "L'approche économique de l'héritage : modèles et tests", *Communications, "Générations et filiation",* no 59, 1994.

ARRONDEL, Luc, and LAFERRÈRE, Anne, "La transmission des grandes fortunes. Profil des riches défunts en France", *Économie et statistique,* no 273, 1994.

ASCHER, François, COHEN, Jean-Louis, and HAUVUY, Jean-Claude, *Luxe, habitat , confort: les références hôtelières,* Paris, Institut français d'urba nisme, université de Paris VIII, 1987.

AUGÉ, Marc, *Domaines and châteaux,* Paris, Le Seuil, coll. "La Librairie du xx siècle", 1989.

AUGÉ, Marc, *Non-Lieux,* Paris, Le Seuil, 1992.

BABEAU, André, *Le Patrimoine aujourd'hui,* Paris, Nathan, 1988.

BABEAU, André, *Le Patrimoine des Français,* Paris, La Découverte, coll. "Repères", 1989.

BABELON, Jean-Pierre, and CHASTEL, André, "La notion de patrimoine", *Revue de lArt,* no 49, 1980.

Banque de France, COB, SBF (Société des bourses françaises), *Les Porteurs de valeurs mobilières,* Paris, Imprimerie nationale, septembre 1994.

BAUER, Gérard, BANDEZ, Gildas, and Roux, Jean-Michel, *Banlieues de charme ou l'art des quartiers-jardins,* Paris, Pandora Éditions, 1980.

BAUER, Michel, and BERTIN-MOUROT, Bénédicte, *L'Accès au sommet des grandes entreprises françaises* (1985-1994), Paris, CNRS, 1995.

BAUER, Michel, and BERTIN-MOUROT, Bénédicte, *Les 200. Comment devient-on un grand patron ?*, Paris, Le Seuil, 1987.

BERTAUX,, Daniel, *Destins personnels et structure de classe*, Paris, PUF, 1977.

BESNARD, Philippe, and GRANGE, Cyril, "La fin de la diffusion verticale des goûts? (prénoms de l'élite et du vulgum)", *L'Année sociologique*, 1993.

BIHR, Alain, and PFEFFERKORN, Roland, *Déchiffrer les inégalités*, Paris, Syros, coll. "Alternatives économiques", 1995.

BLOCH, Françoise, and BUISSON, Monique, "La circulation du don entre générations, ou comment reçoit-on?", *Communications*, no 59 ("Générations et filiation"), Le Seuil, 1994.

BOLTANSKI, Luc, "L'espace positionnel. Multiplicité des positions institutionnelles et habitus de classe", *Revue française de sociologie 14 (1)* 1973.

BOURDIEU, Pierre, "Célibat et condition paysanne", *Études rurales*, no 5-6, avril-septembre 1962.

BOURDIEU, Pierre, and PASSERON, Jean-Claude, *Les Héritiers*, les *étudiants et la culture*, Paris, Minuit, coll. "Le Sens commun", 1964.

BOURDIEU, Pierre, "Les fractions de la classe dominante et les modes d'appropriation de l'oeuvre d'art", *Information sur les sciences sociales*, XIII-3, juin 1974, p. 7-32.

BOURDIEU, Pierre, *La Distinction. Critique sociale du jugement*, Paris, Minuit, coll. "Le Sens commun", 1979.

BOURDIEU, Pierre, "Le Capital social, notes provisoires", *Actes de la recherche en sciences sociales*, no 31, janvier 1980.

BOURDIEU, Pierre, "Le mort saisit le vif. Les relations entre l'histoire réifiée et l'histoire incorporée", *Actes de la recherche en sciences sociales*, no 32-33, avril-juin 1980.

BOURDIEU, Pierre, *Le Sens pratique*, Paris, Minuit, COU "Le Sens commun", 1980.

BOURDIEU, Pierre, "L'illusion biographique", *Actes de la recherche en sciences sociales*, no 62-63, juin 1986.

BOURDIEU, Pierre, and HAACKE, Hans, *Libre-échange*, Paris, Le Seuil / les Presses du réel, 1994.

BOURDIEU, Pierre, *Raisons pratiques*, Paris, Le Seuil, 1994.

BOZON, Michel, "Histoire et sociologie d'un bien symbolique, le prénom", *Population*, 1, 1987.

BRELOT, Claude-Isabelle, "Innocences nobles: la noblesse et la maîtrise de l'espace entre ville et château au XIX siècle", dans *Noblesses et villes* (1780-1950), Université de Tours, Maison des Sciences de la Ville, coll. "Sciences de la ville", no 10, 1995.

CANCEILL, Geneviève, "Les revenus fiscaux des ménages en 1984", *Les Collections de IINSEE*, série M, no 139, 1989.

CANNADINE, David, "L'aristocratie et les villes dans l'Angleterre du XIX siècle: les stations balnéaires", *Urbi*, 1, 1979, p. 33-46.

CASTEL, Robert, *Les Métamorphoses de la question sociale. Une chronique du salariat*, Paris, Fayard, coll. "L'espace du politique", 1995.

CERC, "Les placements des particuliers: que rapportent-ils vraiment?", *Notes et graphiques*, no 6, décembre 1988.

CHAUSSINAND-NOGARET, Guy, La *Noblesse au XVIII siècle. De la féodalité aux Lumières*, Bruxelles, Complexe, 1994.

CHOCRON, Monique, and MARCHAND, Lydie, "Les portefeuilles de titres des personnes physiques à fin 1993", *Bulletin de la Banque de France*, no 10, octobre 1994.

CLAJ-Jeunesse camping, *La Bataille des loisirs. Les années cinquante*, Nice, Éditions Serre, coll. "Actual", 1990.

Conseil des impôts, *Huitième Rapport au président de la République relatif à l'imposition du capital*, Paris, *Journal officiel de la République française*, no 4063, 1986.

CORBIN, Alain, *Le Territoire du vide. L'Occident et le désir du rivage, 1750-1840*, Paris, Flammarion, coll. "Champs", 1990.

COSTON, Henry, *Dictionnaire des dynasties bourgeoises et du monde des affaires*, Paris, Alain Moreau, 1975.

DEBORD, Guy, *La Société du spectacle*, Paris, Gallimard, 1992 (réédition).

DÉSERT, Gabriel, *La Vie quotidienne sur les plages normandes du Second Empire aux Années folles*, Paris, Hachette, 1983.

DION, Jack, and IVORRA, Pierre, *Sur la piste des grandes fortunes*, Paris, Messidor-Éditions sociales, 1985.

DUBOST, Françoise, *Vert patrimoine. La constitution d'un nouveau domaine patrimonial*, Paris, Éditions de la Maison des Sciences de l'Homme, coll. "Ethnologie de la France", 1994.

DUNETON, Claude, *Parler croquant*, Stock, 1973.

DURAND, Georges, "La vigne et le vin", dans *Les Lieux de mémoire*, sous la direction de Pierre NORA Paris, Gallimard, 1993 (tome III, *Les France*, volume 2, p. 786).

DURIEZ Bruno, "La bourgeoisie répertoriée: le Livre des familles du Nord", *Ethnologie française*, 1990-1, janvier-mars, tome 20,

ELIAS, Norbert, *La Société de cour*, Paris, Flammarion, coll. "Champs", 1985.

FAGUER, Jean-Pierre, "Les effets d'une " éducation totale ". Un collège jésuite, 1960", *Actes de la recherche en sciences sociales*, no 86-87, mars 1991.

GOFFMAN, Erving, *Asiles*, Paris, Minuit, coll. "Le Sens commun", 1968.

GOODY, Jack, *La Raison graphique*, Paris, Minuit, coll. "Le Sens commun", 1979.

GOTMAN, Anne, *Hériter*, préface de Marc AUGÉ, Paris, PUF, 1988.

GOTMAN, Anne, "Le vase, c'est ma tante", *Nouvelle Revue d'éthnopsychiatrie*, no 14, 1990.

GOTMAN, Anne, "Déshéritage, dilapidation et filiation: Wittgenstein", *Communications*, "Générations et filiation", no 59, 1994.

GRAFMEYER, Yves, *Quand le Tout-Lyon se compte*, Lyon, Presses universitaires de Lyon, coll. "Transversales", 1992.

GRANGE, Cyril, "La " liste mondaine ". Analyse d'histoire sociale et quantitative du *Bottin Mondain*", *Ethnologie française*, 1990-1, janvier-mars, tome 20.

GRANGE, Cyril, *Les Gens du Bottin Mondain. Y être c'est en être*, Paris, Fayard, 1996.

HALBWACHS, Maurice, *Les Cadres sociaux de la mémoire*, Paris-La Haye, Mouton, 1976 (l'édition 1925).

INSEE, "Les revenus fiscaux des ménages en 1984", *Les Collections de l'INSEE*, série M, no 139.

ION, Jacques, *Tradition touristique et société locale : Aix-les-Bains, station thermale. Contribution à une sociologie du phénomène touristique*, thèse de troisième cycle, 1970.

JOHY, Robert, and CAMPAGNAC, Élisabeth, *Racines historiques du lotissement*, Paris, Secrétariat d'état à la culture, Copedith, 1976.

KESSLER, Denis, and MASSON, André, "Le patrimoine des Français: faits et controverses", INSEE, *Données sociales 1990*, p. 156-166.

KESSLER, Denis and MASSON, André, "Qui possède quoi, et pourquoi?", *Revue d'économie financière*, no 10, 1989.

LAFERRÈRE, Anne, "Héritiers et héritages", *Économie et statistique*, no 214, octobre 1988.

LEPIDI, Jules, *La Fortune des Français*, Paris, Presses universitaires de France, coll. "Que sais-je?" ri' 2424, 1988.

LE PLAY, Frédéric, CHEYSSON, Émile, BAYARD, BUTEL, Fernand, *Les Mélouga. Une famille* pyrénéenne au *XIX siècle*. Postface d'Alain CHENU: "La famille-souche, questions de méthode", Paris, Nathan, collection "Essais et Recherches", 1994.

LEWANDOWSKI, Olgierd, "Différenciation et mécanismes d'inté ation de la classe dirigeante. L'image sociale de l'élite d'après le Who's *who in France*", *Revue française de sociologie*, 15 (1) 1974.

LOJKINE, Jean, "Mauss et l'essai sur le don. Portée contemporaine d'une étude anthropologique sur une économie non marchande", *Cahiers internationaux de sociologie, vol.* LXXXVI, 1989.

LOLLIVIER, Stéfan, and VERGER, Daniel, "Le patrimoine aujourd'hui. Beaucoup entre les mains de quelques-uns...", INSEE, *Données sociales* 1990, p. 167-170.

MAGRI, Susanna, and TOPALOV, Christian, "De la cité-jardin à la ville rationalisée. Un tournant du projet réformateur, 1905-1925. Étude comparative France, Grande-Bretagne, Italie, États-Unis", *Revue française de sociologie*, 28 (3), 1987, 417-451.

MALPOT, Jean-Jacques, PAQUEL, Véronique, and VERGER, Daniel "Que possèdent les diverses catégories sociales?", INSEE, *Données sociales* 1993, p. 385-394.

MANN, Thomas, *Les Buddenbrook*, Paris, Le Livre de Poche, coll. "Biblio", no 3192, 1993.

MARGUERITE, Ber-nard, "Crise du système financier et reproduction de l'oligarchie financière", *Issues*, ri' 12, 2' trimestre 1982.

MASSON, André, and ARRONDEL, Luc, *Facteurs explicatifs de la répartition et de la composition des patrimoines*, rapport pour le Commissariat général du Plan, 1987.

MAUSS, Marcel, "Essai sur le don", *Sociologie et anthropologie*, Paris, PUF, 1966.

MENSION-RIGAU, Éric, "La persistance du modèle du " château ""ou les limites de la fusion des élites dans l'univers de la ville", dans *Noblesses et villes* (1780-1950), université de Tours, Maison des sciences de la ville, coll. "Sciences de la ville", no 10, 1995.

MENSION-RIGAU, Éric, *Aristocrates et grands bourgeois*, Paris, Plon, 1994

MERLLIÉ, Dominique, *Les Enquêtes de mobilité sociale*, Palis, PUF, coll. "Le Sociologue", 1994.

MICHALET, C.-A., *Les Placements des épargnants français de 1815 à nos jours*, Paris, PUF, 1968.

MILÉSI, Gabriel, *Les Nouvelles 200 Familles. Les dynasties de l'argent, du pouvoir financier et économique*, Paris, Belfond, 1990.

MOULIN, Raymonde, "Un type de collectionneur: le spéculateur", *Revue française de sociologie*, 5 (2), 1964.

MOULIN, Raymonde, *Le Marché de la peinture en France*, Palis, Minuit, coll. "Le Sens commun", 1967.

MOULIN, Raymonde, and QUEMIN, Alain, "La certification de la valeur de l'art", *Annales*, novembre-décembre 1993.

PAYS, Bruno, *La Gestion de patrimoine*, Paris, PUF, coll. "Que sais-je?", no 2699, 1992.

PÉRISSE, Xavier, and DUNGLAS, Dominique, *La Privilégiature*, Paris, RMC Édition, 1988.

PINÇON, Michel, and PINÇON-CHARLOT, Monique, *Dans les beaux quartiers*, Paris, Le Seuil, coll. "L'épreuve des faits", 1989.

PINÇON, Michel, and PINÇON-CHARLOT, Monique, *Quartiers bourgeois, quartiers d'affaires*, Paris, Payot, coll. "Documents", 1992.

PINÇON, Michel, and PINÇON-CHARLOT, Monique, *La Chasse à courre, ses rites et ses enjeux*, Paris, Payot, coll. "Documents", 1993 (réédition "Petite Bibliothèque Payot", 1996).

PRETECEILLE, Edmond, *Mutations urbaines et politiques locales*, Paris, Centre de sociologie urbaine, deux volumes, 1990 et 1993.

QUEMIN, Alain, "L'espace des objets. Expertises et enchères à DrouotNord", *Genèses*, no 17, septembre

1994.

QUEMIN, Alain, "Les commissaires-priseurs français: de la tradition à la modernité", *Encyclopaedia universalis*, volume *Universalia* 1994, p. 274-277.

QUEMIN, Alain, *Les Commissaires-Priseurs: analyse d'une profession et de son rôle dans les ventes aux enchères*, thèse de doctorat, Paris, EHESS, décembre 1994.

QUEMIN, Alain, *Les Commissaires-Priseurs. La mutation d'une profession*, Paris, Anthropos, 1997.

SAINT MARTIN, Monique de, *L'Espace de la noblesse*, Paris, Métailié, 1993.

SANDOVAL, Véronique, "La grande bourgeoisie, une planète à explorer", *La Pensée*, ri' 290, novembre-décembre 1992, p. 65-74.

SÉDILLOT, René, *Us Deux Cents familles*, Paris, Perrin, coll. "Vérités et légendes", 1988.

SHALINS, Marshall, *Âge de pierre, âge d'abondance*, Paris, Gallimard, coll. "Bibliothèque des Sciences humaines", 1976.

TEULON, Frédéric, *Vocabulaire monétaire et financier*, Paris, PUF, coll. "Que sais-je?", no 2628, 1993.

URBAIN, Jean-Didier, *Sur la plage. Moeurs et coutumes balnéaires*, Paris, Payot, 1994.

VEBLEN, Thorstein, *Théorie de la classe de loisir*, Paris, Gallimard, con. "Bibliothèque des sciences humaines", 1970 (1re édition 1899).

WAGNER, Anne-Catherine, "Point de vue local, point de vue international: une enquête auprès de la bourgeoisie d'affaires étrangère en France", *Journal des Anthropologues*, ri' 53-54-55, printemps 1994.

ZERAH, Dov, *Le Système financier français*, Paris, La Documentation française, Notes et études documentaires, no 4980-8

Monographies locales

ACACIE, Élisabeth, "La naissance d'une station balnéaire sous le Second Empire", *Villes, histoire et culture, URA CNRS 1010*, no 1, décembre 1994. [Deauville]

ASTRUC, Jean, Le *Raincy*, "*Forêt j'étais, ville je suis*" ouvrage publié avec le concours de la ville du Raincy à l'occasion de son centenaire (1869-1969).

BIANCHINI, Roger-Louis, *Monaco. Une affaire qui tourne*, Paris, Le Seuil, coll. "Points-Actuel", 1992.

CATINAT, Jacques, *Grandes Heures de Chatou et la naissance du Vésinet*, Chatou, Éditions SOSP, 1985 (première édition 1972).

COIGNARD, Jérôme, "Un palais sur la mer", *Beaux-Arts*, ri' hors série: "La villa Ephrussi de Rothschild", 1993.

CONTAL, Marie-Hélène, *1854-1936, Création d'une ville thermale*, Paris, Institut français d'architecture, CEP, Éditions du Moniteur, 1982.

CUEILLE, Sophie, "Une colonie dans une forêt: le lotissement du Vésinet (1858-1930)", *Villes en parallèle*, no 14, juin 1989.

DÉBORDES, Jacqueline, *Vichy, ville-jardin*, Vichy, Éditions du Cygne, 1993.

DELIENCOURT, Roger and CHENNEBENOIST, Jean, *Deauville, son histoire*, S. n., imprimerie Marie, Honfleur, tome 1 : *Des origines à 1914*, 1977, and tome 2: *De 1914 à 1977*, 1982.

"Drouot", n'spécial de *Connaissance des arts*, mai 1988.

GINESTET, Bernard, *Les Chartrons*, Paris, Acropole, 1991.

GRAVELINE, Janine, *Châteaux et manoirs dAquitaine*, Éditions Minerve, 1988.

HERVIER, Dominique (sous la direction de), textes de Laurent ROBERT, photographies de Jean-Bernard VIALLES, *Chatou, Croissy-sur-Seine, villégiatures en bordure de Seine*, Paris, APPIF (Association pour le dével pement de l'Inventaire général), 1993.

KELLER, Eliane, *Arcachon, villas et personnalités. Le temps retrouvé*, Éditions équinoxe, s.d.

LAPARRA-VULLIEZ, Wanda, *Gloire de Biarritz*, Paris, Éditions FranceEmpire, 1979.

Le Vésinet, modèle d'urbanisme paysager, 1858-1930, Cahiers de l'inventaire n' 17 (Imprimerie nationale).

MARTIN, Olivier, *Familles de la bourgeoisie blésoise. 1765-1964. Le rôle d'une ville moyenne dans un processus de mobilités personnelles*, thèse EHESS, 1994.

MARTIN, Roger, "Arcachon, ville impériale", *Nouveaux Cahiers du Second Empire*, no 29, 1992.

NAUDIN, Jean-Bernard, and NICOLAY-MAZERY, Christiane de, *La Vie de château*, Paris, Éditions du Chêne, 1991.

NEU, Jean-Paul, *Enghien-les-Bains, nouvelle histoire*, Saint-Ouen-L'Aumône, Éditions du Valhermeil, 1994.

POISSON, Georges, "Neuilly-sur-Seine, histoire", dans *Évocation du vieux Paris. La banlieue nord-ouest*, Paris, Minuit, 1960.

POISSON, Georges, *De Maisons-sur-Seine à Maisons-Laffitte*, MaisonsLaffitte, Association de sauvegarde et de mise en valeur de MaisonsLaffitte, 1973.

POISSON, Georges, *La Curieuse Histoire du Vésinet*, Ville du Vésinet, 1986.

RÈCHE, Albert, *Dix Siècles de vie quotidienne à Bordeaux*, Paris, Seghers, 1983.

ROCHE, François G., *Les Rothschild à l'abbaye des Vaux-de-Cernay*, Paris, I.D.C. plus, coll. "La vallée de Chevreuse en 1900", s.d.

TULASNE-MOENECLAEY, Annick, *Jean des Monstiers et le château du Fraisse*, Poitiers, Faculté des Lettres, mémoire de maîtrise d'histoire, 1970.

VALETTE, Régis, *Catalogue de la noblesse*, Paris, Laffont, 1989.

WALLON, Armand, *La Vie quotidienne dans les villes d'eaux (1850-1914)*, Paris, Hachette, 1981.

Mémoires et monographies familiales

BEAUMONT, Jean de, *Au hasard de la chance*, Paris, Julliard, 1987.

BERGERON, Louis, *Les Rothschild et les autres... La gloire des banquiers*, Paris, Perrin, coll. "Histoire et fortunes", 1991.

BUTEL, Paul, *Les Dynasties bordelaises, de Colbert à Chaban*, Paris, Perrin, coll. "Histoire et fortunes", 1991.

FAUCIGNY-LUCINGE, Jean-Louis de, *Un gentilhomme cosmopolite*, Paris, Perrin, 1990.

JEANNENEY, Jean-Noël, *François de Wendel en République : l'argent et le pouvoir (1914-1944)*, Paris, Le Seuil, 1976.

MONTESQUIOU, Victoire de, *Je suis née un dimanche*, Paris, J.-C. Lattès, 1990.

PANGE, comtesse Jean de, *Comment j'ai vu 1900*, Paris, Grasset, 3 volumes, 1962, 1965 et 1968.

PRINGUÉ, Gabriel-Louis, *30 Ans de dîners en ville*, Paris, Édition Revue Adam, 1948.

ROTHSCHILD, Guy de, *Contre bonne fortune...*, Paris, Belfond, 1983.

ROTHSCHILD, Guy de, *Mon ombre siamoise*, Paris, Grasset, 1993.

SCH*k* LER, Guy, *Guestier. Souvenirs familiaux et documents*, Bordeaux, Arts & Arts éditeur, 1993.

SÉDILLOT, René, *La Maison de Wendel, 1704-1958*, Paris, RISS, 1958.

SEILLIÈRE, Ernest-Antoine, "La saga industrielle et financière de trois familles lorraines: les Schneider, les Wendel, les Seillière", dans *Les Schneider, le Creusot. Une famille, une entreprise, une ville (1836-1960)*, Paris, Fayard/Réunion des Musées nationaux/écomusée de la communauté Le Creusot-Montceau les Mines, 1995.